S0-AQL-581

WORST TO FIRST

The Story of the 1993 Phillies

The Staff of
The Philadelphia Inquirer

Andrews and McMeel
A Universal Press Syndicate Company
Kansas City

Worst to First: The Story of the 1993 Phillies copyright © 1993 by The Philadelphia Inquirer. All rights reserved. Printed in the United States of America. No part of this book may be used or reproduced in any manner whatsoever without written permission except in the case of reprints in the context of reviews. For information, write Andrews and Mcmeel, a Universal Press Syndicate Company, 4900 Main Street, Kansas City, Missouri 64112.

Library of Congress Catalog Card Number: 93-74221

ISBN: 0-8362-8062-8

Designed by Barrie Maguire

ATTENTION: SCHOOLS AND BUSINESSES

Andrews and McMeel books are available at quantity discounts with bulk purchase for educational, business, or sales promotional use. For information, please write to: Special Sales Department, Andrews and McMeel, 4900 Main Street, Kansas City, Missouri 64112.

CONTENTS

Acknowledgments

The number of names on this page is about what one would expect for a book that draws on several departments of a newspaper. But there's an extra depth to the thanks due these people because of the short turnaround required by the nature of the book, which we wanted in the bookstores as soon as humanly possible—while the glow of a magnificent baseball season was still bright.

The Philadelphia Inquirer is blessed with sports, photo, and graphics departments just bulging with talent. And the work that you see in this book is credited to each of the contributing writers and photographers. But there are a great number of talented people whose work on this book isn't so obvious, and it could not have been assembled without their efforts. They are:

From *The Inquirer's* sports department: Nancy Cooney, Andrew Korbel, Lee Kornmuller, and David Tucker; from *The Inquirer's* photography and graphics departments, Charles Chamberlin, Frank Glackin, Tom Gralish, Gary Haynes, Mike Levin, Bill Marsh, David Milne, Akira Suwa, and Randy Wolf; and from *The Inquirer's* new-ventures department, Ken Bookman, Herbert Kestenbaum, and Vicky C. Lee.

In addition, STATS, Inc., of Chicago compiled many of the statistical tables that appear in Chapter 5.

1
THE YEAR IN REVIEW

As he walked into the Clearwater clubhouse early on the bright and windy morning in February 1993, Pete Incaviglia looked Philadelphian. This kind of swagger, this muscled, macho strut was the norm in hoagie shops at Second and Shunk or at 10th and Fitzwater. These gruff, rasping, monosyllabic sentences could surmount the din in a Frankford Avenue tavern.

Incaviglia was about to spend a first day with his new Phillies teammates. He had watched with an across-the-field fascination in 1992, his first National League season, as these last-place Phils dove and strained and battled for no apparent reason. He liked that. Still, an off-season free-agent signee, he really wasn't sure what made them tick, what locker-room dynamics were at work here.

It wouldn't take him long to learn.

John Kruk, rumpled, limping, and squinting, looking as if he had just awakened from a winter's hibernation in West Virginia, shook Incaviglia's hand.

"Welcome to the [frigging] nuthouse," Kruk said on his first day at camp. "I don't know why anyone would want to come here, but I guess it's too late to change your mind."

Mitch Williams, who had played with Incaviglia in Texas, spotted him. "Inky!" he screamed. "That's all we need, another greaser."

Incaviglia quickly became a part of this club—trading insults, playing cards, irreverent off the field, passionate on it.

The assimilation of Milt Thompson and Jim Eisenreich and Larry

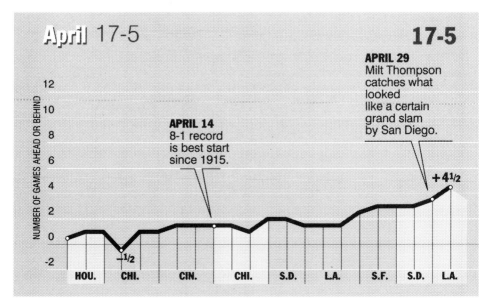

April 17-5

17-5

APRIL 29
Milt Thompson
catches what
looked
like a certain
grand slam
by San Diego.

APRIL 14
8-1 record
is best start
since 1915.

+4½

−½

NUMBER OF GAMES AHEAD OR BEHIND

12
10
8
6
4
2
0
-2

HOU.   CHI.   CIN.   CHI.   S.D.   L.A.   S.F.   S.D.   L.A.

Andersen and David West and Danny Jackson would proceed just as
smoothly. In one off-season, this Phillies club had been transformed
from one whose fringes were populated by untried, quiet, and margin-
ally talented youngsters to a solid collection of like-minded veterans.

"I think," said Incaviglia, "that I died and went to heaven."

And by the time their season concluded 8½ months later, Incaviglia and his overweight and overachieving, spitting and slovenly, hustling and hirsute, joyously demented Phillies, would transport an entire
city wonderfully close to heaven.

They would rush through the schedule's early months with a relentless intensity. With sparkling starting pitching, a consistently pro-
ductive offense, and some memorable defensive moments, they roared
to a 45-17 start. They constructed such a sizable lead over the rest of
the National League East that, despite a few tense moments in July and
September, their first-place margin would never get below three games.

And in a postseason that played out like some Dali dream, they
captivated and tortured their fans before winning the franchise's fifth
pennant in six games over the talented and tested Atlanta Braves. A fascinating World Series with the defending-champion Blue Jays followed,
one that would end for them in the terrible misery of a ninth-inning
Game 6 loss that might haunt this franchise forever.

In the quiet and emotional clubhouse scene that followed Joe
Carter's game-winning home run in SkyDome, Kruk and manager Jim

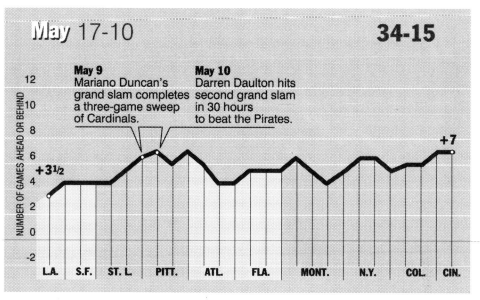

May 17-10   34-15

May 9
Mariano Duncan's grand slam completes a three-game sweep of Cardinals.

May 10
Darren Daulton hits second grand slam in 30 hours to beat the Pirates.

NUMBER OF GAMES AHEAD OR BEHIND

12 · 10 · 8 · 6 · 4 · 2 · 0 · -2

+3½   +7

L.A. | S.F. | ST. L | PITT. | ATL. | FLA. | MONT. | N.Y. | COL. | CIN.

Fregosi, who played his first big-league game in 1961 and had just participated in his first World Series, provided the proper eulogies.

"This game," said Fregosi, still red-eyed and visibly shaken long after the loss, "will break your heart."

Kruk, drinking a beer and, most unusually for this first-baseman who prefers the shadows, talking at his locker for hours after the game, took the broader view.

"This was great," Kruk said. "I never had so much fun. After eight years of getting my ass kicked, this was fun. I think everyone will remember this team for a lot of years."

There was little reason to suspect that would be the case when the Phillies gathered in Clearwater.

If the dreadful 70-92 1992 season had killed the interest of many fans and promised little for '93, it also stung Phillies officials, who attributed the failure to injuries. Club president Bill Giles believed that Philadelphia was not seeing the real Phillies. Despite the last-place finish, he felt the Phils were an entertaining club. Stories characterizing them instead as dull and listless in the '92 season's final days annoyed him greatly.

"I had people at ESPN tell me that we were a team they liked to have on, that we had a lot of characters, players who always played hard," said Giles in the off-season. "I don't think we were dull at all."

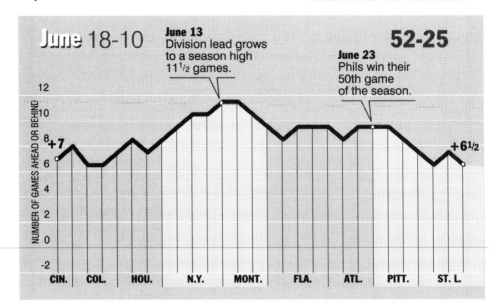

Still, he and Fregosi and general manager Lee Thomas knew they needed help. They took serious runs at two marquee free agents—Kirby Puckett and David Cone. But their were limits on how much money Thomas could—and would—spend, and Philadelphia was quickly out of the running for those prized players.

It was the best thing that never happened.

"At that point, we realized that we needed more than one or two players to turn things around," said Thomas. "So we met and identified our needs and went about trying to fill them with guys who would fit in here."

They went hunting bargain talent, role players who could supplement their everyday nucleus and their young starting pitching. More important, they went hunting players with the kind of hard-nosed personalities that Thomas and Fregosi admired. In other words, the Phillies were looking for chemistry as much as talent.

Thomas signed free agents Incaviglia, Thompson, and Eisenreich to solidify an outfield where Stan Javier and Julio Peguero and Tom Marsh and Braulio Castillo had played in 1992.

"Incaviglia is going to dive for balls and slide headfirst into bases," said Fregosi at the winter meetings. "The fans in Philly are going to love him."

Thomas signed reliever Larry Andersen and traded for David West to help in a bullpen where Jay Baller and Mike Hartley, Wally

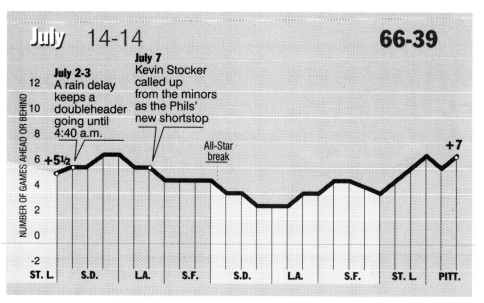

July 14-14   66-39

July 2-3
A rain delay keeps a doubleheader going until 4:40 a.m.

July 7
Kevin Stocker called up from the minors as the Phils' new shortstop

All-Star break

+5½

+7

NUMBER OF GAMES AHEAD OR BEHIND

12 · 10 · 8 · 6 · 4 · 2 · 0 · -2

ST. L · S.D. · L.A. · S.F. · S.D. · L.A. · S.F. · ST. L · PITT.

Ritchie and Cliff Brantley had labored the previous year. He traded for Danny Jackson to add a 200-innings-plus veteran to a rotation where Mickey Weston and Kyle Abbott and Pat Combs toiled in 1992.

They played well in the preseason and, more significantly, they played together. Gone was the sniping of veterans about the "Scranton shuttle" that carried so many youngsters down the Northeast Extension from the minors to Philadelphia. There was no more moaning from hitters about the dreadful pitching.

"I don't know if you call it chemistry or what the heck you call it, but you could sense it in spring training," said Kruk. "By the time we left camp, we knew we had an excellent lineup and some good starting pitching. The year before, when we left camp, we all were saying that we could be contenders. But no one really believed it. We knew we just didn't have enough. This year was different. This was the first time we really felt like we could win it," he said.

The misfortune of others aided them in that faith. One by one, divisional rivals were hit with bad news in the winter and early spring.

The Cubs lost Ryne Sandberg with a broken wrist in the first exhibition game. The Pirates lost Barry Bonds and Doug Drabek to free-agency. The Expos lost their veterans. The Cardinals lost a fight to the Phils in a St. Petersburg beanball war. The Mets just lost their mind.

"It was unbelievable how everything started to go right for us this spring," said third base coach Larry Bowa. "It seemed like every day

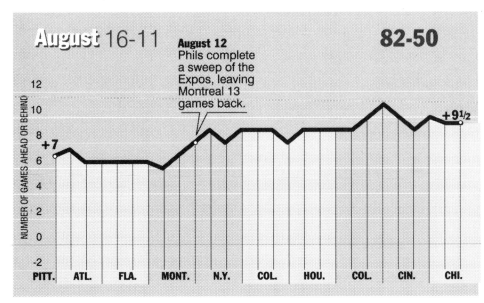

there was more good news for us, more bad news for the other clubs in our division."

The newfound optimism was making these Phillies buoyant. They felt as if they couldn't lose, as if no injury could stop them.

Curt Schilling pitched with a stress fracture in his right leg. Tommy Greene, who was supposed to begin the season in the bullpen after yearlong shoulder problems, was nearly unhittable in Florida. The offense, led by a healthy and super-confident Lenny Dykstra at its top, was generating runs at a scary pace.

On the rainy afternoon before the regular season began, in a tiny Oklahoma City locker room, Phillies veterans were cocky with anticipation. They asked reporters whom they had forecast to win the NL East. Most said they had chosen the Cardinals or Expos. One preseason publication even picked the Phillies last, behind the expansion Florida Marlins.

"That's all right," said Darren Daulton, when hearing that the Phillies were picked down in the division. "We'll show you something. You guys are underestimating us badly."

Actually, these modest forecasts were exactly what the Phillies wanted to hear. Already characterized as fat and scruffy and destined for mediocrity, they had developed the "Us-Against-Them" attitude that would sustain them through the 162 games ahead.

The brawl with the Cardinals showed early that, after serving as

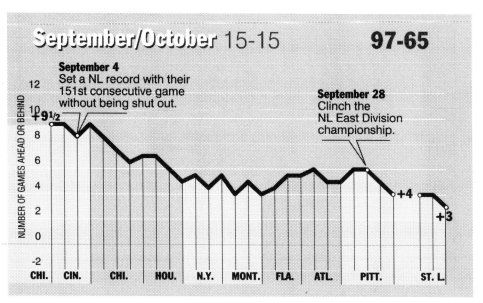

September/October 15-15   **97-65**

September 4
Set a NL record with their 151st consecutive game without being shut out.

September 28
Clinch the NL East Division championship.

NUMBER OF GAMES AHEAD OR BEHIND

CHI. | CIN. | CHI. | HOU. | N.Y. | MONT. | FLA. | ATL. | PITT. | ST. L.

team pincushion for NL pitchers in 1992, they would no longer tolerate such abuse. While the Phils were loose in the clubhouse, they could, with unshaven faces and glaring eyes, appear fearsome on the field. Expos pitcher Dennis Martinez suggested that some pitchers were intimidated by the demeanor and sheer physical bulk in the middle of the Phillies lineup.

Dave Hollins, plunked a major-league-high 19 times in 1992, would be hit by only five pitches in '93.

"I'll tell you what," said Dykstra early in the season. "We've got a lot of mean and intimidating-looking guys on this team. I don't think too many teams are going to be eager to mess with us."

I t looked as if no one could keep up with them either.

They opened the season with a shocking sweep of the Astros in Houston, beating high-priced free-agent pitchers Drabek and Greg Swindell as well as Pete Harnisch.

They were being no-hit through six innings by Harnisch before Daulton's homer in the seventh and little Mickey Morandini's two-run blast in the eighth. They won it on Thompson's hit in extra innings.

"I think we will look back on that home run by Mickey as a turning point in our season," predicted Schilling.

The Phillies raced in front and lengthened their lead. When they won back-to-back West Coast games in April on miraculous late-inning defensive plays by Thompson and Morandini, there was a sense that destiny was at work.

"We were feeling like this was our year," said Morandini, "that nothing could stop us."

On June 15, after winning what would be a season-high sixth straight game, the Phillies led their division by $11\frac{1}{2}$ games over the Cardinals, $12\frac{1}{2}$ over the Expos. They were 45-17.

"You never expect a down time," said Eisenreich. "But they always seem to happen. We're just trying to win as many games as we can for as long as we can."

The down time arrived in just a few weeks. The Cardinals took three of four from them in St. Louis as June turned into July and Daulton publicly criticized Schilling and Greene for timid pitching in the series.

The slide continued. The Giants spanked the Phils in a series at Veterans Stadium before the All-Star break. The Padres beat up on them in San Diego after the break, and on July 19, the Philadelphia lead was at a season-low three games.

"You guys can panic if you like," said Fregosi in response to one too many questions about his team's diminished standing. "I've said all along that no team can play .700 baseball for a whole year. It's a long season, and there are going to be ups and downs. We'll survive this one."

When that West Coast trip concluded for them, with a 5-6 record, the Cardinals, four games behind, arrived in Philadelphia for a three-game series.

"I thought that might have been the time this team showed the greatest character," said Fregosi. "We were coming off a bad West Coast trip and the Cardinals had pounded us pretty good in St. Louis. We had to do something."

They swept the Cardinals.

"They came in here with a chance to put us in a really tough spot," said Schilling. "They could have left here one game back. Instead, they're leaving us in front by seven games."

The Phillies treaded water the rest of the way—they never lost more than four consecutive games in 1993—and when they fought off a late rush by the scorching Expos in September, the race was over.

But not before that Expos charge resurrected Philadelphia's morbid fascination with the 1964 Phillies, the legendary and ill-fated team that blew a $6\frac{1}{2}$-game lead with 12 to play.

Fregosi and his players chafed at the parallels between their shrinking September lead and the 1964 collapse. "I don't understand the mentality of the Phillies fans," Fregosi said often.

The incident reinforced the Phillies' feelings about the dark, negative nature of Philadelphia's fans—a side that surfaced when their ugly loss to Houston on September 12 precipitated loud Veterans Stadium boos. "Most of us weren't even alive in '64," said Daulton. "But for the last few days that's all I've heard about. . . . It will be good to get away."

Finally, on September 28, a cold night in Pittsburgh, the Phillies clinched their sixth NL Eastern Division title.

"There were a lot of people who doubted us," said Terry Mulholland after the clinching. "A lot of people who called us rejects and castoffs. I think we proved something. Not to ourselves, because we always believed in ourselves, but to those people."

There were many more doubters when the NL Championship Series began on October 6 in Philadelphia. The Atlanta Braves had won 104 games, fighting off the Giants in a race made memorable by the consistent excellence of its participants. The Braves had beaten Philadelphia two of three in a late-season series at the Vet. They had the league's best lineup and its best starting pitching.

"Anyone who knew this club knew we weren't going to roll over and say, 'Hey, this was a great season. We can let up now,'" said Incaviglia. "There are too many gamers on this club. We can't play that way."

The doubts seemed justified when, after a 10-inning Phils victory in Game 1, the Braves slammed Philadelphia pitching for 23 runs in winning Games 2 and 3.

But Danny Jackson, the often-ill-tempered lefthander who had scuffled in September, pitched with a fanatical focus in Game 4. Jackson said he was motivated by a desire to "stick it up the media's ass." He was annoyed by questions about the shelling the Braves gave him in the 1992 NLCS, when he pitched for the Pirates, and how he was made to look inferior to Atlanta starter John Smoltz.

His teammates, meanwhile, had other motivation. Atlanta newspapers called them fat and ugly and interviewed Southern women who were disgusted by their tobacco-chewing and other personal habits. "Hide the women and children," screamed one headline.

By then, the scruffy nature of the Phils had become a national fascination. "This ain't a fucking beauty show," said Incaviglia. "It's baseball. All that other stuff don't mind a thing."

Before they could win Game 4, though, Mitch Williams provided another postseason moment of mass hysteria. The maddeningly erratic closer nearly gave away a ninth-inning lead with fielding blunders, but late-inning third baseman Kim Batiste, guilty of several of his own in the postseason, prevented a Williams toss from soaring to the leftfield corner and the Phillies won.

Schilling pitched desperately effective baseball again in Game 5 and again Williams and Batiste gave away a ninth-inning lead. The Phils survived this time when Mark Lemke's one-out liner to left, the winning run at third, tailed barely foul.

"That's when I thought that this might really be our year," said Fregosi. "When I saw Lemke hit that ball, I thought the game was over. It was unbelievable."

The second of the remarkably responsive Dykstra's six post-season homers won it for the Phils in the 10th. They came home uplifted and won the pennant behind Greene, with an easy Game 6 victory. Now they prepared to meet the Blue Jays.

"No one is giving us much of a chance, but that's the way it's been all year," said Kruk. "We like being the underdogs."

The two league champions split the first two games in Toronto and the Jays won easily in Game 3, the first World Series game in a decade in Philadelphia. Then came three emotionally draining games, baseball on the edge.

Dykstra pounded two two-run homers and the Phillies led Game 4, in the rain and mist, 14-9, entering the eighth inning. When Larry Andersen tired, in came Williams. The Jays awoke for six runs, and when Devon White's two-out, two-run triple fell in between Dykstra and Eisenreich, giving the Jays a 15-14 lead, this game and this World Series were effectively over. As Williams left the field to boos, he must have thought his season had hit its nadir.

He would have been wrong.

"It was like a nightmare," said Thompson. "When I woke up the next day, I was hoping it had been a dream. But it was real."

Remarkably, Schilling, pitching with a blatant passion, shut out Toronto the next night, 2-0, and the Series would be concluded in Toronto.

After the 15-14 loss, callers to the Phillies offices began threatening Williams's life. His South Jersey residence was pelted with eggs. The closer slept with a gun, and when the Phils worked out in Toronto on the day before Game 6, he was absent.

Teammates said Williams spent a sleepless night before Game 6 at SkyDome.

"He can't handle things like that, and he shouldn't have to," said one teammate. "He's just a big emotional kid. And as much as he tries to let on that this didn't bother him, I know it did."

This was a Phillies season destined to end with Williams on the mound. Sure enough, after another Dykstra homer had rallied the Phils and left them with a 6-5 lead in the ninth inning of Game 6, in strutted Williams from the rightfield bullpen.

On the Toronto bench, players' spirits were lifted by the appearance of No. 99. "When we saw Mitch coming in, we knew something good would happen," said Carter.

The reaction of most Phillies fans was the opposite. Everywhere in the Delaware Valley, two words were being screamed at inanimate television screens: "Why?" and "Please . . ."

There was one out and two on and Carter was at bat with a count of 2-2. Williams, his fastball having vanished, threw either a slider or a halfhearted fastball—no one was quite sure—at Carter's knees.

Suddenly, the spectacular domed facility quivered with noise. Blue Jays rushed onto the field as a dancing Carter circled the bases gleefully, his Series-winning homer now in the Toronto bullpen.

The '93 Phillies, noisy and raucous all season, left the field for a final time. In silence.

The gloomy conclusion will only add to the legend of the 1993 Phillies. They were a club that fit its city perfectly. They were intense and dogged, they were dirty and gritty, they could not escape their own history, and occasionally they were foul.

They made salaries that row-house residents could only dream about, yet they identified with Philadelphia. And the feeling was mutual—a record 3-million-plus fans crowding the Vet in the regular season, six raucous sellouts in the postseason.

"We're blue-collar," said Schilling, "just like them."

Most of them will be back, but with Atlanta and a young-and-coming Montreal in their revamped division for '94, they will struggle to rebottle the magic.

"I'm not sure there will ever be another season quite like this," said Schilling. "But it was great while it lasted."

Frank Fitzpatrick

2
THE
PHILLIES

The Phillies' dramatic turnaround of 1993 was a result of all the pieces, so painstakingly assembled during the dismal seasons before, fitting together into a team. As well as that team worked together, some of the players stood out for their special talents, for filling a specific gap, or for being just eccentric enough to capture the fans' affections.

Following are profiles of some of the members of the 1993 Phillies.

Lenny Dykstra

He began the game with one of those insolent, arrogant, annoying bases on balls that so infuriate a pitcher.

He struts to the plate in that bantam rooster, cock-of-the-walk stride and then he crowds rudely in, hogging all the room allotted to him and invading the pitcher's air space as well. He is begging to be hit.

He steps out, he steps in, he steps back out. He unwraps his batting glove, he rewraps it. He takes his helmet off, jams it back on. He mottles the tan dirt with dark brown tobacco spurts.

He studies his bat as if seeing it for the first time. He follows each pitch into the catcher's glove with a look of utter disdain, judging each delivery with sneering contempt.

If you are the pitcher, you want very badly to drill the little pest. You want to shout at him: "Quit stalling and step in, you little #@&%&, so I can stick one in your ear!"

Which, of course, is exactly the effect Lenny Dykstra is working for.

He cashed that walk, turned it into a run, created one more instant lead in a golden season.

On a crystal vase of an afternoon in late June, one of those daytime hooky player's delights, the Phillies got to half a hundred in wins. In a season that was still 10 games short of halfway.

The ignitor of it all is Dykstra. The first four times he batted on this day, he reached base. Three walks and a double. He scored twice, keeping a lead he would hold through the season.

The runs, he says, matter more to him than the hits.

"Even when I wasn't hitting early in the season, I was getting on base, and scoring, and that's what the leadoff batter should be doing," he said.

And so it is. Get on. Get on base, get on the pitcher's nerves, get on the other team's psyche. Get on like a rash that only itches more the more you scratch it.

Lenny Dykstra is the man of the moment, which is fascinating in a way because he has survived some big hits, including a scathing portrait of his alleged casino furies.

Either the public doesn't care, or it forgives him because of the raw, earthy abandon with which he plays. Perhaps the public is more lenient because of the times, perhaps because it lusts for a winner. Whatever the Phillies shortcomings may be, their centerfielder covers ground like wall-to-wall shag and infuriates pitchers and then converts that infuriation into runs.

Besides RBI and ERA, perhaps we need another stat: RSP. Runs Scored by Pestering. He'd lead the league.

A s he stepped into the batter's box against the Colorado Rockies one day in late August, Dykstra—as usual—had a plan. In this at bat, in the first inning, Dykstra would not take the bat off his shoulder.

It was a simple, basic way to jump-start the Phillies. Dykstra always has a plan, a design for getting himself and his teammates around the bases and across home plate.

He would come to the plate five times in this game. When it was time to hit the ball, he would be aggressive, but choosy. With his bat cocked and loaded, he would wait not only for a strike, but for his particular kind of strike.

Now, as Rockies pitcher Mo Sanford, a hard-throwing right-hander, finished his warm-up pitches and looked in to catcher Joe Girardi for the sign, he could not have known just how much Dykstra had been studying him.

Studying his pitching record, how many strikes he'd thrown, how many balls, how many strikeouts, how many walks, wild pitches, hits, runs—absolutely everything there was to know about his recent performances, and all in such a detailed way that, at that very moment he stepped into the box in the first inning, Dykstra probably knew more about the pitcher than the pitcher knew about himself.

And yet Dykstra did not stop there with his studying and planning for this at bat. He also had factored in who was catching this day and what umpire was calling balls and strikes and how he himself had been hitting lately. He does this before every game.

"Over the long run," Dykstra says, "over the long haul, if you stick with the plan, daily, you got a much better chance to be successful than if you are just out there hacking away with no idea of what you want to do. I learned that, you know, just from experience. And that's the way I approach the game."

Sanford leaned in for the sign. Dykstra adjusted his helmet with his left hand, cocked his bat aggressively at the pitcher, then pulled it back to his shoulder, loaded, as Sanford went into his motion.

Then Dykstra just waited. He had no intention of swinging.

That was the plan for his first at bat. He was just going to wait. He was going to watch every pitch go by him, no matter what, until he either got a walk or got two strikes on him and, in that case, he would switch to Plan B.

The first pitch was outside for a ball.

He stepped out, adjusted his helmet again, tightened the batting glove on his right hand, stepped back in, pointed the bat at Sanford, pulled it back, and waited some more.

Low. Ball two.

Same routine.

Outside. Ball three.

This time the waiting was easy. He was ahead in the count.

High. Ball four.

Dykstra trotted down to first, the first part of his daylong battle won.

"I know he's got a great arm," Dykstra said of his approach to Sanford. "His numbers were, well, he had a lot of walks, so I was definitely going to take until I got two strikes. I was going to make him throw strikes that first at bat. I wanted to get on base and set the tone early."

Next in the battle plan? Steal second base. "I always have the green light," he said, "and I knew if I could get a good jump, I wasn't staying around."

On the first pitch to Mickey Morandini, Dykstra took off. He slid headfirst into second. Safe. The throw was high, but Dykstra would have beaten it anyway. His 33rd stolen base of the year (he would end up with 37), but to him, no big deal.

"That's my job," he said. "That's what I do to get us an early run, you know."

And anyway, he said, the art of stealing bases is a little overrated. Again, his battle plan for stealing bases is simple and aggressive, a matter of simple and aggressive math: Pitchers take a certain amount of time to wind up and throw to the plate. Runners take a certain amount of time to run from first to second. Lenny looks at each pitcher's time to the plate and, if he can beat him, he runs. If not, he stays.

Morandini popped out to the third baseman. John Kruk singled to right, and Dykstra scored his 114th run of the season. Part one had succeeded. He had helped give his team an early lead.

Dykstra came up again in the second inning. Two men were out and pitcher Curt Schilling was on second base.

He stepped into the box against Sanford, this time with a different plan of attack. No more waiting. Now he'd be aggressive—if he got the pitch he wanted. He adjusted his helmet again, aimed the barrel of the bat menacingly at Sanford, and then loaded it just off his left shoulder.

"I went up there to hit," Dykstra said. "There was a guy in scoring position and I was sitting on an off-speed pitch."

The first pitch was a breaking ball, and Dykstra just ignored it. Ball one.

He stepped out of the box and went through his routine, tightened his right batting glove—uh-oh, not tight enough, so tighten it again—then he got his helmet straight and stepped in, aimed and loaded, and stared at Sanford.

"I'm the type of hitter, I can recognize pitches, you know? So obviously, if I'm sitting on an off-speed pitch, then the fastball is something I just let go by. If he throws it, he throws it," Dykstra said.

"It's a chance you take, waiting for a certain pitch in a certain situation, but I'll do that until I get two strikes called on me."

Many big-league hitters say they just see the ball and hit it. They don't wait for their pitch, they just try to get a good look at the ball and smack it somewhere. Dykstra does not buy that.

"Whoever says he is not a guess hitter is a liar," Dykstra said. "Not only is he a liar, he's an idiot. Anyone who says he is not looking for a certain pitch in a certain situation—that's what hitting is all about. You know? That's what hitting is all about. Recognizing pitches. And sitting on certain pitches in certain counts. That's what hitting is all about."

The 1-and-0 pitch to Dykstra was an off-speed pitch. A change-up, to be exact. Just what he'd been looking for. He lofted it high to left-field for the third out.

"I hit it good," he said. "I just hit it in the air. I hit it real good, in fact. I waited a little longer than I should have on the pitch. Sometimes you have a tendency to do that on an off-speed pitch. You wait because you don't want to get out front. I hit that ball good, and that at bat was over."

Dykstra came up again in the fourth inning with the Phils leading, 4-3, two outs, and shortstop Kevin Stocker on second base.

This time Dykstra decided to use reverse psychology on Sanford. Sanford had been feeding him off-speed pitches, mostly, so this time he would wait for a fastball and swing at nothing else.

First pitch was outside and slow. Ball one.

Second pitch, a curve. Dykstra, of course, let it go right by him and then turned around and looked at the umpire. Strike one.

Another off-speed pitch. Ball two.

Dykstra was ahead now in the count, and he was guessing that the next pitch he saw would be a fastball. He loaded the bat on his shoulder, certain Sanford would try to get a fastball past him.

Dykstra: He Makes the Phils Run

For Dykstra, for the season, the record of the team in games in which he scored no runs, one run, two, and three or more runs.

Dykstra's scoring	Phils record	
	Won	Lost
1 run	35 –	27
2 runs	25 –	2
3 or more runs	9 –	0
Total	**69 –**	**29**
No runs	28 –	35

The Philadelphia Inquirer

"I got the count in my favor," Dykstra said. "I got a fastball situation and I got it and I smoked it to the gap."

Double to drive in Stocker.

Dykstra, at that point, was 1 for 2 with a walk, a stolen base, and a run scored. And still not done.

By the time he got up in the sixth inning, the Phils were ahead, 5-3, Todd Pratt was on second, and Stocker was on first. When manager Don Baylor saw Dykstra stepping toward the plate, he trotted to the mound. Sanford was pulled and replaced by lefthanded pitcher Mike Munoz.

As Munoz took his warm-up pitches, Dykstra went back to the dugout for a minute, came back, watched, and finished his plan.

He was going to swing at the first pitch. The last time Dykstra had faced Munoz, Munoz had started the Dude off with a curve ball, and Dykstra was guessing that he would do the same thing this time.

He stepped into the box. Munoz, pitching from the stretch, bent over and looked for the sign from the catcher. Dykstra cocked the bat at him and then loaded.

Curve ball!

He had guessed right. He took a nasty cut at it and just missed, getting under it a little and fouling the ball straight back. He stepped out of the box and cursed himself, shaking his head. He had guessed right and missed.

Now what?

As it turned out, it didn't matter what pitch he was looking for now. Munoz, apparently feeling he had just gotten away with something on that first pitch to Dykstra, did not throw another one anywhere near the plate.

"He threw me four straight balls," Dykstra said, "and that was that."

Walk. Bases loaded.

Dykstra went to second on a pinch hit by Mariano Duncan that scored two runs and then advanced to third on a wild pitch. He scored his second run of the game on a sacrifice fly by Kruk.

His final at bat was in the eighth inning, and the Phils held a 6-3 lead. Dykstra does not remember much about this one.

"The game was well in hand," he said, "I hit a ground ball to short. It wasn't one of my better at bats. I was looking for any ball to hit. He [lefthander Bruce Ruffin] is throwing really good right now. His ball is really moving, so I was just looking for a ball to hit."

Not one of his better at bats. He hit it to short and sprinted down the line, thighs snapping on every stride, and was thrown out by a half step.

His day's work had come to this. One hit, two runs scored, an RBI, two walks.

Dykstra was happy after the game. Satisfied. His team had won. And he had stuck to his plan.

As usual.

Bill Lyon and Timothy Dwyer

John Kruk

On the late-summer plane ride home from Montreal, John Kruk and Denis Menke talked a little, and, as usual, the talk was of hitting. Kruk was confused. And it showed in Montreal. Once he had hit the ball with flair. Now he just flailed.

He would start his swing the usual way, bat held straight up, and then he'd start to swing, and that's when it got ugly. Like an elephant doing the jitterbug. Arms, legs, wrists, head, and hands all moving in different directions so that by the time he was done missing the ball by a mile, he looked more like a tightrope walker searching for the net than an all-star hitting machine.

In the last game of the Montreal series, he had gone hitless. Oh for four. And the Phillies had lost two out of three in Montreal. Kruk was stuck in what seemed like an oh-for-the-pennant-race slump, failing at the precise moment when his team needed him most.

So he and Menke talked.

"Menke," Kruk said, "I'm sick of making outs."

Next afternoon, Kruk came early to the Vet to take extra batting practice. Menke stood at the cage and watched. "He hit for about 20 minutes," Menke said, "and about 10 minutes into it, he started hitting the ball sharply. Which he hadn't been doing. He had been hitting the ball on the ground, and when he did hit it in the air, it would tail."

Suddenly, Kruk hit one ball after the other. No tail. He turned to Menke and said: "You know what I did?"

Menke shook his head. He had been watching Kruk hit in games and take extra batting practice for a couple of weeks now, trying to help him out of his prolonged slump, seen him make so many adjustments—

feet, hands, bats, hats, helmets—that now he could not tell what adjustments Kruk had made. If any.

"My hands," Kruk said, "I move the bat back into the hands. I've been holding the bat in my fingers, not my hands."

He went back to hitting. One shot after another. That night he had three hits against the Marlins. Next night, three more hits.

Afterward, he was standing in front of his locker, and John Kruk looked like a man who had regained his balance, a man with a new grip on life.

Someone asked about his new, slump-busting grip, and he laughed and said there was nothing new about it. "It's the way I've always held the bat. Somewhere along the way, I changed it and didn't notice. Those things happen."

"It sounds simple," said Menke, "a guy not holding the bat the way he's held it all his life, but once a guy goes into a slump he starts trying everything he can to get out of it, making adjustments here and there, and that's how it happens."

M eet John Kruk, talk-show natural.

"Thanks for fixing yourself up." David Letterman can't believe his eyes. There's his last guest, John Kruk, spread out in the guest chair like a big bag of sand, wearing worn and grungy blue jeans, a black T-shirt that advertised the rock band Steely Dan, and a baseball cap. Of course there was that fashionable two-day-old stubble.

But, hey, it's mid-September and the Krukker's off day, after all. "The Late Show with David Letterman" offered a limo ride to New York and a hero sandwich. That's it. You want him to dress up, too? Not hardly.

As Daniel Kellison, who is called a segment producer, said, "It's like pulling teeth to get John to come to New York. He hates New York. He says the best thing about New York is leaving."

But New York loves Kruk. This big ol' fat guy, as somebody standing in the street outside the Ed Sullivan Theater called Kruk, is a TV star in the making. His new fans loved Kruk. They laughed, they clapped, they waited outside the theater, hoping to high-five the guy.

John Ligato, who had been in the audience, stood behind some police barriers hoping to catch a glimpse of Kruk. Ligato didn't want an autograph or a handshake or anything. He didn't want Kruk to talk to him. He just wanted one thing. "I want to see if close up there is any sign that this guy is for real. I want to see a muscle or something. How the hell can he be a big-time athlete? That's what I want to see. But, man, the guy is a killer. I mean, he's funnier than the guys who are supposed to be fun. Give him a show."

Kruk is the perfect talk-show guest. He tells funny stories. He's not nervous, even for a minute. He shows up, he eats a sandwich, he talks, he leaves, he takes the limo home. A low-maintenance guest if ever there was one. And better yet, a low-maintenance guest in a pennant chase.

Letterman ended Kruk's five-minute segment, the last of the show, with an actual serious and pretty darned heartfelt send-off. "Thank you for coming," he said. "I'd like to see you in the Series."

"We look for personality," Kellison was saying after the show, trying to describe how guests are booked, especially the sports guests, whom Letterman clearly appreciates. "We look for a guy at the top of his game. Kruk, he doesn't have to rehearse. He has a rapport with Dave. He sits down and is the perfect guest."

While Kruk was walking onto the set, Letterman showed a montage of film clips showing the first baseman with sloppy, bulging wads of gum bursting his cheeks out or flowing like a waterfall out of his mouth. Of course, Kruk told gum stories, about how he used to chew tobacco until his teeth started falling out, about how he starts the game with four sticks and keeps adding four more after every inning. Do you spit out the old ones? Letterman wondered. Nope, said Kruk. Unless the Phils are in a bad streak. "Last year I never tasted one stick," Kruk said. Letterman laughed.

Kruk told a story about how he used to be No. 28 until Mitch Williams came along and wanted No. 28, so Kruk got No. 29. "I heard Rickey Henderson got like $50,000 for giving up a number," Kruk said. Williams gave Kruk two cases of beer. Williams wanted No. 28 because his wife had lots of jewelry with 28 on it. That's gotta be classy stuff, Letterman said, those No. 28 earrings. The story continued. Kruk didn't miss a beat. "Yeah, [Mitch] got divorced, and he went to No. 99. The two cases of beer are gone. It's a sad story really." Letterman howled. Kruk kept on talking.

About how he gets to the ballpark at one, talks trash with Larry Bowa, plays cards, spades actually. "Apparently I suck at spades," Kruk said. Letterman winced. The show is on at 11:35 now instead of 12:35. Kids might be watching. "We play for a coupla dollars and I'm in the hole for about $10,000." You gonna get this money back? Letterman wonders. "I'm not paying it," Kruk says.

And there's the story about how Kruk hates playing in Colorado's thin air. He remembers a time he was at first. "There's no air, a 3-2 count, two outs, I gotta run." Dave Hollins fouls a bunch of pitches off. Kruk gets tired of running. He turns to the first base coach, Kruk says, "and I tell him I'm not running no more. Guy tells me I have to." Letterman tells all those kids out there to pay attention because "apparently you don't have to run if you don't want to." But Kruk's got more. Hollins finally gets a hit. Kruk has to sprint for home. He slides. But, "I got no momentum so I kind of stick. Darren Daulton had to pick me up and help me into the dugout." And Letterman is cracking up. "That's an inspirational story," he says.

That's just the kind of guy Kruk is. Inspirational. And here's a final thought for TV execs. You know those pregame playoff and World Series shows? Bag them. Let Kruk do stand-up. He's a natural.

Timothy Dwyer and Diane Pucin

Darren Daulton

It was September 1983, so long ago that Darren Daulton's knees were still healthy. Trembling, but healthy.

Standing in a musty Veterans Stadium corridor that afternoon, gripping his Reading Phillies equipment bag, Daulton was about to become invisible. He inhaled and prepared, for the first time, to enter the clubhouse of the Philadelphia Phillies, soon to be National League champions. Inside, oblivious to the concerns of a 21-year-old call-up, were Mike Schmidt, Pete Rose, Tony Perez, Joe Morgan.

Manager Paul Owens noticed the youngster, saw his uneasiness.

"Kid," he said, putting an arm around a muscled shoulder, "there are four or five future Hall of Famers behind those doors. They might act like you're not even there, but don't be discouraged. Just watch them. Observe. Pick up what you can in the month you're here."

Daulton did. His September statistics read: three at bats, one single, one big lesson learned.

"I learned never to open my mouth," said Daulton. "I never said a word around those guys. It was clear that this was their team."

Now, 10 years later, Daulton has scaled baseball's evolutionary chart. He is the leader of these hellbent and hopeful 1993 Phillies. This is his team.

"We don't really have a captain," said backup catcher Todd Pratt, "but that doesn't mean much. Everyone here knows this is Dutch's team. He's the guy we all turn to."

Of all that befell the Phillies in 1993—the grand slams hit and the grand slams prevented, those 1:40 a.m. starts and those sunrise fin ishes, those Mitch Williams self-administered appendectomies and that record for never being kept off the scoreboard—of all the bizarre and inexplicable, one defining moment stands out in sharp relief, one crossroads instance that righted a listing team and kept it pointed toward a pennant.

It occurred over two games, in St. Louis, on the last night of June and on the first day of July, and it involved two starting pitchers and their catcher.

Jethro: Tommy Greene.

Schill: Curt Schilling.

And Bubba: Darren Daulton.

One after the other, Greene and Schilling were put to the torch by the Cardinals, rocked early, chased into ignominious retreat. It was happening with distressing regularity.

Daulton watched them leave, watched them trudge meekly off, heads down in abject surrender, not a whimper of defiance, not one smoldering ember of anger or disgust, and he seethed.

And then he unloaded.

The Phillies lead had shriveled. For the first time since they'd seized first place on April 11, they looked shaken, tentative, indecisive.

It was their first crisis, and how they responded would determine how they would respond to later duress. On such moments do entire seasons swing.

Privately, and out loud to reporters, Daulton lashed the two starters. He didn't identify them by name, but then that was hardly necessary.

He said they were giving in to hitters. He said they were not pitching aggressively (read inside). He said they looked scared out there. He said they were down on themselves. He said that, instead of reacting to their beatings with renewed determination, they turned tail.

Several things made this remarkable.

For one, that a clubhouse riot didn't ensue. He was, after all, challenging baseball's version of their manhood, and usually this calls for a retaliatory burst of testosterone. Instead, the two pitchers accepted their scalding and agreed that their catcher had a valid point. Either they feared Daulton, who is an imposing specimen, or they respected him, or they were able to recognize the truth when they heard it. Perhaps it was a mixture of all three.

What also made it remarkable was that it was the catcher, not the manager, who did the ripping. Jim Fregosi is strictly a behind-sealed-doors operative. He fiercely, sometimes unrealistically, defends his players in public. Virtually all criticism is meted out in private.

When he doesn't snarl back at a questioner who has so much as hinted at a possible deficiency, then his acquiescence is interpreted as a stinging rebuke of a player. It is why he commands their loyalty, why he is able to play cards and curse familiarly with them one moment and then walk down an aisle the next, with the traffic parting respectfully before him.

You suspect that the catcher acted with both the consent and approval of his manager. It may or may not have been Daulton's idea, but it certainly had the sanction of Fregosi, or it never would have happened.

What is also telling is that Fregosi takes frequent and vocal pride in his knowledge of pitching and considers the handling of pitchers to be one of his strongest assets, yet he condoned Daulton stepping forward.

With 20-20 hindsight, it is possible to look back and see that within a couple of starts after their catcher demanded courage and concentration from them, Greene and Schilling righted themselves.

Greene heated up his heater and dared hitters to catch up to it. He ended up posting the best winning percentage in baseball.

Schilling took to writing messages of combativeness and aggression on the underside of the bill of his cap, dedicated the rest of his season to the memory of Don Drysdale, the side-wheeling knock-'em-down Dodgers star who died in midsummer, and went 13 straight starts without a loss.

Clearly then, Daulton's oratory lit a flame.

The catcher was long ago identified as a leader—no, *the* leader—by the manager.

What, the manager was asked, is the single most important position on a baseball team?

"Among the starting eight, you mean?" he asked, implying that starting pitching was foremost.

Yes.

"Catcher," said the former shortstop, without hesitation. "And I got the best one in the game."

Until 1993, Daulton, who had only three at bats in '83, had never played on a Phillies team that finished within 15 games of first place. Until 1993, Daulton had never even been on a Phillies team that won on opening day.

He'd seen his friendly knee surgeon half a dozen times. He'd seen a parade of mediocre Phillies pitchers that would stretch from here to North Dakota. He'd seen just about everything a guy could see—except the sight he finally witnessed on a cold October night inside turbo-charged Veterans Stadium.

It was the sight of the Phillies—his Phillies—winning a ball game that would send them to the World Series.

They chopped up the mighty Atlanta Braves, 6-3. They finished off the most heralded team in baseball to win a National League play-off series that practically nobody in America expected them to win.

And there wasn't a man in that stadium who appreciated that triumph more than Daulton, the man who thumped the two-run double that put them ahead for good.

"I've never had a feeling like that on a baseball field," said Daulton afterward. "Never. Never. Never. Never. I went crazy out there after the last out. I've never had that kind of emotion. But I looked around, and I saw that house rocking. And that was an unbelievable feeling. You can take the personal accolades home and have pride in them. But this here is something special. This here, you can look in the mirror and say, 'Wow, we really did this.'"

But they never could have done it without Daulton, the guy with the No. 10 on his back—a guy who has truly symbolized the revival of this franchise.

"To me," said pitcher Larry Andersen, "this guy has epitomized the Phillies since he's been here."

Their lowest lows paralleled his lowest lows. As Daulton began the rise from .208 hitter to all-star catcher, Lee Thomas began assembling a nucleus around him. John Kruk arrived. And Lenny Dykstra arrived. And Dave Hollins arrived. And 20 other guys arrived to form the team that completed the journey from last place to the World Series.

But there is no mistaking which guy is the No. 1 leader of this motley crew. He is the man in the shin guards, the man who has lived through it all.

"He's like E. F. Hutton on this team," said Andersen. "When he speaks, everyone listens. He has a presence about him. It's like he's the godfather, and we're all a bunch of thugs.

"But the thing that's made him so important to this team is the respect he gets, the respect he's earned over his career. He earned it just with all he's been through, all the things he's overcome. For what he's endured in Philly, for all the injuries he's come back from, for doing what he's done the last couple of years—that's how you earn the respect he's earned."

And he earned it one more time in the pennant-clincher, with a memorable third-inning at bat against Greg Maddux—a man he called "the best pitcher in the game." In retrospect, it will be that at bat that will stand as the pivotal moment of a game this team will never forget.

Until that at bat, he had not had the kind of series he'd expected out of himself. Just three hits in 16 at bats. Just one RBI—on a solo homer in Game 5. But when he strolled to the plate in the third inning, the numbers didn't matter anymore. The bases were full. The game was scoreless. Maddux was one out away from squirming out of the kind of mess he has made a career out of escaping.

The count went to 1 and 0. And then 1 and 1, on a Daulton foul that sent Deion Sanders scrambling in the Atlanta dugout. And then 2 and 1. And then it happened.

Maddux wheeled and fired. Daulton flicked those wrists. The baseball soared into the rightfield corner for a two-run double. The noise in Veterans Stadium could have drowned out a NASA launch. And the Phillies were heading for the World Series.

"That hit just started us rolling," said Dave Hollins, whose two-run homer off Maddux in the fifth turned that roll into an avalanche. "Before the game, everybody was talking about '91, how the Pirates got shut out the last two games after they went up 3-2 [against the Braves]. So that was a big double. We scored first. It broke the barrier. Tommy Greene was pitching great. That hit took a lot of heat off."

Darren Daulton has performed a lot of feats for this team. He won an RBI title for a last-place team. He became the sixth catcher in this century to drive in 100 runs in back-to-back seasons. He started an All-Star Game.

"But those are personal achievements," he said. "That's something you can only share with yourself. Winning is something you can share with a lot of people. . . . . To accomplish something like this as a team, as a town, and to share it with three or four million people, that's incredible. The way I look at it, the more people you have at the party, the better the party's going to be."

He had 62,000 people at his on this night—every one of them screaming till their lungs hurt, chopping the fallen Atlanta Braves back south. It was a party this town waited the longest decade in its history to throw.

But it never would have thrown that bash without the man who jumped into Mitch Williams's arms at 11:17 P.M. It never would have thrown that party without Darren Daulton.

Bill Lyon, Frank Fitzpatrick, and Jayson Stark

Kevin Stocker

Near 11 P.M. on a midseason Tuesday night, not long after Lee Thomas and Jim Fregosi had watched a half-dozen ground balls hop lazily through the Phillies infield, the telephone rang in George Culver's Scranton office.

"We're calling the kid up," Thomas told the Red Barons manager.

And with those words, the Phillies did something they had hoped to postpone a little longer. This National League East-leading club installed Kevin Stocker, with just three months of Triple A experience, as its starting shortstop.

"I think that the longer we could have gone without bringing him here, the better off we were," acknowledged Thomas. "And the better off he was."

Sometimes, however, the pressure of a pennant race doesn't permit caution.

The story of how Stocker was suddenly summoned to Philadelphia and Kim Batiste returned to the bench is one filled with curiosity and frustration, hopes and error totals both too high to ignore, a little mystery, and some fascinating implications for the Phillies' future.

"I just thought it was time we found out if he can play up here," said Thomas.

"He was the complete package," said Jay Hankins, a Phillies scout who was scouting director when Stocker was the team's second pick in 1991.

Reading reports at his fourth-floor desk in Veterans Stadium in 1992, Thomas, the general manager, noticed Stocker's name appearing more frequently, and in more glowing terms.

"We were starting to get some reports on him, about what a good player he was," said Thomas. "Almost all our people took a real liking to him. Right away, they all said we might have something down the road."

That road became shorter as the reports became better. Over the winter, Thomas decided the time had come for an intense personal evaluation. Stocker, after $1^1/_2$ seasons of minor-league ball, was invited to train with the major-league club in Clearwater, Fla.

"I wanted to see him and I wanted Jimmy [Fregosi] to see him," said Thomas. "And he has the type of mental attitude, I think, that he can handle things a little bit better than most of them. You bring some guys to spring training and when they learn they're not going to make the club, they get a little flustered and let it go to their heads. This kid wasn't like that." Stocker's defense quickly impressed everyone. He had quick hands and, more important, flawless footwork. Fregosi joked that he'd better get him out of camp in a hurry, otherwise he'd be tempted to keep him.

At 23, Stocker also handled the intimidating Phils locker room with ease. "Aggressively quiet" was how coach John Vukovich characterized him. Coach Larry Bowa labeled him a can't-miss prospect, comparing Stocker to himself.

The word was spreading.

"He'd gotten a pretty good reputation, and I guess rightfully so," said Thomas. "Scouts from other clubs had seen him and they probably touted him more to us than we did ourselves. I've had organizations call and say, 'If we make a deal, will you throw Stocker in?'"

By then, Stocker was clearly the shortstop of the future. It was just a matter of when that would arrive. Publicly, Thomas said he needed a full season on artificial turf at Triple A. Privately, with Juan Bell struggling defensively already and a bulked-up Batiste showing he had lost some range, Thomas wasn't sure he could hold out that long.

"Coming out of spring training, I pretty well let it be known that I didn't think there was any way that he should come up here this year," Thomas said. "But in the back of my mind, I didn't rule it completely out."

Bell made two errors on opening day, kicked away a few more balls when the team returned to Philadelphia, and the fans buried him.

When his last error contributed to a painful ninth-inning loss to the woeful Mets, a decision was made.

Bell was placed on waivers and, while Thomas hunted vainly for a shortstop elsewhere, Batiste and Mariano Duncan played at short. The pace of errors slowed, but only slightly. Neither player had the range artificial surfaces require.

Soon after, pitcher Curt Schilling, needing something to boost his battered confidence, got no help from his infield as the Dodgers beat Philadelphia.

For 10 long days, Thomas had been toying with the notion of bringing Stocker up. Culver and everyone else whose counsel Thomas had sought kept insisting he was ready defensively.

Now, in his private box, Thomas made the decision.

"I was probably the last one that wanted to bring him up here," he said. He walked to his office and called Culver. Then he took the elevator down to the first floor, entered Fregosi's clubhouse office, and told the manager he'd be getting a new shortstop.

Stocker showed no signs of stage fright in his first game, a July match against the Dodgers. Playing shallow, with the bases loaded in the ninth inning of a tie game, Stocker short-hopped a ground ball and, off-balance, threw home for an important force out.

"He made an error on a tough play later in the game, but I can tell you one thing. No other shortstop we have makes that play in the ninth inning," said one Phillie.

It's fast, kid. Wicked fast.

"Really?" he says, attentive but not awed.

Oh, yeah. And hard. Hard and fast.

"Really?" he repeats, still leaning back on the stool, still attentive and still unawed.

Uh-huh. As a matter of fact, a lot of veterans consider this the most difficult infield in the National League, what with the grass shaved to putting-green treachery, with the dirt the consistency of interstate. The ball is on you in a blink, and it comes like hot shrapnel, hissing and hoping to cut a chunk out of you.

"Well, then," Kevin Stocker says politely, "I'll be interested to see it."

And he smiles pleasantly, his young rookie face open and eager. And you think you see just the hint of a glint in his eyes, that feral gleam that suggests the fearlessness that it takes to survive in this game, at this level.

He'll be interested to see it, will he?

"Oh, he's cocky," Larry Bowa says, smiling because he's glad the kid's cocky.

"But he's cocky without being arrogant."

Kind of like Larry Bowa was?

"No, I was arrogant," Bowa says, blunt as ever.

Bowa was also the best shortstop the Phillies have ever had, and for the dozen seasons since he left, they had been trying to find his replacement. Without success.

Until now.

Bowa was the first one to champion the kid. Liked him the very first time he saw him. Liked his quick feet and his quick first step and his quick release. Liked his awareness on the field. Liked his eagerness, his instincts, the way he studies situations.

"He knows things that most guys have to be told," Bowa says. "And you have to tell them 10, 15 times, and then tell them 10, 15 more times after that."

Exasperation thickens his voice. But then he thinks of Kevin Stocker, and the sun comes up again.

"I don't want to jinx him," he says, "but . . ."

What Bowa wanted to do was hit a boxcar of ground balls to the kid during batting practice before a hugely important series against the Braves, acclimate him to that infield that is wicked fast and wicked hard.

But it rained. All day. And the Phillies had to take their BP in a dusty cavern under the stands. No infield.

So Kevin Stocker took the field on this August night, a field he had never seen, pretty much flying blind and on his own.

Which he has been doing ever since the Phillies did what they swore they would never do, which was baptize the kid in the crucible of a pennant race.

But every ground ball hit to the left side of the infield caused them to inhale sharply. Juan Bell, Kim Batiste, Mariano Duncan—they weren't the answer to the question: Can the Phils win this division that is begging to be won with just anyone playing shortstop?

The kid has made every play so far.

On this night, the first shot ever fired at him in this ballpark is by Fred McGriff, a tricky short hop up the middle. The kid, cheating toward second, picks and throws. Just like the manual says.

In the third, he gloves Mark Lemke's hard smash directly at him without incident.

In the sixth, with the Phils nursing a 3-2 lead, the Braves put their first two on, but the kid ranges into the hole and gets the force at third.

"What I look for is consistency," Bowa says. "Forget the one-handed jump-throw from the hole. I want a guy who gets the ball that's hit right at him with the bases loaded in the ninth inning and you're up a run."

He is anxious to see how the kid reacts to adversity. They all are. You can see them watching him sideways in the clubhouse, the rest of the team. They are a pitiless, unforgiving bunch, quick to judge.

But he impressed them in spring training. They could all see the potential. And he impressed them again when he came up and took only seven days to come back after turning his ankle on the first-base bag.

"You looked at the replay, you thought it was broken," Bowa says. "And then, like that"—a finger snap—"he's back. That showed them something."

As a matter of fact, in his rush to win them over, he probably came back before he should have. The ankle is heavily taped and braced, and he walks fast to try to conceal the limp.

He's here now, and he means to stick. Already there is a change in the team.

"We'll be in a tough spot," Bowa says, "and Pods [pitching coach Johnny Podres] will be saying, 'Come on, hit it to short. Get the double play.' You never heard that before.

"It affects the way pitchers work, too. When our defense was bad, they'd go for strikeouts when they were in trouble. You do that, get a ball up, it's dangerous. Now they can keep the ball down. You see them on a ball hit to short, they'll be looking over their shoulder, but they'll be walking off the field. That's confidence."

Stocker was standing in front of his locker in the bowels of Shea Stadium, towel wrapped around his waist, talking about how satisfying it was to beat the Mets two out of three games.

Then someone asked the rookie if he was excited about going to Montreal to face the lava-hot Expos in a three-game September showdown, and he smiled a smile as wide as the St. Lawrence Seaway.

"Yeah," he said, "I've never been to Montreal before. A lot of the places I go to with the team now I'm going to for the first time."

Stocker is the rookie. He is also the anchor of the Phillies defense. The Phillies may be taking him places for the first time in his young life, but his strong glove at shortstop and consistent hitting may help take the Phils somewhere they have not been in a long time: the postseason. Then the smile came back, even wider than before.

"I'm excited about playing the Expos, too," he said. "I think the whole team is excited. We've heard all this talk about how hot they've been and now we have a chance to play them."

Stocker has played with poise and assurance since being promoted from Triple A in July. He has a quiet confidence about him that he backs up on the field with sure-handedness and a pretty gaudy .345 batting average.

He said he did not expect to be too nervous before taking the field for the very first time in Montreal. He thinks it's because he really feels like he's a part of the team now—not a rookie trying to win a spot and prove himself, but a guy who goes out and plays every day and has the respect of the team.

"Now I feel good because I feel a part of the team and it's gratifying to know that the guys treat you the same way whether you make a play to win the game or you make an error," he said.

He has earned that with plays such as the one he made in the last game against the Mets. The night before he had committed an error, a bad error because it led to the Phillies losing a game they should have won. After that game, Stocker was there in front of his locker, towel wrapped around his waist, talking about how he had plain messed up, and, yes, it was a bad mistake on his part, and, yes, he felt bad about it, and all he could do about it now was to try to just forget about the whole thing so he could come back and play the next night and not mess up again.

The next night came and he had two hits and two walks and scored a backbreaking insurance run in the eighth inning by making a daring sprint from first base to home on a little base hit to center. He came storming around third, all the while thinking, he said later, that the outfield grass was wet from a rain delay and that might give him a chance. It turned out to be such an unexpected gamble that the Mets infielder caught the throw from the outfield and casually turned toward third expecting to see Stocker there, but instead saw that he was sliding across home plate.

The bold move got him a hero's welcome from his teammates.

And that is the way the Phillies will have to play on Kevin Stocker's first visit to Montreal—bold and sassy, the way they have played all year.

He stood there with the towel wrapped around his waist, and all around him his teammates were getting dressed and heading for the bus that would take them to the airport for the flight to Montreal and their date with the red-hot Expos, and Stocker was talking about how neat it would be seeing places for the first time.

The smile was back, and there was excitement in his voice, and there was no mistaking just how much this rookie was enjoying his wondrous baseball journey.

Frank Fitzpatrick, Bill Lyon, and Timothy Dwyer

Dave Hollins

The body language says it all.

Dave Hollins stands at his locker, moments after a Phillies loss. He bites a fingernail, curses, picks up a can of beer. Curses again. Glares at the uniform he just took off.

Minutes earlier in an early-season game, with the Phils down by 10-7 and two men on base in the ninth, Hollins had blasted a drive 400 feet to straightaway center. It had landed two feet short of the fence, in the glove of Braves centerfielder Otis Nixon.

Almost a hero.

Now, alone in a roomful of teammates, Hollins picks up a bat, tries to squeeze out its sawdust, and lays it down. He sits down, puts his hands over his face, and mumbles.

"Son of a bitch!" he suddenly shouts.

No one comes by to commiserate. His teammates all know better.

Meet Mikey, Dave Hollins's alter ego.

"You stay away from Mikey," warns catcher Darren Daulton, whose locker is just a few feet away. "He'll kill you just as soon as look at you."

On most days, Hollins, the 26-year-old third baseman, is an earnest young man, eager to talk about baseball strategy or his days as a star high school quarterback outside Buffalo. He is the Phils cleanup hitter, their best pure power hitter, and a guy whom teammates would line up behind if a fight broke out.

"A great guy," Daulton says. "A great teammate."

On those days, he is David.

But when things go badly for the Phils, another Hollins shows up. This one broods. This one glares. This one curses.

This is Mikey.

"An 0-for-4 night brings out Mikey real quick," second baseman Mickey Morandini says. "An error, a loss, anything that hurts the club, and Mikey—the evil twin of Dave Hollins—shows up."

Michael is Hollins's middle name. He figures that's how the nickname started. But teammates say it came from the little boy in the old Life cereal commercials. (You know Mikey? He doesn't like anything.)

"Ah, it's been blown out of proportion," Hollins says. "Listen, I have a temper. I take the game seriously. It's a game, but it's my life, too. If we lose or I have a bad day, I don't have much to say. I'm not one for conversation."

Hollins's fuming is rarely aimed at anyone but himself. (Well, maybe an occasional opposing pitcher, too.) His intensity comes from his deep-seated desire to succeed. In a game in which the best hitters make outs two out of three times and the best teams lose 60 times a year, Dave Hollins doesn't accept the statistical realities. He has his own standards.

In 1992, Hollins's first as a major-league regular, he hit .270 with 27 homers and 93 RBIs. How does he feel about the numbers?

"OK, but I can do better," he says. His 1993 average would be slightly better, .273.

Larry Bowa, the Phils third-base coach, calls Hollins "the most intense baseball player I've ever seen." This from a guy who worked alongside Pete Rose and was known to play a few notches above enthusiastically himself.

"If you had 25 guys on the team like David, it would be tough," Bowa says. "They'd all have killed each other by the third week of the season."

Asked to compare Hollins's approach to those of other players, Bowa thinks for a moment and then comes up with the name of Kirk Gibson.

Gibson, the Detroit Tigers outfielder, has mellowed in recent years. But as a young man, he was the swaggering, gung ho, helmet-heaving perfectionist who led Detroit—and later the Los Angeles Dodgers—to World Series victories. Like Hollins, Gibson would steam after losses. And like Hollins, he would approach every game with a tremendous will to succeed.

Hollins is a football player trapped in a baseball player's uniform. "I loved football, but the colleges all wanted me to redshirt as a freshman and warm the bench for two years after that," he says. "I wanted to play right away. Baseball gave me that chance."

Hollins went to South Carolina on a baseball scholarship and became the starting third baseman as a freshman. Despite his success in baseball, despite the two-year, $2.5 million contract he signed in the spring of 1993, Hollins occasionally wonders how far he might have gone in football. In the off-season, he lives next door to Buffalo Bills linebacker Cornelius Bennett, and he maintains a friendship with Bills quarterback Jim Kelly.

"I've gone through times when I've missed football," he says. "But these days, I just block that stuff out. I'm a baseball player."

If Hollins's football mentality has hurt any aspect of his game, it probably is his defense. He is a capable third baseman with decent range and a solid glove. But he made 18 errors in 1992 and would go on to commit 27 in 1993.

The problem, Bowa says, is one of intensity.

"He'll make the great play, the reaction play," Bowa says, "but he has a tough time on the easy throws, the ones where he has lots of time. It's tough for Dave to throw at three-quarter speed. He wants to air it out all the time."

Hollins doesn't disagree.

"I'm not a Gold Glover," he says. "I'll make 20 errors a season. But if I don't hurt the team, that's okay. And I'm trying to work at it. My talent is not that good. I have to really work every day. When I've tried to play relaxed, I stink.

"I just want to come in every night beat and tired and not sit at my locker and think about how I should have run that grounder out. I hate to feel I cheated myself. I have to face myself in the mirror."

Even worse, he might have to face Mikey.

Glen Macnow

Curt Schilling

If the Phillies can't have Roger Clemens, they might as well have the next-best thing: A pitcher whose entire career was changed by Roger Clemens.

Curt Schilling will never forget the day that happened to him. He was working out in the Astrodome one morning in December 1991. As he recalls, he wasn't exactly pushing himself through the American Gladiators workout.

Then Gene Coleman, the Houston Astros conditioning coach, approached him.

"Somebody wants to talk to you," Coleman said.

That somebody was merely the best pitcher on earth. The theme of his lecture was wasting talent. Roger Clemens talked. Curt Schilling listened.

"The conversation lasted an hour, and he didn't just do most of the talking. He did all the talking," Schilling said. "I said 'yes' and 'no' maybe 30 times, but that was about it. Roger went up one side and down the other, saying, 'You're abusing your talent. You've got to remember you're playing the game to put food on the table at home.'

"Driving home that day, I thought about it. I said, 'Here's a guy who might be one of the all-time greats. He didn't have to say anything to me. There was nothing in it for him. He did it for me.' That he actually gave two cents about my career meant a lot to me. And I realized he was right. There had to be some changes made, or I wasn't going to ever get to that level."

Curt Schilling calls that conversation the turning point in his career. If it is, the Phillies won't complain.

In a way, Schilling epitomizes a starting rotation that was finally ready to keep the Phillies in a pennant race. Not long ago, he was somebody else's disappointment, somebody else's case study in potential unfulfilled.

Then Lee Thomas made another one of his famous pitching trades, swiping Schilling from the Astros for Jason Grimsley in April 1992. Like the other four members of the Phillies starting rotation, Schilling started somewhere else before growing into his Phillies job. He was passed along from the Red Sox to the Orioles to the Astros to the Phillies by the time he turned 26. "We're the Drifters," Schilling said of the starting pitchers. "We're all from different organizations, brought here in Lee Thomas's trades. We all drifted in here at the right point in our careers, looking for someone to help us turn the corner."

Before Schilling drifted into the Phillies three days before the end of spring training in 1992, he was like a thousand other guys in this game—so much talent, so little to show for it. And he knows now that he had nobody to pin that on except the guy he looked at in the mirror every morning.

"I was a malcontent for a long time," he said. "I did my own thing. I hung out with the boys. I made my own hours. I did the minimal amount of work. Basically, as much as I could avoid, I avoided. My arm alone got me to Triple A and got me a couple of shots in the big leagues. But I had to learn that no matter how hard you throw, it isn't enough to get you places."

Well, actually, it was. It got him to a lot of places—Boston, Baltimore, Houston, Philadelphia. For six years, his career was one big tradefest.

Each of those deals was supposed to be his big opportunity. But in those days, by his own admission, Curt Schilling didn't take the game seriously enough to know how to take advantage of his opportunities—until three things happened: a trip to the minor leagues, a conversation with Roger Clemens, and an all-expenses-paid trip to Philadelphia.

"There's no question that was a turning point for me," Schilling said of the chat with Clemens. "That conversation opened some doors for me, as far as being able to focus. Last year, for the first time, when I came to the park between starts, I was as focused on the work I had to get done as I was on the game itself.

"I knew I had to get to the park, I had to run, I had to do this and that, and then I had to watch for all nine innings. I wanted to go into every game knowing how I was going to pitch every hitter. There's no substitute for preparation. I finally learned that. And that had a lot to do with my success last year."

Beyond that, the local pitchin' magician, coach Johnny Podres, added the big old roundhouse curve ball to Schilling's repertoire. Then the manager, Jim Fregosi, gave him a chance to start games—and to finish them without looking over his shoulder. And when all that came together in 1992, Curt Schilling pitched as well as any starting pitcher in the game.

It would make 1993 the year the Phillies would count on him big-time, the year they'd ask whether Curt Schilling would just be known as a man who once got berated by Roger Clemens, or whether he would be known as a guy who pitched like Roger Clemens.

The relationship between fathers and sons and baseball is so celebrated that it has become part of this country's mythology. At Veterans Stadium for Game 1 of the National League playoffs, there was a poignant reminder of the essential truth behind the myth.

Schilling saved a seat for his father, Cliff. The stadium was packed, but Seat 9, Row 4, Section 314 remained empty throughout the game.

Clifford E. Schilling died in 1988 of a heart attack, complicated by cancer, at age 55, and the seat was left vacant in his honor and in his memory.

The pitcher's mother, Mary, sat next to the unoccupied seat. Her immediate neighborhood was inhabited by John Kruk's father and Dave Hollins's brother, and assorted parents and in-laws and cousins, all with some strain of Phillies blood running through their veins.

Nobody made a move toward Seat 9. Everybody understood. When Mary Schilling laid her coat on the seat, her daughter, Allison, said, "Mom." The coat was immediately removed.

During the regular season, Schilling signs a sheet before each of his starts, leaving the name of Cliff Schilling on a list for a courtesy pass. During the playoffs, that courtesy is not extended to the players. Each player is allotted 12 tickets for home games, and the tickets must be bought. During the season, Schilling's action is chiefly symbolic. Not this time.

"He'll be with me in spirit," Schilling said. The night of that game was "something we dreamed about for a long time. It just doesn't feel right that he won't be here with me."

Schilling's father was a big man, like his son, an army sergeant and a paratrooper who grew up in Somerset, in western Pennsylvania, where he played football in high school. But baseball, Mary Schilling said, was his abiding love, and he taught his only son the pleasures of the game at an early age.

After serving in the army for two decades, Cliff Schilling worked as a night auditor for the Ramada Inn chain, but open-heart surgery in 1977 forced him to retire. From then on he devoted himself to his son and two daughters, all three of whom were at the ballpark for the game. Cliff Schilling was particularly devoted to seeing the fulfillment of his son's dream, to become a big-league pitcher.

Curt played one year in college at Yavapai Junior College, a two-hour drive from the Schilling home in Phoenix, and his father never missed a game. When Schilling's father died, the coach, Dave Dagler, went to the funeral, and there he saw a side of the young pitcher he had never witnessed.

"As a kid, Curt was not the most mature person in the world," Dagler said. "But the eulogy he gave at his father's funeral was amazing. Up to that point, he had never shown me the ability to be composed, to be serious. But he did then. He said things from the heart, things that touched everybody. Baseball was their link. As I recall it, they were playing 'Take Me Out to the Ball Game' when we were coming in. That death left a big void. To his credit, Curt survived."

When he's in a pitching slump, Curt thinks of his father.

"I think he thinks of his dad particularly when he does badly, because that's the person he would want to talk to," Schilling's wife, Shonda, said as she sat with other wives of players in Section 314. "His father would always know what to say. He can talk to me, but it's not the same. I haven't seen every pitch of his career. His father saw all the development but never a major-league game. He never saw him in the majors."

Mary Schilling was on her feet as the first inning began, eating her knuckles and tugging on the brass buttons on her elegant black blouse. Her son was pitching in the opener of the National League playoffs. Nothing in his career had ever remotely matched the experience.

He struck out the first batter he faced. He struck out the second. He struck out the third. Swing, swing, swing. His stuff was good. His mother was a wreck. She spoke of her husband.

"Curt and Cliff were always baseball, always, always, always," she said, dabbing her eyes with a ball of tissue.

She was asked what her husband would have thought of seeing his son pitch in the opening game of the playoffs.

"He is watching," the pitcher's mother said. "He's watching, he's watching."

When you think of October MVPs, you think of Reggie Jackson filling the night with home runs. You think of Rickey Henderson, wreaking havoc. You think of Orel Hershiser, starting and relieving in the same series.

You don't think of a pitcher whose record reads: no wins, no losses.

But the man who was voted the most valuable player of the Phillies' stunning playoff triumph over the Atlanta Braves was a pitcher with no record at all.

What Curt Schilling did in that series was hardly reflected by his record. From the moment he struck out the first five Braves who batted in the playoffs, you began to sense that something special was happening.

And though he never wound up with an official win, he left his mark on the series like no one else—twirling 16 brilliant innings in two landmark starts in Games 1 and 5.

"I didn't even think about [winning the MVP award] until someone brought it up tonight," Schilling said after Game 6. "And then I tried to flush it out of my head right away. All I wanted to think about was that we needed that fourth win. The award wasn't something I was able to think about. I was more focused on whether I might have to pitch [in relief in Game 7] if they needed me."

But hours later, Schilling was standing on a podium in a champagne-soaked clubhouse, accepting a trophy unlike any other jewel in his heretofore-modest trophy case. And he could only shake his head at the thought of it.

"Yeah, I don't think any of the others can stand next to that one," he said, nodding toward the trophy. "That thing weighs more than I do."

What he did along the six-month marathon that brought the Phillies to the Series was invaluable. But what he did in his two starts against the Braves may have changed the entire course of his career.

"I'd say finishing third in the junior-college World Series doesn't really measure up to being National League champions," he said. "But I owe everything I've done to many different people."

And one of those people, needless to say, was his late father, Cliff. "My father is the reason I'm standing here tonight," he said. "He taught me discipline, determination to succeed, and how to pick myself up after getting down. I've spent my life trying to pay him back for what he taught me, and I don't think I can.

"It's such an unbelievable feeling, I can't even begin to describe it."

Jayson Stark and Michael Bamberger

Tommy Greene

Waiting for the first pitch of the first game of a critical mid-September road trip, manager Jim Fregosi sat on the edge of the dugout bench, arms folded tightly, rocking rhythmically, back and forth, back and forth, looking for all the world as if he were willing his team forward inch by bloody inch.

This is what happens to managers during pennant races. They can't hit, field, or throw the team out of its troubles. They just get to rock back and forth and think too much and wait for the funk to end and try not to overmanage or in any way add to the pressure that gathers around their club. And go nuts. Quietly. With as much dignity as possible.

Sometimes the pressure gets lifted in the most unexpected, circuitous ways—in ways a manager could never have predicted in a million years.

A rude fan says something to a player. The player hears it and is stung by the remark. He starts thinking about what the fan said. The remark spurs him to take action. So he decides to give advice to a younger player. The younger player, insatiably curious and always eager for advice, hangs on every word from the veteran, takes each word to heart, and the next day pitches a glittering, pressure-stanching shutout.

That's how Tommy Greene's fine pressure-shedding shutout had come about a couple of nights earlier.

It started on September 12 in Philadelphia when the Phils finished a dismal homestand and got something from fans they have rarely heard this season—boos.

"When I was walking in from the dugout after that game on Sunday," relief pitcher Larry Andersen said, "a guy in the stands yelled at me: 'Hey! Get it together, you bums!'"

It was nasty stuff—even for Philadelphia—and the players looked forward to the refuge of the road, to three games with the worst team in baseball, the Mets, before they headed on to Montreal for three games with the Expos, who were loudly nipping at the Phillies' lead.

Andersen said the fan's remark made him wonder about the state of the team. It seemed to him that the Phils had lost their way, had forgotten that they were still in command of the National League East.

"We were still in the driver's seat, but it was like we lost our map," he said.

So the next day, he walked into the dressing room and saw Greene sitting by himself at his locker, and Andersen decided that he should hand Greene a map.

"I've been trying to talk to some of the younger guys because it is something that Lefty did for me and helped me with," Andersen said, referring to Steve Carlton. "He always told me that a thought should always precede an action. Whatever your thoughts are before you do something is important. Your mind will always tell your body what to do. So every pitch, you take a second and tell yourself what you're going to do."

When Andersen arrived at the stadium, he had not planned on talking to Greene. It was an instinctive decision made when he happened to see Greene sitting there by himself. He said he doesn't usually bother to talk to pitchers on the day they are scheduled to start, but he knew that Greene was a willing and eager student of the game.

"When I was with Atlanta," Greene said, "Ted Simmons once told me: 'Don't be afraid to ask questions and don't be afraid to shut up and listen.' And that's one of the biggest lessons I ever learned in baseball."

So with the boos of Philadelphia 90 miles away, the relief pitcher sat down with Greene and unfolded his map. He told Greene that when he looked in to Darren Daulton for the sign, he should take the moment after he nods to picture in his mind just where he wanted that pitch to go.

·   "I told him he didn't have to take a delay-of-game penalty—it just takes a second," Andersen said. "And when he's pitching from the stretch, I told him to look over at the runner at first after he got his sign and take that moment. It's something that I started doing about eight years ago and it sounds easy, but I still don't do it all the time because I don't focus enough or rush."

He told Greene to try putting this into practice while he warmed up in the bullpen. And if it worked, to carry it into the game.

Andersen did not have any grand scheme for the team to regain its balance. He was not looking at the big picture, just one night in a 162-game season, just one step back to where he thought the team should be, to where it had managed to stay for most of the season.

"We had lost our sense of direction, our aggression, our intensity, our focus, and we had stopped having fun," Andersen said. "With Greene going out and doing what he did—you can only hope that it carries over to the rest of us as a team thing."

So as the game began, Fregosi was back in the same spot. He was rocking a little less intensely, though, and a little less willfully after a victory that came about in a way you will never find diagrammed on any chalkboard.

D amon Berryhill and Mark Lemke had just singled, and a murmur arose from Veterans Stadium's restless fans. Tommy Greene, a tantalizing two outs shy of a shutout, knew his night was over even before Jim Fregosi's red satin jacket cleared the dugout.

In 1991, 1992, even earlier in 1993, Greene's reaction would have been as sure as a sunrise. Those massive shoulders would sag. He would paw at the mound dirt in frustration, shake his head in self-loathing.

This time, though, Greene was unmoved. Looking Fregosi in the eye, he handed him the ball and, head high, bounced off toward the dugout.

That moment on September 24 explained, as much as anything

else, why 1993 was Greene's breakthrough season, why this sensitive young pitcher with awesome stuff had the major leagues' second-best winning percentage (.800, with a 16-4 won-lost record), why he would be starting for the Phillies against Greg Maddux in Game 2 of the National League Championship Series.

"That's always the way I was taught coming up," Greene said on the last weekend of the regular season, in St. Louis. "Not to let things get you down. I guess it just took a while to sink in.

"You know it's the mental process that's tough up here," he said. "You have to know how to concentrate out there. That's the big key. That and staying healthy."

Getting the mind in sync with the arm. That has always been the key for Greene, a simple young man from an unsophisticated town in rural North Carolina. He is the stereotypical country hardballer. Fastballs, not philosophy.

"When he has his head in the game," Darren Daulton said, "with that kind of stuff, he can be as good as anyone."

But too often, a bad pitch or a bad game would cause Greene to doubt himself. It was transparent, even though the pitcher tried hard to fight it.

"It happened. But the only times I would get really bothered out there was when I would give up a two- or three-run homer," Greene said. "I can live with giving up hits or solo home runs. If a guy hits a home run and there's nobody on base, I'll tip my cap to him. Sometimes you've got to give the hitter some credit too. But when there are a couple of men on base and I give up a home run, then I'm letting the whole team down. That's why I get mad."

Yet there are those who will tell you there is nothing wrong with pitchers displaying some emotion.

"That's okay," said pitching coach Johnny Podres. "I can remember Sandy Koufax one day gave up three home runs and he came back to the dugout and threw his glove up in the air."

Shocking.

When the 1993 season began, it seemed as if Greene had only to throw his glove on the mound to beat teams. He was the National League's best pitcher for two months. On June 5, he was 8-0 with a 1.89 ERA.

"There were times early this year, when he had that slider working to go along with his fastball, that it was a mismatch between him and the hitter," Daulton said.

However, starting with a June 10 game in New York, Greene's arm and spirit weakened. "My arm just had a couple of dead spells this year, and the deadest one started in that game in New York," he said. "Things just didn't feel right."

By July 16, he was 11-3, his ERA swollen to 3.61, his catcher criticizing him after a particularly bad game in St. Louis.

In five starts beginning June 10, he was knocked out before completing five innings three times—once in the second, once in the third, and once in the fifth.

"He got real high at the start of the season and then he fell back," Podres said. "Who knows why? Maybe it was pitching nine innings a lot. He had a lot of complete games. But everybody goes through stretches like that."

By mid-July, Greene's arm was restored to life. "I just went a couple of days without even picking up a ball," he said. Then a groin injury interrupted his recovery.

Finally, by the time September dawned, the righthander was feeling healthy and strong.

Between September 3 and September 24, with the Phillies clinging to a lead over the fast-charging Expos, Greene made five starts. He went 4-0 with a 1.97 ERA. There were two complete games and a shutout in that stretch, not to mention two huge victories over the Braves in Philadelphia and the Mets in New York.

"I didn't look at them as anything extra-special," Greene said. "That would have been putting too much pressure on myself. I just went out and did the things I always try to do, trying to get them to hit the ball to my fielders."

And he appeared to get stronger deeper into those games.

"The last couple of times out, I felt better in the fifth, sixth, seventh, and eighth innings than I did early," he said.

Greene is as serious about conditioning as any Phillie, religious about his between-game running sessions. He throws between starts, but, unlike the pitchers with his former team, the Braves, not every day.

"I was talking to [Atlanta pitching coach Leo] Mazzone the other day," he said. "He had me in the minors there, and we were talking about conditioning and whatnot. When I used to try to throw every day like that, I just didn't rebound well between starts."

The Braves, noticing that, traded him to Philadelphia. He has won 34 games and lost just 17 since then.

Timothy Dwyer and Frank Fitzpatrick

Terry Mulholland

You wait a lifetime for this day to come.

It was just yesterday, or so it seems, that you were driving your boy to Little League games, catching him at neighborhood sandlots, screaming at umpires at his high school games.

When the scouts started coming by, dropping papers on your kitchen table and talking about the pitching coach in the instructional league, you tried to be nonchalant with the old baseball men. You mentioned college, the value of a degree. But you were already imagining this day, the day your boy would be pitching in a World Series game.

"Terry's living out every wish and dream I had as a child, but never fulfilled," Terry Mulholland said before Game 2 of the World Series. He was talking about his oldest son, also named Terry, who was the starting pitcher for the Phillies in that game.

The senior Mulholland looks nothing like his son. He's a large, large man, with thick hands and a broad nose. On this night, he wore, as he usually does, sneakers, a golf shirt, a baseball cap, and a green hooded windbreaker; if you put a whistle around his neck, you'd have a high school football coach out of central casting, circa 1956.

He sat in the stands while the Phillies finished batting practice, sipping a beer from a Styrofoam cup, perspiring in the humid warmth of Toronto's SkyDome.

Terry Mulholland, the pitcher, grew up in Uniontown, Pa., a coal town in the shadows of Pittsburgh's foundries, the town where his parents still live. The senior Mulholland is a familiar figure to regulars at Veterans Stadium, and he's also known to stadium ushers in Pittsburgh, Cincinnati, and New York.

For the playoffs, against the Braves, Terry and Patricia Mulholland motored their way to Atlanta, a 16-hour drive.

Mulholland is between jobs now; he had been selling diesel engines. In he early 1960s, when Mulholland was a third baseman on the St. Vincent's College baseball team, in Latrobe, Pa., he was still clinging to his dream of the majors. Not that he was a big-time talent. He wasn't an all-American or anything.

"Neither was Terry," the father points out.

Mulholland's father, the pitcher's paternal grandfather, sold uniforms for Oliver Brothers Knitting Mills, a Philadelphia company, and managed a Pittsburgh sporting-goods store owned by Honus Wagner.

One of his jobs was to drive the Hall of Famer, long retired, to Forbes Field every afternoon.

"Maybe he could've been a big-leaguer, too," Terry Mulholland said of his father. "It was different then. You had to know somebody, had to get a break."

Pat and Terry Mulholland have five sons: two are golf professionals working at clubs, one is an architect, one is a salesman, one is a pitcher. The family is close, and people tell Terry Mulholland all the time how unusual it is for a father to count his sons among his friends.

"I don't think that's really the case," the father said. "I just think we're a little more visible than other families. Terry and I have a good friendship. But he doesn't tell me his deep, dark secrets. If he does that, it's with his brothers."

When Terry Mulholland pitched in the playoffs, he was shelled and he took the loss, but his father enjoyed watching the game.

"I can't explain it," he said. "I was much less nervous for that game then I would've been for a regular game. I'm just hoping I can enjoy this game."

The game began: A father watched his son pitch in the World Series. He wore a microphone, placed by the producers of "This Week in Baseball." He wasn't worried that the show would record his moments of angst. "They said they'll edit it," the father said.

"I know Terry's delivery," the senior Mulholland said, "but I don't talk to him about it. That's for him and Johnny Podres to talk about, a professional pitching coach." He took a sip of his beer, overwhelming the tiny cup with his massive hand.

"I was his first coach," the father said proudly.

Michael Bamberger

Danny Jackson

The end came in the eighth, in Atlanta, after Danny Jackson had gotten Fred McGriff to strike out on a wicked slider that nicked the corner of the plate and made McGriff's heart bleed. Then, on the very next pitch, he made Terry Pendleton ground out to shortstop Kevin Stocker so that things looked easy. Except that David Justice and Damon Berryhill both singled, and that was it for Jackson in the crucial fourth game of the 1993 National League Championship Series between the Phillies and the Atlanta Braves.

Phils manager Jim Fregosi came out with a purpose, motioning for Mitch Williams before he spoke to Jackson, his starter. Jackson knew it was time, knew he had pitched with everything he had, with all the smarts and power and luck that he had, and left the game with the Phils leading the Braves, 2-1. The guys in the dugout gathered to honor Jackson as he walked in, and they should have. This pudgy, maligned 31-year-old was the star of the game, win or lose for the Phils.

And, well, it wasn't easy. It was a grueling effort summoned from sheer gut and heart. The Braves went 1 for 12 with runners in scoring position against Jackson, who seemed to be constantly in trouble, constantly ready to give way, to surrender to the incredibly talented Braves. But Jackson proved that sometimes desire can beat talent.

The fifth, sixth, and seventh innings were all noise and boos and Braves baserunners and Jackson heat.

In the fifth, there was John Smoltz, the Atlanta pitcher, on second, and that was sure Jackson's fault because Smoltz had coaxed a walk off the Phillies pitcher. So one out, bottom of the fifth, Phils barely in the lead, 2-1, and Jackson pounded his glove and spit. All anyone talked about was how Jackson had gotten pulverized in 1992 by the Braves when he was pitching for Pittsburgh in the NLCS.

Jackson heard that criticism. Geez, had he heard it. Wrapped up in ice and tape and venom, he said he had pitched angry in the game. "Nobody gave me a chance," he said. "All you guys—nobody gave me a chance. Smoltz hadn't pitched any better than me, but what I heard was I had no chance. Pretty much, I wanted to go out and stick it up your rear ends. When you hear time and time again that you're no good, that kind of puts you off. But I believed in myself, and my teammates believed in me."

So that was an angry Jackson facing Jeff Blauser, and he threw impossibly hard and Blauser swung at the first pitch, a fastball, and hit the bottom of the ball if that's possible.

It went up high, high, high, and slow, too, so that leftfielder Milt Thompson could take his time and wait for the catch. That was the second out, but trouble was still around. Ron Gant was next. Jackson wiped his brow, fiddled with his cap, and threw. Ball one, ball two. Oh, about 52,000 people stood up now waving sponge tomahawks, neon tomahawks, fists, mittens, and gloves even, and Jackson threw a strike that Gant just looked at. And another that Gant fouled off, which only got the crowd cheering louder and only made Jackson throw harder. Harder than ever, a smoking fastball that might have heated up the ex-president (Jimmy Carter) and the ex-actress (Jane Fonda) sitting behind home plate. Gant swung and never came close. Jackson was walking off the mound when Gant finished his swing.

Everybody just expected that Danny Jackson would blow up at some point. In the sixth inning, after Jackson gave up a leadoff double to Fred McGriff, the guys on TV talked about how the Phillies shouldn't have left 10 guys on base so far because they were going to need a lot more runs than a measly two. Okay, so they didn't complete the thought, which was that Danny Jackson would not go unclobbered.

And so that McGriff double, of course, was the beginning of the end in the bottom of the sixth what with Pendleton and Justice due up next. Pendleton had been a killer all through this series, and Justice finally had found his hitting range. Pendleton just scorched a 1-1 pitch. You looked for it to land somewhere deep in right and couldn't figure out what happened to the ball until John Kruk held up his glove and found the ball stuck in it.

Justice took a good whack, too, and the ball hung in the night awhile, but in the cold wind it didn't carry. Thompson had another easy putout. The danger past, Jackson hit catcher Greg Olson in his ample tummy.

Strike one and strike two came immediately on Mark Lemke, then ball one and ball two came just as quickly. Both pitches were close. On both, Jackson had the fist raised, ready to pump again, but he couldn't, and the next pitch was almost disastrous. It was a high fastball. Lemke hit, the ball traveled low and hard, an uncatchable line drive, only it was foul. Jackson picked up the rosin bag, dropped it, picked it up again, then got Lemke to fly out easily to Jim Eisenreich.

Think the seventh was easier? Pinch-hitter Francisco Cabrera led off with a single, and Deion Sanders came in to run. That can distract a pitcher, having a guy on first with all that blinding gold and blinding speed, but Jackson ignored Sanders, never threw to first base. Otis Nixon sacrificed, a bunt that Kruk bobbled. Kruk's throw barely beat Nixon, and maybe it didn't. The crowd was furious and booing the whole time Jackson got Blauser to ground out and Gant to strike out again.

When the inning was over, Jackson pumped his fist. He had gone far beyond what anyone expected of him. Soon he would be handing the ball over to "Wild Thing" Mitch Williams. Soon he would be in a position to say he told you so.

And you know what? After all this time, he would tell them so. First chance he got. Yes, he would!

Diane Pucin

Mitch Williams

The score is always close, the stakes and emotions high, whenever Mitch Williams struts to the mound. Sometimes those moments are too difficult for Jim Fregosi to witness unaided, and the Phillies manager retreats to the dugout runway for a cigarette's comfort. Inactive infielders like John Kruk lower their heads and paw lazily at the dirt, pleading, not always silently, for strikes. In the stands, fans' emotions race up and down like a cheap stock.

"He doesn't have ulcers," said Fregosi. "But he's one of the biggest carriers there is."

He infuriates. He upsets. And, more often than not, Williams succeeds.

What was so disturbing about Mitch Williams on a night in late May was not merely the way he pitched against the Mets, which was terrible, but the way he reacted after being yanked.

Williams had come in with a runner on first and nobody out in the ninth. He retired the first batter he faced, then gave up Jeff Kent's sharp single to center, a bases-filling walk, and Dave Gallagher's two-run line single to right.

With the bases loaded, one out, and the 4-1 Phillies lead that Williams had inherited trimmed to 4-3, manager Jim Fregosi had seen enough.

What he saw, most of all, was a seemingly sure victory over the punchless, last-place Mets suddenly slipping away. So Fregosi made a pitching change, bringing in David West.

One of the most impressive things about the 1993 Phils was their approach to the game. They helped one another out, gave themselves up to move runners along. They thought and acted and played as a team.

Williams, accustomed to Fregosi living or dying with him in save situations, was stunned by the hook. He kicked dirt. He stormed off the mound. He acted as if it was his birthright to be given the opportunity to pitch his way out of the tight spots that he so often pitches his way into.

He looked like a spoiled little child, too caught up in himself to consider what was best for the team. It was not a pretty sight.

"Yeah, I saw Mitch," Mets manager Dallas Green said after his team had pulled out the improbable 5-4 victory. "I thought he was going to kill himself. He jumped halfway into the dugout. I was hoping he broke his toe. . . . No, he was not very happy when he left, but he earned that unhappiness."

West, on the other hand, had earned a shot at cleaning up Williams's mess by stringing together some solid outings as a setup man in the bullpen. So Fregosi gave him a chance to save the game.

And if Juan Bell hadn't botched a potential double-play grounder, or if first baseman John Kruk had been able to hold Vince Coleman's line drive—for another potential double play—West would have succeeded. Instead, Charlie O'Brien, batting .162 as he strode to the plate, lined a two-out, two-strike, bases-loaded double to left to win it for the Mets.

"I don't think that clubhouse is feeling too good over there right now," Green said of the Phillies.

No, and Williams didn't help matters any. He was still fuming— not so much over the loss, it seemed, as over being removed from a game with a save, however shakily, still within his grasp. Usually, he is most willing to talk to reporters after a game, whether he saves it or blows it. Not this time.

"Don't come down here," Williams warned. "I've got nothing to say."

Actually, he had a lot to say later, but that came behind closed doors in Fregosi's office. If we can judge by the raised-voice expletives that could be heard on the other side of the door, Williams did not go in to apologize for his childish behavior. He was furious about being lifted.

Frankly, it's about time he grew up.

The bottom line is, Mitch Williams has stopped overpowering enemy hitters. He's throwing more strikes than the "Wild Thing" we've come to know and tolerate, but not striking out as many people.

A startling statistic: Of the last 54 batters Williams had faced before this game against the Mets, only two went down swinging. Three others took sliders, a pitch Williams is using more frequently, for called third strikes.

One scout who attended the fiasco said that Williams's fastball was in the 84-to-85 m.p.h. range, about 5 m.p.h. slower than a year before.

Williams's velocity was "a little off," Fregosi acknowledged at his postgame news conference. "I did not think he was throwing the ball well."

The results would seem to bear that out.

It was an excruciating loss for the Phillies, who appeared to be breezing to a sweep of the three-game series until Williams breathed life into the moribund Mets.

"It takes 27 outs to win a game," Green said. "The game ain't over till it's over. Somebody from New York said that, if I'm not mistaken."

That's the way it goes after a game like this: The winning manager makes jokes; the loser holds a stormy closed-door meeting with his ace relief pitcher.

For the Phillies, it was a loss that focused attention on the lingering headache of a relief pitcher who needs to remember that he's part of a team.

Mitch Williams vs. The First Batter

If you held your breath every time Mitch Williams trotted to the mound in the ninth inning, take heart. His 1993 numbers were a lot better than his 1992 totals. In fact, Williams had 1-2-3 innings 14 times. A look at how he fared vs. the first batter he faced.

	1993	1992
Average	.204	.286
At-bats	54	49
Hits	11	14
Doubles	2	2
Triples	0	0
Home runs	1	1
Runs batted in	1	3
Walks	10	16
Hit by pitch	1	1
Strikeouts	14	14
On-base pct.	.338	.470
Slugging pct.	.296	.388

The Philadelphia Inquirer

While his teammates danced around a sodden clubhouse after the Phillies won the National League pennant, Mitch Williams headed for the spot where he would feel most comfortable talking about what had happened earlier in the night. He was backed deep into a corner, the deepest corner of the raucous, champagne-soaked room.

He is happiest in corners. In corners, he often sounds and acts—how shall we say this?—gracious, genial. Even charming.

On this night, he was all that. And he was proud of what the Phillies had done this season, this series: proud of how they had gone from a dead-end, last-place team, to a safe house for baseball's castoffs, to division champs, to you-had-to-see-it-to-believe-it National League champs.

"It's awesome," Williams said.

He was holding an unopened bottle of champagne

in his hand. Around him, the stuff was flying through the air like anti-aircraft spray, and Mitch Williams stood and talked about his very unusual appearance in that night's clinching Game 6.

You knew the Braves had to be licking their chops, waiting. Williams had two wins in the series before Game 6, but those were miracle wins, start-the-fire-and-get-a-medal-for-alerting-the-neighbors wins. So in Game 6, with the Phils holding on to a 6-3 lead, Williams came in to the game, and the crowd waited for the smoke.

"I did not want to put that first man on," Williams said. "I wanted to go right after him. When you got that three-run lead, you can't let them get that first guy on, because then they start thinking they can beat you."

Not that this is any different from the way that Williams usually thinks. But sometimes his best intentions lead to bases loaded and nobody out.

The first hitter was Damon Berryhill, and Williams struck him out.

On the mound, Williams could hear unusual sounds coming from the crowd. Cheers. He was two outs away from clinching the National League championship, and he kept telling his wild side to just slow down, slow the whole thing down, and don't let anyone get on base.

And for once, Mitch Williams listened to himself.

Williams got the second hitter he faced to hit a fly ball out to Lenny Dykstra in center. With the fans on their feet cheering the man they had booed all season long, he struck out the final hitter. Swinging.

Now he was in the corner of the clubhouse.

"We're a bunch of misfits," he said. "I've spent most of my life trying to prove to people that they were wrong about me. People who said that Mitch Williams could be a closer for an expansion team, but never for a contender. Well, they can go piss up a rope."

Frank Fitzpatrick, Frank Dolson, and Timothy Dwyer

Jim Fregosi

It's the time when you find out about a manager. Not when a team is doing everything right, getting those clutch, two-out hits, making spectacular, game-saving catches, winning all those extra-inning games, the way the Phillies were a month or so before.

But, in a mid-July swoon—when the big hits are few and far between, when the defense falls down in critical situations, when a seemingly insurmountable lead in the division race becomes eminently surmountable—this is when Jim Fregosi really has to earn his pay.

He is doing it by being himself, acting and managing and communicating with his players the same way he did weeks before when the Phillies were on a roll.

Walking into the clubhouse before a game these days, you wouldn't know if the Phillies were hot or cold, running away from the opposition or struggling to fight off the then-onrushing Cardinals.

Nothing had changed—except the standings. There was Fregosi, engaged in a heated card game with Larry Bowa, John Kruk, Mickey Morandini, and others. And there was Bowa, looking over at Kruk after Fregosi had pulled ahead, saying, "Okay, John, there's only one guy to get—the leader of the ship." And then, noting Fregosi's dirty look, barking at him, "Who should I let win?"

"Let your conscience be your guide," Fregosi retorted. "It depends on what you want to do the rest of this summer—barbecue in the backyard at home or work. Hey, anybody can coach third base."

And they all laughed, the way they would have weeks before when the Phillies were winning at a .700 clip and leading by 11½ games.

Don't underestimate the role a manager and his coaches play at a time like this.

"As a manager, you have to stay this way," Fregosi said, moving his hand in a straight line. "I stayed this way when we were playing good. I'm going to stay this way when we're playing bad."

That's the secret. Don't change. Don't add to the pressure the players are feeling by showing them how worried you are. Fregosi learned that as a young manager.

"It's not any easier now," he said of going through a slump, "but you know how to handle it."

"Let me tell you about managing," said Tom Lasorda, a Norristown, Pa., native in his 17th year as the Dodgers manager. "No matter how tired I might be, no matter how dejected I might be, no matter what problems I might have when I walk through that clubhouse door, I've got to put on a new face—a winning face, a happy face, an enthusiastic face. If my players see me walk in with my head down, what's the attitude and the atmosphere going to be?"

When you're struggling, Lasorda said, "that's when the job of the manager and the coaches becomes very, very important. Anybody can be happy when you're winning. Listen, I feel for Jimmy because I hate to see him lose that lead like that!"

But they all go through slumps. Those who learn how to deal with them stick around.

The key to getting a team through a bad period, Phillies coach John Vukovich said, is being yourself. If that means hugging your players after a home run or being relentlessly upbeat, the way Lasorda is, so be it. If that means getting engrossed in a pregame card game with coaches and players, trading obscene one-liners and laughing uproariously, that's fine, too.

"Jimmy's remained the same," Vukovich said. "He's probably remained the same more than anybody in the room. It takes a strong guy to do that. His philosophy has always been to make the players feel comfortable and enjoy playing. He knows it worked for three months. He's not about to change things because we struggled for a couple of weeks."

So life goes on. No signs of panic. Maybe you have to work a little harder at times like this, as Lasorda said, but whatever you do, be yourself.

"I think players read you if you're 'real,' if your real personality is there on a consistent basis," Vukovich said.

That's the key. Look at Fregosi dealing those cards, trading those wisecracks, and you'd never know his team was facing a crisis. Through it all, he has remained outwardly optimistic. Perhaps that's one reason his players have stuck together.

"I think they've been very good toward one another," Vukovich said. "That's the thing we, as coaches, have to keep together. There's been no finger-pointing.

"You can set the tone in a lot of ways. I don't think there's any one style of personality that's the way it should be, but the one thing that comes to the front—whatever your personality is, stay with it."

Fregosi has.

Frank Dolson

How The Team Was Built

Draft

1980

Darren Daulton • Twenty-fifth round pick.

1983

Ricky Jordan • First-round pick.

1987

Kim Batiste • Third-round pick.

1989

Dave Hollins • Selected from San Diego in Rule 5 draft.*

1988

Mickey Morandini • Fifth-round pick.

1991

Todd Pratt • Selected from Baltimore in Rule 5 draft.*

Kevin Stocker • Second round pick.

Free Agents

1991

Mariano Duncan
Signed in December.

1992

Larry Andersen
Signed in December.

Pete Incaviglia
Signed in December.

Milt Thompson
Signed in December.

1993

Jim Eisenreich
Signed in January.

*Players not among the 40 a team can protect during the off-season can be claimed by any other team for $50,000.

Trades

1989

John Kruk • Acquired from San Diego with Randy Ready on June 13, for Chris James.

Lenny Dykstra • Acquired from New York Mets with Roger McDowell and Tom Edens on June 18, for Juan Samuel.

Terry Mulholland • Acquired from San Francisco with Dennis Cook and Charlie Hayes on June 18, for Steve Bedrosian and Rick Parker.

1990

Tommy Greene • Acquired from Atlanta with Dale Murphy on August 3, for Jeff Parrett, Jim Vatcher, and Victor Rosario.

Wes Chamberlain and **Tony Longmire** • Acquired from Pittsburgh with Julio Peguero on August 30, for Carmelo Martinez.

1991

Mitch Williams • Acquired from Cubs on April 7, for Bob Scanlon and Chuck McElroy.

1992

Curt Schilling • Acquired from Houston on April 2, for Jason Grimsley.

Ben Rivera • Acquired from Atlanta on May 28, for Donnie Elliott.

Danny Jackson • Acquired from Florida on November 17, for Matt Whisenant and Joel Adamson.

David West • Acquired from Minnesota on December 5, for Mike Hartley.

1993

Roger Mason • Acquired from San Diego on July 3, for Tim Mauser.

Bobby Thigpen • Acquired from White Sox on August 10, for Jose DeLeon.

3

THE SEASON

The First Half

A nyone who believes that on Opening Day the hearts of all ballplayers pound like boom boxes never met Terry Mulholland.

The laid-back Phillies lefthander takes a steely focus to the mound.
He can block out bad weather, daunting foes, even unfriendly ballparks.

So with a first-night crowd of 44,560 bringing a new season's optimism to Houston's aging Astrodome, with an ex-president seated in
his sights, with a nationwide television audience observing, Mulholland
hardly noticed.

He limited the Astros to four hits and a single unearned run as the
Phillies defeated Houston and nemesis Doug Drabek 3-1, for their first
season-opening victory since 1984.

"Even before I got to the ballpark, I knew there was going to be a
crowd here," Mulholland said dryly when asked about a third straight
Opening Day start. "I also knew I'd be facing big-league hitters. But I
did that for the last four weeks of spring training, anyway."

Mulholland moved closest to tension in the bottom of the
eighth when a two-out double by pinch-hitter Chris James and Juan
Bell's second error of the night left Houston with the tying run at third
base.

As Gov. Ann Richards, ex-president George Bush, and thousands
of less-famous Texans stood and yahooed, Mulholland merely waved

his hand toward his infielders, appealing for calm. He then got Steve Finley on a grounder to second.

Said catcher Darren Daulton: "I went out to talk to him [after Bell's error], and I said, 'Mo, it looks like we're going to give them five outs this inning.' He just said, 'Don't worry about it, we'll be okay.' When he is focused out there like that, he just doesn't let anything deter him. That was one of the best games I've ever seen him pitch."

It was another Bell error, with two outs in the first, that had given Houston its only run and a brief 1-0 lead. But Mulholland remained unaffected after the sometimes erratic shortstop's second error.

"You can do two things in that kind of situation," he said in an even, controlled voice. "You can say, 'Why me?' That's not doing yourself any good, and you're sure not doing the guy who booted it any favors. Or you can tell yourself that you know he didn't mean to throw it away and go on from there. I had a good spring, and I told myself that I'm not going to let anything distract me from my goal, and that's to get myself and my team into a World Series."

They won't get there after a lone victory, of course. And they probably won't get there until they can answer the questions about shortstop that lingered through training camp.

"Hey," manager Jim Fregosi said, reluctant to cast a negative light on his club's debut victory. "You might find this hard to believe, but even I made an error or two."

Frank Fitzpatrick

They've persuaded Mickey Morandini to hit down on the ball. Sometimes, though, he just can't resist.

It was April 8, the third game of the regular season, and the unlikeliest Phillie slugged a game-tying two-run homer off junk-tossing reliever Doug Jones in the eighth inning, then scored the winning run as the unbeaten Phils rallied for a 6-3 victory in 10 innings and a sweep of their season-opening series with Houston.

"You can't chop down on the ball all the time," Morandini said.

Pete Harnisch had stifled the Phillies on one hit through seven innings before Morandini's homer.

Jose DeLeon escaped a bases-loaded, two-out fix in the ninth when Steve Finley lined out to Milt Thompson. The Phils then went ahead in the 10th when Thompson's line-drive double cleared the bases and gave them a 6-3 cushion.

"It was nice to be able to contribute," said Thompson, who was 2 for 3 after going 0 for 4 in the opener. "I didn't do much in that first game the other night."

Mitch Williams picked up his second save in as many nights with a scoreless 10th.

So, these surprising Phillies will play their home opener at a sold-out Veterans Stadium having started a season with a 3-0 record for the first time in 23 years. The beginning is even more improbable, since the Phils had to beat Doug Drabek, Greg Swindell, and Harnisch—in a park where they traditionally scuffle for runs.

"Realistically, I would have been happy to have started out with two out of three," said Phils manager Jim Fregosi. "This was very nice."

Philadelphia, which had come back from a 3-0 deficit on Morandini's homer and an earlier one by Darren Daulton, missed chances to take a 4-3 lead in both the eighth and ninth innings—first when John Kruk was thrown out at the plate, and then when Luis Gonzalez, who also had a pair of homers and a single, grabbed a Lenny Dykstra bolt at the wall in left-center.

The bullpen, a spring trouble spot for the Phils, almost gave the game away in the ninth. David West yielded a single to Gonzalez and, two outs later, DeLeon hit pinch-hitter Chris James and walked Craig Biggio before retiring Finley on the liner to a perfectly positioned Thompson with two outs.

It was a third straight strong starting effort by a Phillies pitcher. "Our starters are really doing the job," said Morandini, "but it seems like whoever we bring in is contributing in some way or another."

Frank Fitzpatrick

The rightfielder was missing for 2¹/₂ hours. The manager's door crashed shut. Fans booed the shortstop during the pregame introductions and the starting pitcher a few rocky innings later.

This was the Phillies home opener, and it wasn't supposed to turn out like this. This was to be a day of raucous welcomes, not slammed doors. A day when a sellout crowd at Veterans Stadium was supposed to cheer its 3-0 team all day, not leave early.

The Phillies' 11-7 loss to the Chicago Cubs began in cheerful sunlight and concluded beneath sullen clouds. Yet, unbeknownst to the largest opening-day crowd ever at the Vet—60,985—there had been dark clouds hanging over the game long before the gates opened.

Wes Chamberlain overslept and didn't arrive in the Phils clubhouse until 1:51 P.M.—1 hour, 14 minutes before the scheduled start and 2 hours, 11 minutes after he was supposed to be in uniform.

"Everybody was in a good mood, we were 3-0, and then I had to go and let everybody down," Chamberlain said. "I feel like hell."

So instead of enjoying the opener's pregame atmosphere, Phils manager Jim Fregosi was left with a lot of unpleasantness. He had to insert a new rightfielder into his lineup (Pete Incaviglia), find Chamberlain, fine Chamberlain, and then deal with whatever clubhouse commotion Chamberlain's tardiness created.

And while players were reluctant to discuss the matter openly, some said privately that they expected an apology from Chamberlain—one that the benched rightfielder promised he would deliver.

Fregosi's mood improved briefly after the game began. The first of two home runs by Darren Daulton—a potent wind blowing toward rightfield helped the two teams combine to tie a stadium record with eight—provided the Phils with a 3-0 lead in the first inning.

"He's really swinging the bat so well now," Fregosi said of Daulton, who collected five RBIs with his second and third homers of the season.

But Phils starter Ben Rivera never looked like himself in his brief but painful first 1993 outing. With the hitter-friendly jet stream howling toward right, Jose Vizcaino, the Cubs' weak-hitting second baseman, tied the score with a three-run shot of his own in the bottom of the second.

With one out in the third, Rivera, reluctant to use his rising fastball because of the wind, permitted a single to Mark Grace (2 for 4 with a two-run homer), a homer to Derrick May (3 for 4 with two homers and five RBIs), a triple to Sammy Sosa, and an RBI single to Steve Buechele.

That was it for Rivera. And as those long strides carried him off the field, the crowd, which booed Juan Bell both during introductions and after a strikeout, did the same to the soft-spoken righthander.

"I felt like I had good stuff, but you couldn't throw a high fastball because of how the wind was blowing to rightfield," Rivera said. "You had to try to keep everything low, and sometimes I didn't do that."

Neither did Cubs starter Frank Castillo, who, in addition to Daulton's first homer, gave up two more—to John Kruk and Lenny Dykstra—before leaving with one out in the fifth and a 6-5 lead.

Trailing by 9-5, the Phils closed to within two runs in the eighth, when Daulton clubbed a two-run homer to right off Paul Assenmacher, who usually stifles him.

But the bullpen, which figures to be a lingering question mark for a team with division-title aspirations, let the Phils down again. This time, it was Tyler Green, making his big-league debut. He allowed Grace's two-run homer in the ninth for the game's final runs.

Frank Fitzpatrick

They are a team that can look like the Big Red Machine one minute and like so many frightful Phillies teams of the past the next.

There are so many things about the current Phillies that get your hopes up. But they aren't exactly perfect, either. Their bullpen definitely can make you squirm. And it is hard not to notice that their shortstop went into the first weekend of the regular season with more errors (two) than hits (none).

Their trainer's room is a lot emptier now than it will be in six months. And as much fun as that three-game sweep in Houston was, it was only the beginning of a season that stretches way off into the distance.

Nevertheless, there still is reason to believe that this Phillies season might be different from so many of the seasons that came before it. In fact, there are a lot of reasons. So here they come—Nine Reasons Why This Year's Phillies Might Be for Real:

1. The Division. It would be one thing if this team played in the National League West, with the Braves and the Reds and the Astros and the Barry Bonds Giants. But the Phillies play in a division with a bunch of teams that don't look a whole lot better than the clubs around them. It is not going to take 105 victories to win the NL East. So you don't have to be a super team. You just have to be a good, solid team—which the Phillies are eminently capable of being. "We play the West so many times, I think whoever plays the West better could wind up winning this thing," Curt Schilling said.

2. The Schedule. If ever the Phillies had a schedule designed to get them off to a good start, this is it. No road trips longer than three games before April 28. Fourteen of the first 20 games at home. Lots of games early against teams that figure to bring up the rear in the NL West—the Padres, Dodgers, and Giants. Only three games in April against the Reds and none against the Braves. In fact, the first three games of the season in Houston looked like maybe the Phils' toughest series of the first month, and they wound up sweeping that—which didn't hurt their frame of mind any.

3. The Offense. The Phillies were second in the league in runs scored in 1992, with Lenny Dykstra playing only half a season. So with Dykstra back and the bench much deeper, there is almost no question that the Phillies will score more than enough runs to win. "What's good about our lineup," John Kruk said, "is that most of us have guys hitting behind us where you can't pitch around any one of us and get to the next guy—because there's danger in facing any one of us, just about."

4. The Catcher. Everybody thought Darren Daulton had a career year in 1992. He has given every indication this year, right from the first day of spring training, that he might be ready to have even a better year—assuming that no one steamrolls him at the plate any time soon. "He's more confident than ever before," hitting coach Denis Menke said. "I don't think last year was any fluke at all. I think he's just going to get better. You could be looking at an MVP, I think."

5. The Bench. "Last year," Kruk said, "when we lost Lenny and some other guys, we couldn't replace them. This year, I think we're more prepared to handle an injury. God forbid, if something happened to Lenny this year, we've got someone to take his place." If there is one big difference between this Phillies team and the teams of the last few years, Terry Mulholland said, it is that "now we have 25 major-league ballplayers on this club. You look at the roster last year and a lot of guys were here just because you need to carry 25 guys."

6. The Chemistry. Chemistry alone may not get you to the World Series. But it doesn't hurt. "This is as close a ball club as I've ever seen," said Menke, who is in his 34th season in baseball. "They just fit. They belong with each other. They're perfect for each other. We've got some veteran guys in here who weren't here before, and this team just got together right at the beginning, and it's stayed together."

"It has a lot to do with the guys they went out and signed this winter," Schilling said. "I think they had in mind the type of players they wanted. And those guys fit like a glove on this club. It's not necessarily the best team that wins every year. Sometimes it's the team with the best chemistry."

7. The Rotation. Okay, so the Phillies can't run five proven starters out there every night like the Braves. But outside of the Braves, who can? The one thing the Phillies have going for them is that at least their rotation now is made up of five guys who have had success in the big leagues at some time or other. "At least we're not putting any high expectations on someone who hasn't done it before," Schilling said. "No one's expecting us to do anything we haven't shown we're capable of doing."

8. The Law of Averages. After all the things that have gone wrong for this team since the 1990 season, wouldn't you think it's almost due for something to go right? "Yeah, but the problem with the law of averages," Mulholland said, "is that if you're looking for the law of averages to help you, now you're trying to rely on luck. And I believe you make your own luck. That's the difference when you have a deep team. No matter how strong your No. 4 hitter is or your No. 1 starter is, you're only as good as your weak links. To me, we have no weak links."

9. The City. One final thing this team might have going for it that other Phillies teams haven't had is a town full of people who actually are ready to (gulp) like it. Compare them with the other teams in this town and the Phillies suddenly will look downright lovable if they win at all. "To me, this team personifies this city," Schilling said. "It personifies the blue-collar, hard-work ethic of this city. We go out and try to earn every penny we make. There are no loafers, no Cadillac-ers on this team—because no one on this team will let that happen."

Of course, if all eight regulars break their legs or the bullpen self-destructs, none of this will matter. But if the Phillies proved one thing in the season's first week, it is that they offer legitimate reason for hope. And it sure hasn't been every first week of a season that you could say that.

Jayson Stark

Six players had at least two hits. The rightfielder, with the game scoreless, threw out a runner at home with a one-hop strike. The starting pitcher went six solid innings.

For the Phillies, it was another typically successful night at Veterans Stadium—typical for the young season, but not for the franchise. The Phils, after the April 14 game, were 8-1 for only the second time in the team's 111-season history. The other time was in 1915, the year the Phillies won their first pennant.

With Ben Rivera pitching six shutout innings and Wes Chamberlain and Mariano Duncan each delivering three of the team's season-high 16 hits, the Phillies defeated the sagging Cincinnati Reds, 9-2, before 21,111 at sometimes-rainy Veterans Stadium. They completed their first sweep of the Reds in Philadelphia since 1968, back in the days of delightful Connie Mack Stadium and dreadful baseball teams.

With their 8-1 start, the Phillies have:

■ Made people forget that their starting pitchers had the second-worst ERA (4.11) in the league in 1992. Thanks to Rivera's six scoreless innings in this game, the starters' ERA was 2.63.

■ Moved seven games over .500 for the first time since May 27, 1990.

■ Increased their winning streak to five. In 1992, they didn't have a five-game winning streak until late September.

"We're 8-1, and the chemistry's working," said Chamberlain. "Everyone is so anxious to get to the ballpark; everybody's coming nice and early."

It was Chamberlain, of course, who arrived late and was benched for the home opener. But no one has the heart to bring up the matter any more.

Sam Carchidi

Meat Loaf's lusty screams exploded out of Curt Schilling's CD player. Larry Andersen screamed along. Wes Chamberlain, clutching a postgame pitcher of beer, danced across the clubhouse floor toward his locker. Laughing players stuffed belongings into red-and-blue suitcases that all of a sudden bore the logo of a first-place team.

A 5-1 homestand successfully completed, the Phillies giddily prepared, for the first time in most of their memories, to take just a little swagger with them on the road. When they arrived in Chicago's O'Hare Airport on April 14, this club of experienced losers owned baseball's best record.

"It will be nice to go into a town not wagging our tails between our legs," said general manager Lee Thomas.

In April 1992, on their initial trip to Chicago, it was a downcast and tail-wagging Phillies team that showed up for a four-game series. When their chartered plane touched down late that Easter night, the Phillies season was, for all practical purposes, already over. They were 4-7, and their leadoff hitter and most of their rotation were hurt. In last place, they were 5 $\frac{1}{2}$ games back. That afternoon they had been beaten by the

Pittsburgh Pirates 11-0, their fifth straight loss. And, after the embar-rassing defeat, Thomas delivered a locker-rattling clubhouse sermon.

"I remember that, man," said Mariano Duncan. "I couldn't even sleep once we got to Chicago. All you did was think about how bad we were playing. It was a terrible time."

Things didn't get much better on the rest of the Phillies road trips. A Phils visit to any city was met by the intense lack of interest that only a last-place club can generate.

"It's nice to be able to walk into any clubhouse, on the road or at home, and be able to hold your head up," said Mitch Williams, so dis-couraged during a 2-11 West Coast trip in '92 that he blasted team management.

"Last year we couldn't hold our heads up anywhere we went," he said. "I don't know if you noticed, but we were not featuring a real pretty team here last year."

Now, the Phillies locker room is frequently as raucous and relaxed as it used to be dreary and downbeat. In '92, the only songs heard regularly were the mournful wailings of Williams's favorite country artists. Now, Schilling's cranium-crashing rock music dominates the atmosphere.

"You never heard it like this last season, did you?" Schilling asked, pointing toward the CD player's overworked volume control.

The marked change is, of course, due to the improved fortunes of the 8-1 Phillies. But Williams contended that the new atmosphere was also a by-product of a lesson imparted by the painful '92 season.

"If you don't learn to hate losing," he said, "you can never learn to love winning."

This buoyant mood, like their winning streak, is a fragile thing, though. It is likely to vanish and reappear many times during the long, long 162-game season.

"The atmosphere is great in here now," said Darren Daulton. "But we've got to remember it's a long season. You never know, we could lose seven games in a row."

Frank Fitzpatrick

The Phillies blew another ninth-inning lead with their bullpen ace on the mound. They went seven straight innings, from the sixth through the 12th against five San Diego pitchers, without getting anything close to a hit. They walked the leadoff Padres batter in the 12th, and again in the 14th. They failed to turn what had the look of an easy double play on Tony Gwynn's sharp grounder to second in the 14th, and let Gwynn steal second and third with one out and Gary Sheffield coming up.

And still they won.

This must be the Phillies' year.

From the time Darren Daulton lined an RBIs single to right with one out in the fifth until Milt Thompson rifled a single to center with one out in the 13th, 28 Phillies went to the plate without getting a hit. When Thompson finally delivered his, Padres centerfielder Derek Bell was so surprised by the sudden show of offense that he let the ball scoot through his legs for a two-base error.

And even then, with the winning run on third and one out, the Phillies were unable to bring the marathon to an end, stymied by Jeremy Hernandez, who smothered Mariano Duncan's hot smash that appeared headed for centerfield and victory, turning it into the inning-ending out.

Frustration after frustration, goose egg after goose egg, inning after inning. Sure, nobody said winning the division was going to be easy. But is beating what's left of the thrift-conscious Padres supposed to be this hard?

Not to worry. With the natives settling in for an all-nighter, Phillies manager Jim Fregosi flashed another hit sign on 3 and 0, this time for John Kruk's benefit.

Kruk connected. The ball took off toward right centerfield, high and deep. On a night when nothing seemed to be carrying—where's Wrigley Field when you need it?—the fans held their breath.

But this one had the distance, landing against the Pirates logo. Another extra-inning victory was in the bank. Jubilant Phillies came tumbling out of the dugout to thank Kruk for letting them go home to their wives and children.

"You play 162 games, you're going to have some bad games," Lenny Dykstra had said before taking the field. "The key to winning in this league is being consistent over the long haul. It's not just a one-day thing. . . ."

Nope, sometimes it's a two-day thing. But hey, the harder you work for it, the sweeter it is.

The feeling around this Phillies team, Dykstra said, was similar to that of the world champion '86 Mets—a feeling "that we're better" than the other team. "That's the way we feel in here," Dykstra said. "We believe we're going to win when we come to the ballpark every night. The thing is, it's somebody different all the time. That's what it takes."

Frank Dolson

The best catcher in baseball was dressed like a downhill racer. Darren Daulton's base clothing layer for an April 23 game against the Dodgers consisted of metallic blue tights, apparently pasted on. Goggles, and he would have been dressed to schuss down a mountain.

One by one, from the sitting position, he hefted four burgundy-colored bats, testing them, searching them for hits. A quick chop, and maybe a line single can be squeezed to the surface. Two wrist cocks, and perhaps a double in the gap can be coaxed.

He chewed his gum and he smiled and he went through the burgundy bats and he strode down the chute to batting practice, with just the right swagger, his stride one of anticipation. Game time could not come soon enough.

These are promising nights for the Phillies and the best catcher in baseball. For the first time in seasons without end, they have that certain unmistakable look.

"Uh-huh," Darren Daulton confirmed. "You can feel it. For the first time, we expect to win, every night."

They radiate that feeling, too. Nothing spoken. No, you sense it in their manner, their bearing, their body language. Gone is the dour gloom of clubhouses past, of players sullen and sulking. Those teams had the heavy, stooped gait of a chain gang. They came to work expecting to lose. Rarely were they disappointed. "Not a good feeling at all," Daulton said, frowning at the memory.

But now . . .

"Now we never feel we're out of a game," he finished.

You cannot precisely identify this look, or give a name to all of its components, but you have seen it before. It is a look that usually finishes a season sprayed with champagne.

Darren Daulton resolutely works his gum and hefts his burgundy bats, and he nods his understanding. He knows exactly what it is that you fumble to explain. This time a year ago, the Phillies were, typically, already below .500 and sinking, the season over before it ever began.

"And six and a half out, too," Daulton said, smiling.

Of course, it is impossibly early yet. And April is the month of mirages. April roses have a way of turning into withered dandelions by August. The Phillies had played only 15 games, which meant that something on the order of 10/11ths of the season remained. No other sport offers more sustained opportunity for self-destruction than baseball. And no other team has sustained such an unremitting run of crippling injuries, especially to its pitching staff.

You could argue that they are overdue for favorable fortune.
Jim Fregosi played in 1,902 games and has managed more than
1,200. So he is qualified to identify that certain look. He leans leisurely
back in his chair, in the slow, measured manner of a man who has run
this marathon many times before.

"They are surprised when they don't win," Fregosi said, and then
slowing his speech for emphasis, added: "And they're upset when they
don't."

That has not been the case at the Vet for most of a decade.

"All the signs so far have been positive," the manager affirmed.
"They're a close-knit group. The atmosphere in the clubhouse is more
important in baseball than any other sport." True enough, but talent
helps, too.

You have to search harder than usual to find holes in the Phillies
now. There appear to be only two obvious ones, at shortstop and in the
bullpen. Neither is necessarily a fatal flaw but could become one, especially if the team finally comes to a September of significance.

On April 23, Mariano Duncan became the third different shortstop
to start, and it was his bat that got him that. But then, aren't the Phillies
always looking for a shortstop? When you think about it, they have never
satisfactorily replaced Larry Bowa. They think they have uncovered his
successor at last, but Kevin Stocker is young and just getting acclimated
to artificial turf in Scranton.

As for the bullpen, Fregosi said, it has been more than satis-
factory so far. Still, age and question marks lurk behind the Plexiglas
of the rightfield fence. Other than that, the Phils seem sufficiently
equipped.

Of course, their starting pitching could blow up again.

And they have not yet encountered a sustained stretch of misfortune, which is inevitable, and which, finally, will be the acid test of
whether this is of lasting substance or just another false spring.

Bill Lyon

On the night of April 26, San Francisco reliever Bryan Hickerson
snatched Wes Chamberlain's bullet out of the damp air for the third
out of the sixth inning and spiked the ball. If he intended it to be a triumphant gesture, it didn't work.

Aroused when Hickerson slammed down the ball at a point in the
game when they trailed by 8-3, the Phillies rallied for six runs in the

next four innings to record a remarkable 9-8 victory in 10 innings at Veterans Stadium. At one point, they had trailed 8-0.

"It fired up a lot of guys," Dave Hollins said. "It was one of those times when a team is sleeping and you don't want to try to wake them up. That got a lot of guys pumped on our bench."

Giants manager Dusty Baker said he didn't believe that his reliever had intended the spike to show up his opponents.

"He wasn't spiking the ball at them; he was spiking it at himself," Baker said. "If the opposition takes it the other way, that's their prerogative."

The Phils' comeback victory, their fourth straight win and their 14th win in 18 games, was their most improbable in this so-far improbable season. It required 4 hours, 33 minutes. It came despite 14 walks by six pitchers and three errors by Hollins.

"It was 10 on 8 out there tonight with me playing for us," Hollins said. "We're just lucky they didn't hit a ground ball to me at the end."

The winning run scored in the 10th after both clubs had exhausted their supplies of position players and used most of their relievers.

Juan Bell, who had walked to start the inning, moved to third on Jim Eisenreich's single off reliever Gino Minutelli and a throwing error by shortstop Royce Clayton. Then, with Hollins at bat, Minutelli unleashed a wild pitch, and Bell scampered home to a tumultuous welcome.

"That was unbelievable," said the Phils' Curt Schilling. "That's one of those games you can live on for a while."

Trailing 8-0, the Phillies had begun their comeback in the sixth with three runs. Mariano Duncan's double and Pete Incaviglia's single were the big hits. Chamberlain's line-drive out, with runners at second and third, temporarily halted the rally. But Thompson's two-run single sparked a four-run seventh. Then, in the eighth, Mickey Morandini tripled with one out and Eisenreich poked his second RBI single to tie the game.

Once again, the Phils bullpen, roughed up early in relief of an ineffective Ben Rivera, stifled the opponents in the late innings. David West struck out three and permitted no hits in the eighth and ninth.

The first 2½ innings lasted 90 minutes, and the score was 4-0. The game was without electricity, and suddenly, the stadium appeared to be moving in that direction, too. A large bank of lights atop the roof in rightfield went out in the third inning. Play, unfortunately, continued, and power, if not interest, was soon restored.

Jose DeLeon continued the Phils walkathon in the Giants fourth.

Matt Williams and Barry Bonds (for a third time) drew bases on balls. With one out, Hollins's second error—he booted Robby Thompson's ground ball—loaded the bases. Clayton's single made the score 5-0, and Kirt Manwaring's sacrifice fly made it 6-0.

While rain fell just hard enough to further annoy the scattered fans but not hard enough to cause a delay, the Giants continued to take laps around the bases. Their lead grew to 8-0 in the sixth on a walk to Thompson—the 10th walk issued by Phillies pitchers—Clayton's triple and Jeff Brantley's second RBIs single.

The Phillies started to roll in the sixth. Morandini walked. John Kruk singled him to third, then limped off the field. Hollins scored Morandini with a sacrifice fly. After Darren Daulton walked, Incaviglia singled in pinch-runner Eisenreich.

After Duncan's double, pinch-hitter Chamberlain scorched a line drive that found Hickerson's glove. Hickerson took the ball and spiked it. That seemed to infuriate the Phils. When Incaviglia walked to the outfield, he glared at the Giants.

The aroused Phils got four runs in the seventh on three walks, an RBI single by Eisenreich, Thompson's two-run single, and an error by Mike Benjamin at second base. That left them trailing by 8-7 as the game plodded toward four hours.

Morandini's triple with one out in the eighth and another RBI single by Eisenreich tied the score.

Frank Fitzpatrick

M onths later, people would still be talking about "The Catch" of April 29 in San Diego.

The ball left relief pitcher David West's hand and jumped off Bob Geren's bat toward the leftfield seats like a well-struck Titleist. Centerfielder Lenny Dykstra took a few reluctant steps before his shoulders sagged. Back in the infield, Mariano Duncan quickly assessed the situation.

"Uh-oh," the second baseman said.

There were two outs in the bottom of the eighth, the Phils ahead by two runs. But San Diego runners filled the bases—and the ball kept soaring.

Suddenly, like some late-arriving superhero, a streaking Milt Thompson appeared at the base of the leftfield wall. He leaped. His left hand reached above the top of the Jack Murphy Stadium fence, above the orange stripe there. The ball descended, going over the fence. Thompson's large glove snapped shut on it.

That's how a potential game-breaking grand slam became instead the third out of the eighth inning. And that's how the Phillies held on to defeat the Padres, 5-3.

"It's unbelievable," Duncan said. "Every day, every game, it's something different."

On this day, it was Thompson, who entered the game hitting .185. He not only pulled off the game-saving catch, he also had three singles, including one that sent home two runs in the Phils' four-run third.

"It's been a long, rough, emotional road," said Thompson, who fretted publicly about his offensive ineffectiveness after many early-season games.

"You've got to relax, but mentally it was tough to do that. But I've been through these kinds of things before, and I know you just have to be patient."

Thompson's catch came in a spot where, in 1992 for sure, the game would have slipped away from the Phillies.

"I knew [Geren] hit it good, but I was still going to try to get it," Thompson said. "I can't explain how I caught it, I just did."

After the play, he pumped a fist and jumped excitedly into the air. Dykstra, shocked and ecstatic, bear-hugged him. Phillies players emptied the dugout. The Padres were dead even before Mitch Williams came in to pitch a one-two-three ninth for his ninth save.

Frank Fitzpatrick

Darren Daulton and Lenny Dykstra, frustrated and perplexed by long funks, awoke on the night of April 30 as the Phillies rolled merrily along with another amazing victory, this one by 7-6 over the Los Angeles Dodgers.

Daulton drove in three runs, and his two-run homer in the eighth inning—his first since the season's opening week—broke a 5-5 tie. Dykstra singled, doubled, walked, and scored three times in the first five innings.

This latest remarkable victory was preserved in vintage Mitch Williams fashion. Williams allowed one run, loaded the bases, and left the mound for several minutes to replace a broken shoelace.

Then pinch-hitter Mike Sharperson appeared to have won the game for the Dodgers when he ripped a shot back through the box. But

Mickey Morandini made a great diving catch and doubled off Mike Piazza at second.

Williams then retired Brett Butler on a grounder to short to record his 10th save and third in three days.

Ho hum. Just another evening at the ballpark.

Frank Fitzpatrick

Welcome to life with the first-place Phillies.

Torn away is the mask of relative obscurity that consistent losing provided them. With baseball's best record as May dawns, Phillies players and coaches are stopped on the street for hugs and handshakes. There are fewer hours of sleep and more phone calls. Fans, reporters, charities, collectors all want their thoughts, their autographs, their time.

"Life is all about winning," explained Lenny Dykstra. "When you're winning, everyone wants a part of you. That's just normal."

Perhaps it is for Dykstra, who underwent this same experience with the world-champion New York Mets in 1986. But for many with these Phillies, life at the top is an unusual experience.

"I was at a PAL awards dinner the other night," said Phils president Bill Giles, "and for the first time in years, people were coming up and congratulating me."

"I love it," said Curt Schilling. "People are more interested in what we do, and that makes it more enjoyable. But in some ways it makes everything a little harder, too. I mean, I'm the kind of person who can't say no to anyone. And that can put some demands on your time."

Larry Bowa, who lived through one of these bursts of baseball excitement $1\frac{1}{2}$ decades before with all those division-winning Phillies teams, said busy players need to beware.

"On our days off now, there are always people looking to do clinics and that kind of thing," Bowa said. "But the players have to learn to limit themselves. You can't go out on every whim. It will wear you out.

"I remember in 1980 we could have gone out every day and done something," he said. "There were some guys who tried. They pay top dollar for some of these things."

If baseball players are becoming heroes again in Philadelphia, on the road, this first-place club filled with characters is an irresistible curiosity.

In 1992, the last-place Phillies were nearly invisible outside of their home city. This year, in each road stop, more and more red Phillies caps are sprinkled around the stands. Like visitors to a zoo, writers, television crews, and broadcasters crowd around players' lockers for a close-up look at the grungy and gritty Phillies.

"There are times when that can be an inconvenience," said pitcher Terry Mulholland. "Like when you're all showered and dressed and rushing to catch a bus to the airport and someone walks over to your locker and starts asking you a lot of questions."

"That all goes with the territory," said coach John Vukovich. "It can be a distraction, sure. But it's a heck of a lot easier to answer questions about why you're playing well than why you're in last place."

Frank Fitzpatrick

When things looked bleak for him in spring training, when it looked as if his playing time would be curtailed and his at bats limited, Mariano Duncan put on a hopeful face.

"I will get my playing time," he said publicly. Was he really that confident? "To tell you the truth, no," Duncan said on May 2. Whatever the genesis of his prediction, it has been proved correct. By that date, Duncan had started 12 games for the Phils, including nine of the previous 10.

With Juan Bell and Kim Batiste struggling, Duncan became, temporarily at least, the everyday shortstop, giving the Phils what Bell and Batiste could not—good solid defense.

"I think Dunc is doing a great job at short," said Phils manager Jim Fregosi. Which is no surprise to Duncan.

"No, it's not a surprise at all," he said. "I came up as a shortstop. I might not have the range I had then, but I think I'm a little smarter."

Frank Fitzpatrick

In less than a week on the West Coast in early May, the Phillies preserved one win when Ricky Jordan made a ninth-inning scoop, another when Milt Thompson snatched a potential grand slam, and a third when a lunging Mickey Morandini latched onto a bases-loaded line drive.

Those eager to discern the causes of the Phillies' 18-6 start often look to the club's starting pitching, its improved bullpen, and its balanced lineup. But, as the play so far has shown, defense might be the biggest reason of all.

"Defense is the name of the game," manager Jim Fregosi said after an error-free 9-1 Phils victory over the Dodgers in Los Angeles. "It makes everything better. It makes your pitching staff better if you don't give away any runs."

For most of the last decade, the Phillies usually had made errors at a pace that ranked them at or near the bottom of the National League.

"There's been a knock against us that we're not a very good defensive team," Morandini said. "I think we are now. We're not only making all the routine plays, but we're making the occasional great ones, too."

Indeed, only one National League team—Atlanta—has made fewer errors than the Phillies' 15 at this early point of this season.

"Last year, we gave the other team four and five outs an inning all the time," said Mariano Duncan, whose solid play at shortstop has strengthened the defense. "There is just no way you can win ball games when you give a team that many chances."

Why the improvement this year?

"Better players," coach John Vukovich said.

Thompson and Jim Eisenreich, a pair of newcomers, provide the Phillies with help where they needed it most in 1992—in the outfield. Morandini is blossoming into one of the league's better second basemen.

Frank Fitzpatrick

One month down, five to go, and the Phillies are 19 and 7.

Say it slowly. Savor it. Nineteen and seven. A year before at the same point they were 12-14 on the road to last place. A year before that, they were 11-15. Now they're 12 games over .500 and they haven't had a chance to fatten up on the Florida Marlins or the Colorado Rockies. Or, for that matter, the New York Mets.

With each passing day the feeling grows that these Phillies aren't merely early-season wonders, but true contenders, maybe even the team to beat in the National League East.

The difference between the 1992 Phillies and this team is like night and day.

In 1992, the Phillies pitching staff had a 4.11 earned-run average, worst in the National League. The opposition hit .257 against them. This year's staff ERA is 3.50, and opponents are hitting just .235 against them. In contrast, the Mets, once renowned for their superlative pitching, have been rocked at a .280 clip.

Frank Dolson

A fter a successful West Coast trip that confirmed that their fast start wasn't a fluke, the first-place Phillies returned to Veterans Stadium on May 7 to see if their early-season magic was still working.

Phillies 4, Cardinals 3. The magic-carpet ride continues.

Despite committing three errors, despite going 0 for 8 with runners in scoring position, and despite falling into an early two-run hole, the Phillies outlasted the Cardinals before 33,739 spectators.

Dave Hollins delivered three hits, including a two-run homer that gave the Phils the lead for good in the fifth, and winner Tommy Greene pitched 7$\frac{1}{3}$ innings to pace Philadelphia. After three rocky innings, Greene (3-0) allowed just two hits and struck out five in his final 4$\frac{1}{3}$ innings.

"We played sloppily at times, but even when we were down early, you knew they could come back," manager Jim Fregosi said. "You could feel it on the bench."

Mitch Williams, looking better than he had in several rocky outings on the West Coast, pitched a one-two-three ninth to nail down his 12th save, tops in the majors.

Sam Carchidi

I t's as if they are determined to erase all memories of the past decade's misfortunes and mistakes with one glorious run of reality-stretching baseball.

And as Mariano Duncan watched his game-winning grand slam smack against a brown seat in Veterans Stadium's left centerfield stands in the late afternoon of May 9, the 43,648 stomping, screeching fans were not thinking about the nine lost years that preceded this one or the 777 lost games that filled them.

"Things are different around here now," said Duncan. "We want to make people forget about last year and other bad seasons."

If the previous day's emotion-pounding, 6-5 victory over the St. Louis Cardinals didn't do that, it is doubtful that anything ever will.

Duncan's eighth-inning slam off Lee Smith gave the scorching Phillies yet another remarkable win and a three-game sweep of their sinking divisional foes.

"We've already played a number of games that have been amazing," said Phils manager Jim Fregosi. "This was just one more."

As they have several times these past few weeks, the Phillies looked dead. Cardinals starter Bob Tewksbury was in front 5-2, and seemingly in command as he got two quick outs in the eighth inning.

"He was making us look bad," said Duncan.

But Darren Daulton kept the lights on with his third hit, a single to right. Wes Chamberlain doubled into the rightfield corner, sending Daulton to third. St. Louis manager Joe Torre then lifted his starter and summoned the towering Smith from the bullpen.

The Cardinals had not had many recent save opportunities, so Smith hadn't pitched for about 10 days. The big leagues' all-time saves leader loaded the bases by walking Milt Thompson, his backdoor slider on a 3-2 pitch barely missing. That brought Duncan to the plate.

"After he walked Milt Thompson, I didn't think he would be throwing me any breaking balls," said Duncan, now 8 for 15 lifetime off Smith. "I was looking for a fastball on the first pitch."

At third base, Daulton and coach Larry Bowa, having experienced so many spectacular and illogical victories of late, were not at all superstitious about raising the possibility of a game-turning slam.

"That's exactly what we were talking about," Daulton said.

Duncan got his first-pitch fastball and he crushed it. "I knew it was gone as soon as I hit it," Duncan said.

A roar, at first disbelieving but ultimately ecstatic, grew with each foot the drive traveled. Midway between first base and second, as the ball dropped into the stands, Duncan pumped his right fist in the air.

On the mound, Smith didn't look quite so large anymore. "I usually throw him breaking balls," said Smith.

Frank Fitzpatrick

The next night, the game was tied in a seventh inning that was home to more strange plays than off-Broadway. The inning's first break went against the Phillies. So did the second. Surely fate, so long enamored of this club, was ready to turn its back. Surely this was the night the miracles ended.

Not.

Darren Daulton belted Philadelphia's second game-winning grand slam in 30 hours with two outs in that seventh inning to end the tie and give the unconscious Phillies a 5-1 victory over the Pittsburgh Pirates.

"Don't analyze it, boys," coach Larry Bowa shouted to Phillies players as he exited the postgame clubhouse. "Just let it ride. We're in the zone."

It must be the Twilight Zone. There is a surreal quality to the way the Phils are playing these days. It's as if winning any game within reach is part of their destiny. They seem to know it. And their reawakening fans—29,712 of whom loudly summoned Daulton from the dugout twice—know it too.

"It's awesome," said Pete Incaviglia. "It's a great, great feeling."

"We come here every night expecting to win," said Daulton.

Lately, it has only been a question of how. Each game produces a late-inning Hero du Jour. In this game, it was Daulton and starting pitcher Danny Jackson (now 3-1).

"I can't say enough good things about Danny Jackson," said manager Jim Fregosi. "He had command of all his pitches tonight."

Jackson, his fastballs consistently in the 90s, turned in his best outing as a Phillie, limiting Pittsburgh to four hits and walking only two while striking out six in eight solid innings. David West finished up for Philadelphia with a scoreless ninth.

So a bit more than a month into the season, the first-place Phillies have won four in a row, 13 of 16, and lead the National League East by a stunning seven games.

This latest winning rally was born in an abnormal seventh inning. It started when Fregosi allowed Jackson to hit for himself in the 1-1 tie. He grounded out, but Lenny Dykstra followed with an infield single. Shortstop Jay Bell then gloved Mickey Morandini's bouncer up the middle, but a headfirst-sliding Dykstra avoided his tag. Bell, off-balance, tried to get Morandini but flipped the ball into the stands behind first.

Third-base umpire Eric Gregg held Dykstra at third, but home-plate ump Greg Bonin signaled him home. If Dykstra were at second before Bell's throw, he would have been awarded third and home. Finally, the four umpires gathered alone in the infield and decided Dykstra should stay at third.

John Kruk was walked intentionally to fill the bases. Kevin Young scooped up Dave Hollins's ground ball and fired home. His throw was high, and as Don Slaught returned to earth after grabbing it, he swiped at Dykstra. Bonin called him out. Dykstra erupted in all of his considerable frenzy. Fregosi and John Vukovich struggled to restrain him.

"From where I was sitting, it looked like he tagged him in the shoulder," said Fregosi. "But Lenny didn't think so."

Now there were two opportunities squandered, and two outs as well.

Loser Bob Walk (now 3-3) fell behind Daulton 3-0. The Phils catcher, stuck on 16 RBIs for quite some time, watched the next pitch for a strike.

"I was not swinging there," said Daulton. "That was not really a green-light situation. . . . On the 3-1 pitch, I was looking for a fastball. That's about all he could really throw in that situation."

Daulton got it, and he smoked a 402-foot drive into the right centerfield seats that was, except for its location on the opposite side of centerfield, exactly like Mariano Duncan's the day before.

Frank Fitzpatrick

You were starting to believe they couldn't lose, weren't you? You almost forgot about bad bullpens and stumbling rightfielders, didn't you?

The Phillies' 8-4 loss to the Pittsburgh Pirates on May 11 may serve as an antidote to some of the overconfidence that has been racing through Philadelphia like a new flu.

Mark Davis and Jose DeLeon, in relief of Ben Rivera, turned a tie game into a rout, and rightfielder Wes Chamberlain misplayed a couple of balls and added a few misplaced throws as the Phils ran out of dramatic finishes, disappointing a Veterans Stadium crowd of 32,871.

Pittsburgh scored a total of six times in the sixth, seventh, and eighth innings—three off Davis and one off DeLeon—to end the Phils' four-game winning streak.

Frank Fitzpatrick

They could have won three, they could have lost three. They could even have tied all three, if baseball allowed draws.

Instead, what the Phillies take with them to Florida is a one-run win and two enthralling losses to the two-time defending National League champions—and the belief that they have survived their first chance to be exposed as early-season mirages.

On May 14, 15, and 16, they played three taut, entertaining games with the Braves and were neither intimidated nor cowed. Twice they came from behind in the middle of the game, and twice again in the finale. The Phillies have grit.

But it is also true that in each of the three they failed to hold leads. Partly this was due to the Braves, who are no worse than the second-best team in baseball until proven otherwise, and partly this was due to the Phillies bullpen, which still looks too much like flammable liquid and not enough like extinguisher.

But the starting pitching remains promisingly solid and the team itself shows not a whiff of give-up. They were anxious to demonstrate that to the Braves. It was important to the Phillies to earn respect.

"Confidence-wise, everything-wise, this was an important series for us," manager Jim Fregosi affirmed.

They are 25-10. It is still the best record in the bigs. "If our starting pitching stays healthy, I think we should be able to avoid long losing streaks," said Lee Thomas, the general manager.

And so they should. But a slump, somewhere, is inevitable. So what the Phillies are doing is buying insurance. They are building a cushion on which to land once they do fall.

"We're building a margin for error," Thomas agreed.

They have been inventive for six weeks now, and in the last game with the Braves, they manufactured another intriguing way to win. Their leftfielder, who used to be regularly replaced for defensive purposes by his former employer, canceled two runs with his arm.

Milt Thompson threw out two Braves at the plate. This was a triumph for accuracy over velocity. Thompson is not known as a flinger of laser beams, and both his throws home were on arcs, not lines. But they were true, and Darren Daulton was impenetrable.

"You don't think," Thompson said, "that they might be trying to score. You just get to the ball, get it out of your glove, and get it there the fastest you can."

Fourteen games before, in San Diego, it was Thompson on a pogo stick retrieving a would-be grand slam from beyond the leftfield wall. And now he throws out two at home—first Mark Lemke, whom Daulton decoyed guilefully, and then Tony Tarasco, who uprooted the catcher but couldn't dislodge the ball.

The Braves played textbook, 90-feet-at-a-time baseball against the Phillies. They sacrificed three times and plated two of their runs on sacrifice flies. They also threw two Cy Young winners at the Phillies, and some serious leather afield. And Terry Pendleton had a smoking series.

But the Phillies never backed down; indeed, they seemed to be spoiling for a fight. They interpreted every Braves move as a challenge or a provocation.

They are chesty and full of themselves, and this series was their first Saturday night on the town. They wanted to get rowdy. They were eager to measure themselves. They left town feeling they had, and feeling that their suspicions about themselves had been confirmed.

Bill Lyon

The ball was a hissing projectile and, in the sultry Florida spring evening, a trickle of sweat crawled into John Kruk's eye. He blinked. And in that instant lost the ball.

"I figured I'd better bail," he said.

Bryan Harvey's fastball, which regularly sets red 95s to winking on the radar gun, was tailing toward the batting helmet that partially covers Kruk's cranium. Kruk sprawled in the dirt, arose, rearranged himself, and then got his fifth base hit of the game.

In the Marlins half of the inning, their first batter was Alex Arias. David West curled a sweeping hook in on him. There was no way to escape. Arias could only twist away and accept it on the back.

It was the most revealing pitch of the May 17 game, one of the single most revealing pitches of this season.

It was one more illustration that these Phillies are different from Phillies of the recent past. These Phillies have sand. These Phillies abhor defeat, will not accept it without impassioned resistance, and are quick to defend their own.

In the timid past, Phillies hitters, most notably Dave Hollins, would be sprayed with fastballs from sneering opponents and no retaliation would be forthcoming. Those passive Phillies pitchers never enforced baseball's macho code of justice that requires a conked noggin for a conked noggin.

"All I'll say is I was just doing my job," said the coy West, who has blossomed in the Phillies' bullpen after abortive efforts with the Mets and Twins. His ERA is now measured in tenths of a run, but that one pitch did more to endear him to his new team than all his scoreless innings.

For the record, Bryan Harvey apologized to Kruk for the knockdown, said he was trying to go up and in, but not to decapitate.

When West drilled Arias, both dugouts boiled onto the field. But there was only aimless milling about. The expansion Marlins were about to finish absorbing a 10-3 flogging and haven't yet gotten the knack of how to work up a good case of righteous outrage.

It was, by one estimate, the fourth time in a season barely six weeks old that swift retribution has been dealt by a Phillies pitcher.

This is a team that may or may not win the National League but, unlike its undistinguished predecessors, it will not be cowed. The dugout is eager to erupt. The team has an unmistakable swagger. It aches to prove its new self at every provocation, even one that might be imagined.

Bill Lyon

The rain drummed down on the infield tarp, and if you listened closely you could hear the drops click-click-clicking like a calculator.

And the readout made you blink. The Phillies, it said, can win 100 games. This season. The math is this: They started 25-10. They play 38 games against the two dreadful expansion teams—the Marlins and the Rockies—and the Mets, who are playing like the dreadful expansion team they once were. Is 30-8 an unreasonable expectation? Not the way the Phillies are playing.

That leaves 89 games. If the Phillies do no better than 45-44 in them, they win 100. And their division.

All of this overlooks only four things. In order, those things are: June, July, August, and September.

All of this also assumes that Curt Schilling, Tommy Greene, Terry Mulholland, and Danny Jackson do not break down. And that a fifth starter can be found. And that whatever David West now has in his left arm becomes contagious in the bullpen.

The players don't want to hear talk about 100 wins. The manager claps his hands over his ears if you suggest it. Like all athletes, they are ragingly superstitious. They believe that to make projections is to anger the gods and invite a visitation of toads and fire.

Bill Lyon

Pete Incaviglia drove in five runs with a grand slam and a single on May 20 as Curt Schilling and the Phillies thumped their closest competitors, the Montreal Expos, 9-3, in the opener of a four-game series at Veterans Stadium.

He is a very intense player, and such intensity loathes inaction. Since the burly outfielder has been platooned this season, you might have expected him to be of little value. But while his playing time has been limited, his production has not.

"I have a lot of respect for Jimmy Fregosi," Incaviglia said of the Phils manager. "And as long as we're winning, I'll do whatever he wants. I just have to go out there each chance I get and play my hardest."

That is rarely a problem for Incaviglia. In addition to his long slam—his fifth homer and second in two nights—and an RBI single, he also dove headlong into first trying futilely to outrace a seventh-inning grounder.

The leftfield foul screen probably prevented Incaviglia's rocket from reaching the upper deck. The night before, in Miami, he smashed one off the upper-deck facade at Joe Robbie Stadium.

"He hit that one in the first inning so hard that parts of the ball were probably missing when it hit the net," Schilling said. "I told people here that when Inky gets hot, he can carry a ball club."

Actually, the first-place Phillies don't require too much lifting these days. The victory, their fourth in five games, increased the Phils lead in the National League East to 6 ½ games. It improved their best-in-baseball record to 28-11.

Frank Fitzpatrick

I magine a kid who was expecting Nintendo awaking on Christmas morning to find a checkers set under the tree. That's about how Phillies fans, eager for a David Cone or a Kirby Puckett, reacted to the off-season signings of Milt Thompson, Pete Incaviglia, and Jim Eisenreich.

The three outfielders, though, might well be the big reason these Phillies are the best-looking team in the National League East right now.

Incaviglia, Eisenreich, and Thompson were hitting a combined .269 with 41 RBIs before the May 20 game with Montreal, when Incaviglia drove in five more runs.

Even when they're on the bench, the three outfielders give opposing managers a lot to think about.

"I think the big thing that we bring to this ball club is our experience," Eisenreich said before the game. "Each of us has been in the league for about seven years. I think that's what the Phillies saw in us. That and the fact that they could get us cheap."

Eisenreich has become the rightfield closer, coming in late for Wes Chamberlain. He also has 16 hits and 8 RBIs in his previous 35 at bats (.457). Thompson is hitting .379 with runners in scoring position and has saved at least two wins with his glove. Incaviglia has 18 RBIs on just 20 hits.

And all have accepted their part-time status—a task made easier, of course, by the Phils' racehorse start.

Frank Fitzpatrick

R adar guns have trouble identifying some of Frank Tanana's pitches as moving objects. Hitters can hurt themselves in their wild efforts to club his barely breathing offerings great distances.

In his 40²/₃ innings before facing the Phillies on May 24, the Mets lefthander had allowed just one home run. Not surprising, since hitting one requires either perfect timing or basketball-size biceps. In his season debut against the Phils at Veterans Stadium, Tanana's weakling pitches met the Phillies' twin hulks. Pete Incaviglia homered twice and Dave Hollins belted a three-run shot as Philadelphia defeated the Mets, 6-3.

The three home runs kept Tommy Green unbeaten at 6-0. Hollins's fifth-inning blast, following infield singles by Lenny Dykstra and Mariano Duncan, allowed Philadelphia to overcome a 2-1 deficit.

It was the first-place Phillies' second straight win and their 30th of the season. That they achieved that total in just 43 games is somewhat remarkable when you consider that the Phils' 30th victory of 1992 did not come until June 20, in game 65.

The first 1993 meeting between these divisional bookends left the last-place Mets 15½ games behind the Phillies in the National League East.

Surely, the Phillies and their fans recalled all those painful nights when the high-riding Mets would swagger into Veterans Stadium accompanied by thousands of vocal New York supporters?

Well, the Mets have lost much of their swagger—as well as 27 of their 41 games. Some of their turnpike-traveling fans still made the trip to the Vet for this game, but their numbers were as diminished as the franchise's fortunes.

Frank Fitzpatrick

This is the inscription on the Phillies' tombstone: E-6.

On May 26, their shortstop made two errors, one on a room-service double-play bouncer in the ninth inning that helped turn a cruise-control 4-1 triumph over the certifiably bad Mets into a toad-ugly, coyote-ugly, warthog-ugly 5-4 loss.

It is becoming a disturbing habit. The infield gives away outs. The closer closes doors on his own fingers. And the Phillies have met the enemy, and it is themselves.

At every infield position not attached to the end of first base, the Phillies defense is a series of flashing red danger lights. But the biggest sieve of all is at shortstop.

It was Juan Bell's turn to kick away a game at Veterans Stadium. He butchered a tailor-made, 6-4-3 game-ending, streak-preserving ground ball.

So instead of jetting off to Colorado on the giddy wings of a four-game winning streak, buoyed by the prospect of three games with a bad expansion team in a stuffed ballpark that is a shooting gallery, the Phillies sullenly filed home with the ominous knowledge that they desperately need an everyday shortstop.

Not Ozzie Smith's clone. Not ruffles and flourishes and curlicues. Just a warm body with a glove that suctions up what he can get to and an arm that throws with reasonable accuracy.

But unless and until they acquire one, they are a threat to themselves and to what has appeared to be their manifest destiny this year—100 wins, a division title, a place in the playoffs.

The Phillies have tried to spackle and plaster over that gaping wound between second and third, but whatever they stuff in there eventually dries and crumbles and falls out, usually taking a sure victory with it.

And while shortstop is in flames, the bullpen is smoking suspiciously.

Mitch Williams, summoned with one on and none out in the top of the ninth, retired one hitter. He lost the plate more frequently than he found it. Manager Jim Fregosi could take no more.

Williams left, lengthening his stride with every step, and at the top of the dugout he catapulted himself up the runway to the clubhouse. David West followed. Bell fielded the game-ending grounder, fumbled it, double-clutched, and finally had to eat the ball. There followed a two-run double.

The Mets scored four in the ninth. The Mets. The 16$\frac{1}{2}$-games-out-of-first-place Mets.

And Rusty Staub, now a paid shill for the Mets, waddled by deadline-fuming literati and cackled: "Sorry you got to rewrite all your leads, boys."

The Phillies wasted eight brilliant, persistent innings by Danny Jackson, running the starting pitching's remarkable run to 26 consecutive innings. In hindsight, maybe Jackson should have been left in. He couldn't have done worse.

The last three Phillies losses have been leads they couldn't hold, either because the defense threw it away or the bullpen couldn't preserve a mummy, or a combination of futility by both.

It is easy to overreact here. It is easy to forget that the Phillies are still in first place, still possess the best record in baseball, still are 17 games over .500, and still have 32 games remaining against the Marlins, Mets, and Rockies.

But they blew a sweep against the Marlins and repeated against the

Mets. And good teams, in any sport, win championships by beating up on the weak teams and splitting with the strong ones. It is a flawless formula.

Frankly, the Phillies haven't met anyone yet who could beat them straight-up consistently. Most losses, the Phillies can find the reason in the mirror.

Bill Lyon

He was ambling in from centerfield after batting practice when the voice from across the field caught his ear.

"Hey Pods," Mets coach Bobby Wine was shouting at Johnny Podres. "You're a genius, Pods. You're a genius."

Johnny Podres stopped, put his hands on his hips, and stared in mock disgust.

"Oh no," Podres shouted back. "I'm no genius. Not me. Tommy Greene is a genius. He's the genius."

If ever one slice of baseball life illustrated the essence of Johnny Podres, the Phillies' brilliant, semi-invisible pitching coach, this was it.

He is practically single-handedly responsible for turning the Phillies starting rotation into the force that has made this whole crazy first-place joy ride possible.

Does he get much credit? No. Does he want much credit? No. And does he enjoy being called a genius? Yikes. He'd rather be the personal publicist for his favorite umpire, Bob Davidson.

"But he is a genius," said fellow coach John Vukovich, "because he probably gets more across with fewer words than any coach I've ever seen. I told him this year, 'John, the rest of the coaching staff got better because we've got better players in our areas. But you're the only coach I've ever seen who just made your area better.'"

And Johnny Podres has, with his astonishing, instinctive feel for pitching and his never-ending behind-the-scenes passion for his work. Yet for all the good he has done since the Phillies hired him in 1991, to hear Podres himself talk about it, you would get the impression he thinks of himself as an innocent bystander.

"Isn't it amazing how all of a sudden you get a group of guys that come together as a pitching staff and pitch as good as these guys have pitched?" Podres asked, as if he had nothing to do with that. "Makes you sit back and say, 'Why couldn't they pitch that good till now?'"

Why? Maybe because they hadn't come in contact with Johnny

Podres. Just contemplate what the Phillies starters had done before Podres came into their lives:

Curt Schilling: B.P. (Before Pods) had as many trades on his résumé (four) as wins, a 4.15 career ERA, and a 4-11 record. But A.P. (After Pods) he's 20-12, with a 2.47 ERA.

Tommy Greene: Had four big-league wins in six pro seasons and a 4.75 career ERA, B.P. But A.P. he's 24-10, with a 3.38 ERA and might be a month away from starting an All-Star Game.

Terry Mulholland: Career B.P. record: 16-25, 4.06 ERA. But A.P. he's 35-29, 3.76, with 25 complete games and six shutouts.

Ben Rivera: Once was looked upon as just a big, hard-throwing guy who never won (B.P. pro record: 31-42). But A.P. he's 11-5, 3.22.

Danny Jackson: Went a combined 21-35, with a 4.60 ERA, in his last four seasons B.P. But A.P. he's 4-2, 3.77, and the Phillies are 8-3 in games he has started.

Could it be some remarkable coincidence that all these guys miraculously put it together in Philadelphia? Or could it be that their 60-year-old pitching coach, with his endless supply of Brooklyn Dodger stories and his classic Buster Keaton gaze, has touched them all with his special magic wand?

"Aw, I'm not pitching," said Johnny Podres, waving his hand furiously to fight off another unwanted barrage of universal praise. "They are."

But the people around him know the real story.

"I don't think this organization should take lightly what they have in him," said Mulholland. "There aren't a whole lot of Johnny Podreses out there. He'd be a very tough individual to replace. And I'd like Lee Thomas and Bill Giles to be aware that we all know that."

"Look at what he's done," Vukovich said of Podres. "He completely changed Ben. He completely changed Schilling. He completely changed Tommy. What they throw now—variety of pitches, quality of pitches— is totally different from what they threw when they arrived here. And that's all Pods."

Yet two things stand out about the way Johnny Podres went about transforming these guys—the swiftness and the simplicity with which he did it.

His first spring training as a Phillie, in 1991, Podres watched Greene throw in the bullpen one day. Then, Greene recalled, "he said, 'Hey, I want to try something.'" That something merely would turn around Tommy Greene's whole career.

Podres asked Greene to throw 20 fastballs—10 sinking, two-seam fastballs (Greene's big pitch until then) and 10 rising, four-seam fastballs (the pitch that would change his life).

"Then," said Greene, "he asked the catchers, 'Which one's better?' They all said, 'The four-seamer.' Then he asked me. And I said, 'Well, the four- seamer's got more life.'"

And bingo. That fast, that simply, Podres handed Tommy Greene the strikeout pitch that has made him a dominant pitcher. But Podres also revamped Schilling's repertoire in one afternoon. And he changed Rivera from a sidearm slinger to an over-the-top power pitcher practically overnight, too.

The genius of Johnny Podres, though, is that he could do all that without ever uttering any mumbo jumbo about keeping the shoulder tucked or stopping the shoulder from flying open, or any of that other impressive pitching-coach jargon.

"John uses the simplest method of teaching you can use," said manager Jim Fregosi. "His theory is, you don't have to show your players how much you know. To him, getting your point across in the easiest manner you possibly can is all that matters."

But maybe Podres's greatest contribution is that he hasn't just changed his pitchers by teaching them his fabled circle change-up or by tinkering with their pitch selection. He has changed the very way they think of themselves on the mound.

"He's made me a winner," said Schilling, "just with all the confidence he's instilled in me."

He has ingrained a special feeling in Mulholland, too, just by observing that Mulholland reminds him of himself—"and I take that as a very, very high compliment," Mulholland said. "I don't consider myself a great baseball historian. But I know Johnny Podres was a hell of a pitcher."

The men who pitch for him now are too young to remember Johnny Podres on a pitcher's mound. But Podres's fellow coaches remember. He gave up Denis Menke's first career hit and Mike Ryan's last hit. And Fregosi says, "I usually tell him once a week about the home run I hit off him."

But in between those hits, Johnny Podres got a ton of outs in 15 memorable seasons. He won an ERA title. He made three All-Star teams. He once struck out eight straight Phillies in a game in 1962. He was a postseason terror (4-1, 2.13 ERA in six starts). And he was the man on the mound when the Brooklyn Dodgers won their only World Series in 1955.

Later, Podres was the pitching coach in Boston, where he broke in John Tudor, Bruce Hurst, and Bob Ojeda. Then he worked five seasons for the Twins, where he taught Frank Viola the change-up that won Viola a Cy Young award.

But what's forgotten is that, in Minnesota, Podres also turned Mike Smithson into a 15-game winner (twice). And turned Ken Schrom into a 15-game winner. And turned Bobby Castillo and John Butcher into 13-game winners.

Despite all that, however, Podres spent five years out of the big leagues after the Twins let him go in 1985. Even he can't explain why.

"When I got let go by Minnesota," Podres said, "I went right to work for the Dodgers [as a minor-league instructor]. And I might have said something in the papers, like, 'I'm back home again, and this is where I want to be.' Maybe people thought I wasn't interested in going back to the big leagues. I don't know. And I really don't care."

But when Phillies general manager Thomas called in the fall of 1990, Podres was ready to get back to the big leagues—until he saw his first Phillies pitching staff in spring training.

"We were just getting killed every day that spring," Vukovich recalled. "We were giving up 8, 10, 11 runs a game. And I remember him sitting in his chair, looking in his locker, saying: 'Fifty thousand. Fifty thousand. Ten on. Seven off. Fifty thousand.'

"We said, 'Pods, what the hell are you talking about?' And he said, 'I had it made—$50,000 a year with the Dodgers. Worked 10 days. Then took seven off. I gave that up. What did I do?'"

"Yeah, I remember that first spring," Podres said, laughing. "I was saying to myself, 'What the hell did I get myself into?' But what the hell. Everything turned out good."

Yes, it has all turned out great—thanks to a certain Phillies pitching coach who would prefer to keep his own genius the best-kept secret in baseball.

Jayson Stark

In the crazed dance that is the Phillies' locker room, Jim Eisenreich is the wallflower. He stands apart from the bedlam.

A lone raisin in this bowl of flakes.

"My first day here, I didn't say anything to anyone," said Eisenreich, "and as I was leaving, Dave Hollins said, 'Nice talking to you.'"

He has since found easy acceptance off the field from his noisier teammates. On the field, he always fit as snugly as Jim Fregosi's uniform.

On June 6, Eisenreich went 3 for 4 with three RBIs, lifting his average to .361, as the Phillies pounded Rockies pitching again in an 11-7 victory at Veterans Stadium.

Curt Schilling improved his record to 7-1, but did so with a sloppy five-inning performance that left the righthander confused and bothered.

"I'm just not pitching with a lot of confidence," Schilling said. "I don't know why. I'm searching."

The victory was the Phils' 10th in 13 games as they increased their lead in the National League East to 7 1/2 games over the Montreal Expos and gave themselves an 8-0 record in Sunday games. And their little two-weekend, six-game set with the rocky Rockies concluded with the Phils owning a significant advantage—5-1 in games, 57-21 in runs.

This latest win, in a sluggish 3 hours and 24 minutes, was more difficult than it needed to be. Darren Daulton's bases-loaded triple off loser Andy Ashby (0-4) and RBI singles by Eisenreich and Mariano Duncan (4 for 5 with a homer and two RBIs) gave Schilling a 5-0 advantage in the first inning.

But Schilling never found a rhythm. "Curt Schilling didn't have his best stuff," said Fregosi. "He was getting the ball up in the zone. . . . We just outscored them."

That was possible because Ashby turned in the kind of performance that might drive more sensitive pitchers to a premature retirement—or grave. The former Phillie's line was frightening—$3^2/_3$ innings, 13 hits, 9 runs (all earned), and 2 walks. Numbers like that made it difficult for Ashby to achieve what, he said later, was his pregame intention.

"I wanted to stick it [to them]," said Ashby, left unprotected by the Phils in the November 1992 expansion draft. Eisenreich had all three of his hits off Ashby, singling in the first and third and clubbing a two-run double off him in a four-run fourth as the Phils lead expanded to 9-2.

"My confidence level is real high right now," said Eisenreich. "I had heard this was a fastball league and that hasn't proven to be true. I've been able to do some things offensively."

And this 34-year-old's hitting philosophy is as simple and direct as his unassuming manner. "See the ball," he said, "hit the ball."

It was one more game when the value of Lee Thomas's off-season acquisitions was on display, this time in front of the season's second-largest crowd, 55,714.

In addition to Eisenreich's contribution, Pete Incaviglia was 2 for 5 with another long home run (his ninth) and two RBIs (his 35th and 36th in just 127 at bats). And reliever Larry Andersen squelched a minor Colorado uprising in the seventh, after Colorado closed to within 11-7 on the second homer of the game for good-looking rookie Chris Jones (3 for 5 with 4 RBIs).

Among the 18 Philadelphia hits were four more by Lenny Dykstra, who now has his once anemic average up to .276.

Frank Fitzpatrick

Bobby Bonilla swung at the first pitch, and the baseball jumped off his bat, soaring high and far over Jim Eisenreich's head and over Shea Stadium's right centerfield fence before plummeting to earth deep in the Mets bullpen.

Tommy Greene, the man with the all-winning record and the 1.87 earned-run average, had given up two runs before getting three Mets out.

Take the game's hottest pitcher, a guy who has won eight straight decisions, completed his five most recent starts, held opposing hitters to a .184 average, and not given up more than three runs in any of his 10 starts, send him out against the worst-hitting team in the big leagues, and what happens?

A 418-foot home run happens. A succession of three-ball counts by a pitcher who has made a habit of getting ahead of the hitters happens.

Four singles, three walks—the last a four-pitch job to Bonilla with the bases loaded—and the quickest KO of a Phillies starter this season happens.

Greene hadn't walked a batter in his first 21⅓ innings. Suddenly, on June 10, facing a Mets lineup that hasn't worried anybody in 1993 except Mets management, he couldn't throw strikes. The Mets killed him, figuratively speaking, of course. Bonilla's first-inning blast started his night to forget. A two-out, line-drive single by Todd Hundley on a 3-1 pitch with a runner on first, and back-to-back walks to Eddie Murray and Bonilla ended it.

The pitcher who had such remarkable command through 10 previous starts and one early-season relief appearance had no command at all on this night.

His final pitch, the bases-loaded 3-0 delivery to Bonilla, sailed inside by a considerable margin. As the Mets runners advanced behind him, Greene walked in a few steps, snatched angrily at the baseball that Darren Daulton returned to him, retreated to the back of the mound, and awaited the arrival of Jim Fregosi.

No complete game this time. No ninth straight victory that would have put him within one of the all-time Phillies' record for season-opening wins—the 10 in a row recorded by Hall of Famer Grover Cleveland Alexander, 80 years ago.

Greene walked slowly to the dugout, carrying his glove in his right hand, and plopped down on the bench. Even on a night like this, he didn't do what so many pitchers would do: rush off to the clubhouse, tear off his uniform, and take a shower. Instead, he sat there, watching as Tim Mauser completed the second inning. And he kept sitting, and watching, and rooting for the rest of the game.

It was Tommy Greene's night to struggle, the night his ERA jumped to a still-terrific 2.27. A preseason question mark, he had turned himself into an early-season exclamation point, the league's "pitcher of the month" in May, impressing one and all.

One of those most impressed was Mets manager Dallas Green, who had followed the pitcher's progress as a scout before returning to the dugout.

"If there's a noticeable change," Dallas said, "I think it's his demeanor and approach on the mound. He's a bulldog now. He doesn't [mess] around out there. He's got a purpose in mind with every pitch. He looks like he's got one thought in mind, and that's to get the hitter out. I didn't see that before."

On this night, the question was whether the Mets' sad-sack relief-pitching corps could keep the Phillies from erasing the deficit to get Greene off the hook.

"Relief?" Green said before the game. "There isn't any. . . . It's awful. We can't wait to give up a run, and it doesn't matter who I put out there."

Indeed, after starter Bret Saberhagen had to leave after five innings because of shoulder problems, he put lefty Eric Hillman out there, and Tommy Greene's teammates set about trying to give their ace another chance in his pursuit of Grover Cleveland Alexander.

Indeed, two Mets relief pitchers and one awesome Pete Incaviglia moonshot later, and Greene's winning streak was still alive. The Phillies hungrily tore into New York's weak bullpen for seven runs in the sixth and seventh innings, and stunned the dispirited Mets, 7-6.

Frank Dolson

A team without many defeats suffered a major loss on June 11. Third baseman Dave Hollins, one of two players the first-place Phillies could least afford to lose, will miss four to six weeks because of a broken bone in his right hand.

"Six weeks. That's a big deal," Darren Daulton said. "You hate to see that happen. Things were going so well, almost too well."

Hollins will undergo surgery on June 15 in Philadelphia.

For the moment, Kim Batiste will fill in for Hollins. Batiste, however, cannot be expected to provide anywhere near the offense Hollins had been providing. Hollins was hitting .288 with nine home runs and 47 RBIs.

Frank Fitzpatrick

A s Mariano Duncan scooped up the madly rolling ball, his red cap nearly brushed against three yellow numbers that read "330."

Those numbers were on the rightfield wall. Duncan was the second baseman. This was the first inning. Need you ask how the rest of the Phillies' night went?

It was June 17, and Duncan was chasing down a first-inning triple by Orestes Destrade that skipped past a diving Pete Incaviglia. Two runs scored on the play. There would be more.

By the time it was over, Florida's Chris Hammond had beaten the Phillies 4-1, in the Marlins' first appearance in Philadelphia.

"As soon as I saw him dive and the ball get past him, I knew that if I didn't get there it would be an inside-the-park home run," Duncan said. "That's how things go sometime."

That's not how the Phillies had come to expect things to go. Now, suddenly mortal, the Phils have lost three straight for the first time this season. Their still-substantial National League East lead over the hot St. Louis Cardinals has slipped to 8 $\frac{1}{2}$ games.

"Like I've been saying," said Lenny Dykstra, "you're going to hit some ruts in a long season, some peaks and valleys. The schedule is set up so that good teams and weaknesses will be exposed over 162 games."

Frank Fitzpatrick

T he ball, descending from baby-blue skies, fell softly into Kim Batiste's waiting glove. As the third baseman squeezed David Justice's ninth-inning pop-up, the Phillies had an 8-3 victory over the Atlanta Braves.

Before 57,903 fans at Veterans Stadium on June 23, on a day nearly as perfect as their season has been, the Phils picked up their 50th victory—and did so nearly two months earlier than they had in 1992.

Surely, even Jim Fregosi, never one to express surprise at a turn of events, could not have envisioned two score and ten wins with a week left in June.

"No, I'd have said it was a little unrealistic," the Phils manager acknowledged, "especially since it took us until August 18 last year to get 50 wins."

The 50th victory was easier than most, especially after Braves starter John Smoltz (now 6-7) left the game. Until the seventh inning, Smoltz and Ben Rivera (now 7-3) had been locked in a duel that the Phillies led, 2-1.

In the seventh, though, Atlanta relievers couldn't find the plate, and the Phillies used five walks, three hits, and an error to score six times. In all, Braves pitchers walked 10 Philadelphia batters, and the Businesspersons' Special dragged on for 3 hours and 9 minutes.

The 50th season win was the Phillies' fifth of their last six games, including two of three in a series with the two-time National League champions. As they head into the traditionally tough cities of Pittsburgh and St. Louis, they will take along a 9½-game lead over the second-place Cardinals.

Frank Fitzpatrick

Much has been written about Larry Andersen's marvelous mask collection and his booming belches. The time he spray-painted his head and the radical alterations he's performed on teammates' clothing have been chronicled. So have his one-liners.

But there's a lesser-known side of Larry Andersen. His pitching.

Sometimes, Andersen says, he thinks all that other stuff overshadows his performance on the mound. "But that's all general-public stuff," he said. "I don't think my peers overlook what I can do on the field."

On the field, the Phillies righthanded setup man is enjoying a remarkable season. Remarkable, especially for a 40-year-old who throws the slider almost exclusively.

If you wonder about his success, think for a minute that you are a hitter and you have two strikes on you. You watch Andersen closely before the pitch and you watch his hand visit more places than a tourist with time to kill.

"I'll go to my forehead, the back of my cap, my sleeve," he said. "I'll rub the ball up a lot, so I make sure the hitter sees me."

Now you are wondering if Andersen is cheating. The pitch is on its way, and even though all the evidence suggests it will be a slider, it looks as if he's trying to sneak a fastball by you. You swing, but as you do the ball plummets away from you. You are out. Shaking your head, grumbling to yourself as you return to the dugout, you wonder if he scuffed, scraped, spit on, or otherwise lubricated that final pitch.

Andersen insists that what he does is perfectly legal. If hitters prefer to believe he is lying, that's fine with him. He is in his 16th big-league season, after all, and he throws basically one pitch. He needs an edge. That—if nothing else—he learned from Gaylord Perry when the two played together at Cleveland in the mid-1970s.

"A lot of hitters have it in their heads that I'm cheating out there," Andersen said. "And that works in my favor. It just puts one more thing in their heads for them to think about. I learned that from Gaylord. Get them thinking as much as you can."

Whatever his methods, there can be no denying the results. Andersen has been the Phillies' most consistent reliever this year. He has come into games and held leads for Mitch Williams, or kept the Phils close enough to rally.

The pitcher credits a change in his delivery for his recent setup success.

"For five years I was able to throw the slider when and where I wanted," he said. "But just before I went on the disabled list, I wasn't able to do that."

So Andersen, who was on the disabled list in May with an inflamed right shoulder, began toying with his mechanics.

"I opened up my feet a little more," he said. "That kept me from rotating my hips too much. I've got kind of a big delivery, with a high leg kick, so I just cut it all down a little."

Still, the fact that Andersen consistently gets hitters out when he throws the slider so often is extraordinary.

"It's no secret they're going to get the slider," he said. "I probably throw it about 90 percent of the time. When I talk to hitters on new teams, and I've changed teams quite a bit, they tell me that it's tough to pick up the rotation on the pitch, that it looks like a fastball coming up there.

"I mean I'd like to say that the reason I keep getting people out with it is because the slider is that good. But that would make me sound like an overconfident prima donna."

Then why do hitters look fooled so often when the odds are nearly 10 to 1 they will be seeing a slider? "I think that when I fall behind in the count, 2-0 or something like that, hitters just naturally expect to see a fastball. That's just how they think," said Andersen. "And if I get ahead of them, say 0-2, they have to guard the plate and they're more likely to chase a pitch that breaks out of the strike zone."

Frank Fitzpatrick

A group of yellow-shirted visitors from Russia stood and waved pompoms as the ball screamed toward their leftfield seats. No language barriers could obscure the drama of the moment.

As Don Slaught's game-tying 10th-inning home run dropped in front of those Russian fans, Mitch Williams walked off the mound and chastised himself furiously. The words would probably defy an easy translation.

Slaught's leadoff homer off the Phillies closer tied the game at 3-3, and Kevin Young's bases-loaded single five batters later gave the Pirates a 4-3 victory on June 27, sending the Phillies to St. Louis with a shrunken divisional lead, a two-game losing streak, and an ill humor.

"I stunk," said Williams, staring at the floor, clutching a plastic cup of beer that failed to console him. "I made a stupid damn pitch to Slaught. And I didn't get the rest of the guys out, either."

Williams tore away at his clothing. He scooped up the red spikes he had been wearing and handed them, obviously cursed now, to a clubhouse boy. "Throw them out," he said. "Throw them away."

The Phils' bitter loss, their first in 12 Sunday games, came after they had scratched out a go-ahead run in the top of the 10th on Lenny Dykstra's double, a sacrifice bunt, and Pete Incaviglia's broken-bat sacrifice fly.

Pinch-hitter Slaught worked the count to 2-2. Williams, who has become increasingly enamored of his slider, threw him one. A bad one.

When Williams and the Three Rivers Stadium crowd calmed themselves, the reliever allowed a Jay Bell single. Lonnie Smith's bunt, an intentional walk to Jeff King, and an unintentional one to Lloyd McClendon preceded Young's game-winning hit over a drawn-in Ruben Amaro in right.

"Mitch just didn't get the job done," said Phils manager Jim Fregosi. "He's got it done quite often this year, but he didn't get it done today."

The Phillies' 11½-game lead of June 13 has been reduced to 7½ games by the fast-approaching Cardinals.

Frank Fitzpatrick

For the first time, the Enchanted Season has come to a fork in the road.

For the first time, for the Phillies, for whom every move has been the right one, for whom showers of magic dust are a daily bathing ritual, peril looms.

They just lost the kind of game they routinely win, lost it in extra innings, lost it in brilliant sunshine, lost it after losing three different leads, lost it after stranding runners at third four different times.

They lost the kind of game that leaves the clubhouse mute as a tomb, the only sound the mocking clack of bats being racked and packed.

And the Cardinals, who probably couldn't pass a rabies test right now, won again, although beating the Mets these days should only count for half a game.

So now, on June 28, for the first time since the Enchanted Season began almost three months before, the Phillies are confronted with a reasonable facsimile of jeopardy. Now they play four in a row against their nearest pursuer, in his yard. It may be exactly what they need. For if they are as good as their record says, if they are as good as they think they are, then they should welcome this series.

They should welcome it eagerly, as a chance to validate themselves, as a chance to squash all hope in their division, as a chance to destroy their closest competition and cow the rest of the NL East into unconditional surrender.

By week's end, they could begin setting up their pitching rotation for the playoffs. Or they could be in flames.

And if they should happen to get swept, then the alarmists, the doomsayers who have been waiting for a collapse, can thumb through their yellowed morgue files and dredge up 1964.

But more than anything else, the Phillies should take perspective with them to St. Louis.

The Enchanted Season is not even half done. The magic number still holds at 82. All this represents is a series that finally holds the promise of some excitement in a race that hasn't been a race since the first week.

And it is not as though they face withering pressure. They need do nothing more dramatic or heroic than win two games. That would preserve their lead, which presently represents just over one week's worth of wins, and keep them four weeks over .500.

"Oh, I think we can do it. Definitely," said Ruben Amaro, the latest Phillie to shower in magic dust during the Enchanted Season.

Called up from the minors, Amaro was an unending spool of highlights during the weekend just ended in Pittsburgh. In all, he reached base 10 times in the three games against the Pirates—eight hits, two walks. The only time he was retired in five at bats in the last game was when he gave himself up to sacrifice Lenny Dykstra to third.

That was in the 10th inning, and sure enough, Dykstra then scored on Pete Incaviglia's splintered-bat sacrifice fly. But Mitch Williams gloriously self-destructed in relief, and Ruben Amaro's weekend of joy had a crimp put in it.

When the Phillies lose, they are genuinely surprised. When they lose two in a row, which they have now done, they are struck almost dumb.

They wasted their usual splendid starting pitching in this series. After Tommy Greene was shelled, Curt Schilling yielded only three runs and Terry Mulholland only two. But the team that leads the league in scoring totaled only five runs in its last two games.

In the series finale, Williams couldn't preserve what would have been a sweet 3-2 win in 10. Manfully, he was there to be grilled afterward, however, and while he was in the midst of berating himself for throwing pitches that he described as "stupid," Incaviglia muscled through the crowd and reached in to pat the back of Williams's neck.

"Forget about it," he told Williams. "It's over and done with."

Sage advice, certainly, and definitely applicable in the Phillies' current circumstances. The worst thing they could lug with them to St. Louis would be the latest loss.

Besides, they should be flattered. The Pirates played, and Jim Leyland managed, as though these were the playoffs.

"They look," Leyland mused of the Phillies, "like they're having one of those seasons."

He is in a position to know, having come off three consecutive Enchanted Seasons.

Now the Phillies have the chance to reaffirm that this is, indeed, The Enchanted Season.

Bill Lyon

They were lonely marathoners for a couple of months. So far in the lead, so far from the finish, there was nothing to do but run on.

"It's been a long time since we played an important game," Phils general manager Lee Thomas said before the first of those four in St. Louis, on June 29.

As the race nears its halfway mark, though, there suddenly are footfalls to the Phillies' rear. The St. Louis Cardinals are coming. Fast.

The Cardinals used two slightly tainted first-inning runs to defeat the Phillies, 3-1, at Busch Stadium in the opener of the four-game series between the National League East's first- and second-place teams.

The scalding Cards' fifth consecutive victory, their 17th in 21 games, reduced the Phillies' division lead to 6 $\frac{1}{2}$ games, five games fewer than it was 15 days before. Philadelphia has lost three straight games for just the second time this season.

"We're not worried," said John Kruk. "It's no big deal. We just lost a game, that's all. We haven't been hitting, and you know we're going to hit. Our pitching's been fine."

It was not a pleasant night for Kruk, or many of the other left-handed hitters in the lineup. Lefthander Rheal Cormier (now 5-4) beat Philadelphia for a fourth time in five career decisions.

"We've faced four lefthanders in a row," Fregosi said, "and some of our lefthanded hitters are a little messed up. Kruk's been struggling and so has [Darren Daulton] and Lenny Dykstra. Those are the three key guys in our lineup."

Kruk, Daulton, and Dykstra went 1 for 12 in this game.

"I've never gotten a hit off Cormier," Kruk said. "I couldn't hit him last year when we were in last place. What makes you think I can hit now just because we're in first place?"

"The last four games the pitchers have really been getting ahead of me," said Dykstra (3 for 15 in that span). "But when you've walked 61 times already, they're going to start getting ahead of you."

It was four hours before game time, and there was Dave Hollins, sitting bare-chested in front of his locker waiting for word on whether he'd get the okay to play and killing time by working over his glove with enough intensity to raise the dead.

First he'd spit, and then he'd pound with his right fist, spit and pound, spit and pound, over and over again until the black leather finally bent to his will.

"I feel good," Hollins said. "I'm ready."

Hollins, who had surgery on his right hand just two weeks before, was still waiting for permission to play from team doctor Phillip J. Marone. He had already taken batting practice under a hot afternoon sun, and when he was finished he said there was no pain. None. Nothing at all.

Marone was skeptical. After all, his patient still had stitches holding together a long scar on the palm of his hand, and that, along with Hollins's tough-guy reputation, had Marone wondering whether the third baseman was just trying to slip one by him about this pain thing.

"He swore to me that he was not lying," Marone said.

So, just after he finished working over his mitt, Hollins, one day shy of a two-week anniversary with the surgeon's blade, got medical clearance to play for the Phillies again. He was back at third and hitting cleanup.

Frank Fitzpatrick and Timothy Dwyer

On June 29, after looking like offensive weaklings against a series of soft-tossing lefthanders, Phils hitters exploded against St. Louis righthander Rene Arocha and several relievers to post a significant 13-10 victory over the second-place Cardinals at Busch Stadium.

"That was one of those games you really don't like to have," said Phils manager Jim Fregosi. "But I thought it showed something about the character of this club."

Philadelphia collected 17 hits, and four errors by an unusually porous Cards defense contributed to the carnage.

Lenny Dykstra was 3 for 4 with three runs scored and an RBI. Jim Eisenreich had a double, triple, and three RBIs. Mariano Duncan had two hits and two RBIs, and Milt Thompson and John Kruk each had three hits and two RBIs.

"It was just a matter of time till we started hitting," Eisenreich said. "We all know we can hit. It took us 3½ hours to play the stupid game, but at least we came out of it with a win."

Frank Fitzpatrick

Even before he threw his first pitch of game 3 with St. Louis, Tommy Greene had uncomfortable questions clinging to him the way his sweat-soaked uniform would be a few innings later.

Would we see the pitcher who was 8-0 with a 1.92 ERA on June 5? Or the one whose ERA was 8.62 in four starts since then? Was he healthy? Was he mixed up mentally? Mechanically?

The answers the Phillies got were as unsettling as the final score. The Cardinals bruised the slumping Greene for nine hits and six runs in five innings on their way to a 9-3 victory at Busch Stadium. The defeat trimmed the Phils' National League East lead to 6½ games as they lost for the fourth time on this seven-game trip.

Greene's fifth consecutive bad start permitted the Cardinals to take a 2-1 lead in the four-game series.

Frank Fitzpatrick

Their TWA charter touched down in Philadelphia about 7:30 P.M. on July 1. The Phillies had fallen to earth considerably earlier. Considerably harder. The blessed three-month journey through an unfamiliar land of wins and wonder officially ended in rancor for the Phils.

The reborn Cardinals had pummeled a helpless, harried Curt Schilling for 11 runs in 2⅔ innings as St. Louis leaped forcefully back into the National League East race with a 14-5 drubbing of the Phillies.

"I embarrassed myself," Schilling said after the game.

And after this 2-5 road trip ended there was not only understandable concern about the way Schilling and Tommy Greene have pitched lately, but a slightly veiled anger.

As Schilling sat at his locker in a shirt and tie, staring aimlessly, a group of veterans in underwear huddled near Darren Daulton's locker.

"That was the most embarrassing game I've ever been a part of," said the catcher. "I've been on some bad teams and I've been a very, very, very bad player. But that's the most embarrassed I've ever been."

Asked to assess his team's mood during the game, Daulton said: "I would say pretty pissed off."

St. Louis produced all of its season-best run total in three innings off Schilling and Mark Davis, who, after an ill-timed John Kruk error in the third inning, permitted Brian Jordan's torture-topping grand slam.

There were some subtle and not-so-subtle postgame comments, statements, and suggestions that, in their recent struggles, Schilling and Greene have lost their aggressiveness.

"It's only July 1; I don't think there's any need for pressure," said Daulton. "But I think a couple of guys might have felt it. I would not think that four games against a contending team would cause guys to change the way they've been going about things, but maybe it has. And I'm not talking about everybody.

"We've got one guy who was 8-1 (it wasn't clear if he was referring to Greene or Schilling), and in his last five decisions except for maybe one game, he hasn't shown up.

"The other guy . . . I don't know if they're tired, nervous, scared, worried, feeling the pressure, or what," said Daulton. "I don't think this is the time for it."

It was as if all the bad fortune they had avoided in compiling baseball's best record visited the Phillies on one hot and overcast afternoon. They committed two errors, Kruk's leading to seven unearned runs. When it mattered, they swung the bats feebly against the bent and corner-hugging offerings of Bob Tewksbury (now 9-6). And they allowed the Cardinals 15 hits and three walks. In the final three games of this road trip, Phils pitching permitted St. Louis 42 hits and 33 runs, with 22 of those runs coming off the starters.

By winning three of four in what was for them a crucial midseason series, the Cardinals drew within 5 $1/2$ games of first-place Philadelphia, which now has lost five of six.

"If they don't think we're going to chase them now, they're doing us a big favor," said Tewksbury. "They better feel like this is a race now. I know we do."

Frank Fitzpatrick

Yes, the Phillies admit they have played lousy baseball of late. Yes, catcher Darren Daulton felt the need to call the first closed-clubhouse, players-only meeting of the season on July 2. Yes, the theme was that the Phils should start behaving like their surly, malevolent old selves again.

But no, the Phillies are not panicking, shortstop Mariano Duncan said. They just had to clear the air, pitcher Curt Schilling said. It was simply time for the Phils to regroup, Daulton said.

The meeting was no big deal, they all said. Really.

When the 31-minute meeting ended, Daulton, who had been sharply critical of Phillies pitchers Curt Schilling and Tommy Greene after back-to-back lopsided losses to St. Louis, did say that he called the meeting, and reluctantly added that the meeting was constructive and upbeat.

"You know, guys, I really don't want to talk about what we talked about," Daulton said to a dozen reporters who gathered at his locker. "It was just a little regroup, and that's all I have to say."

Without getting too specific, others said the tone of that little regrouping session was simple: Start playing fearless, intimidating base-ball again. Take it a game at a time again. Forget about the pennant race.

"We're good enough to get a big lead, and we're good enough to keep it," Schilling said.

Daulton did not apologize for his remarks. He suggested that Greene and Schilling were feeling the pressure of a pennant race that had barely begun.

Schilling said Daulton had been right to chew him out. "That's his job," Schilling said. "He's one of our leaders."

It was clear that this once supremely confident, rollicking, profane team had lost a little of its sparkle after its 2-5 road trip. The clubhouse was as somber as a Christian Science reading room, with players keeping to themselves and the stereo above Schilling's locker switched off for a full hour after the meeting was adjourned.

(Later, after the stereo had been turned on, it was turned off again for a time as players, learning of the release of Mark Davis, commiserated with the departing reliever.)

Dave Caldwell

The rain came and went, came again, went again. It washed away the fireworks. It drove off the crowd.

And still they played ball at Veterans Stadium.

The clock struck 11 P.M. on Friday, July 2; midnight, Saturday, July 3, then 1 A.M. At 2 A.M., a sleeping seven-year-old caught a bouncing foul ball in the gut. At 3 A.M., the remaining fans—the few, the loyal, the committed, the oughta-be-committed—did the Wave. At 4 A.M., the lower deck boogied to "Twist and Shout."

And still they played ball at the Vet.

The people came when the bars let out, when their shifts ended. They came with no tickets, only the desire to see the Phillies win and the sun rise simultaneously. The foursome from King of Prussia had tickets, but left the park and the rain. The foursome drove home, changed clothes, turned on the television, then drove all the way back.

And there they were, still playing ball at the Vet.

The Phillies and San Diego Padres had said, "Let's play two," and the umpires were holding them to it. Once the action starts in major-league baseball, only the men in blue have the authority to halt it.

"There are no curfews," crew chief Dana DeMuth, fresh out of the shower, said at five in the morning. "It was scheduled as a doubleheader, and our job was to get in the doubleheader. There are no rules or guidelines for canceling because it's late, just for bad weather. We played that first game, and the rain was stopped, so you've got to roll right into the second game."

Some players understood the plan. Some didn't. Pete Incaviglia, the burly Phillies outfielder, was undressing at about 1 A.M., anticipating a warm shower, when coach John Vukovich told him that there would be a game 2.

"I couldn't believe it," he said. "I had no clue."

The fans were kept in suspense until 1:04, a minute after the final out of a 5-2 Padres victory. "The second game will start at 1:25," the stadium announcer said firmly and calmly. Delirium ensued. T-shirts, still soggy from six hours of rain, came off their owners' backs and went twirling in the air—a salute to the disembodied voice. One man turned his back to home plate and bowed repeatedly in the direction of a stadium skybox.

Meanwhile, Incaviglia pulled his shoes back on, grabbed a glove, and reported to leftfield. The first pitch was delivered at 1:28; the final play came at 4:40. Incaviglia crossed the plate in the bottom of the 10th inning, giving the Phillies a 6-5 victory, completing a rally from a 5-0 deficit, averting a doubleheader sweep and ending the latest day in major-league history.

All that remained was for relief pitcher Mitch Williams to take a curtain call. Sent up to bat for himself in the 10th because the Phillies had used up every pinch-hitter, Williams singled home Incaviglia. It was his first at bat of the season and the third hit of his major-league career. In a place where common sense took a vacation and everyone else worked overtime, a Mitch Williams RBIs in the 10th inning at nearly five in the morning seemed perfectly natural.

"My family was here but left after the first game," Williams said. "I'm sure my mother is asleep by now. My father went to sleep in my truck" in the parking lot.

But now it was over, 12 hours and 5 minutes after the scheduled start. "Shortest doubleheader in history," someone said later in the Phillies clubhouse. "4:35 to 4:40."

The culprit was three rain delays totaling 5 hours and 54 minutes, which set a team record and made the groundskeepers heroes on a par with Williams. The 16 men, seven full time, nine part time, pulled up the infield tarps four times—once on a false alarm. The rain returned before the players, and the crew members retreated to their tunnel behind home plate.

At 11 P.M. Friday night, Mark "Froggie" Carfagno, the dean of groundskeepers with 23 years' experience, put on his fifth dry shirt of the day. Two of his mates played catch in the dark, drizzly corridor leading to the field. Dave Raymond, temporarily out of his Phanatic costume, cruised by, trying to think of new ways to amuse the crowd.

"Let's go out there naked," he suggested. Before long, Raymond was in green feathers again, leading cheers, discouraging boos, and starting water-gun fights with the Padres. He would stay till the end, indefatigably upbeat.

Back in the tunnel, the grounds crew watched the second game with three employees of their favorite after-work haunt. "Tonight," Carfagno said, "the bartenders had to come to us."

The ninth ended, and crew members talked of staying straight through the Saturday night game. Home-plate umpire Larry Poncino motioned to the tunnel, and the men sprang to action. "Get the umpire some water, he wants some water," dugout security guard Nick Palmer hollered over his shoulder. Then he turned back toward Poncino and asked: "How do you like your eggs?"

The stadium ushers were released somewhere around midnight. About 20 supervisors stayed behind, enforcing minimal rules. No drinking, smoking, or fighting. Sit wherever you want.

The crowd, about 3,000 strong, clustered in the lowest level. Joe Krause and his buddies were there. They had left a bar in Feasterville to catch the last hour and a half. So were Bill Shank and Gerald Lee, Fishtown neighbors who are regulars at rain-delay freebies.

Lew Clark, an Archbishop Carroll senior, also made a return trip. He and three friends drove back from King of Prussia, toting a blanket and a pillow stuffed into a navy blue sham with ruffles.

When Phanavision played a tape of Mike Schmidt's 500th homer at 2:23 A.M., the fans acted as if they'd just seen it live. Ricky Jordan's three-run homer in the fifth brought the kind of ovation usually reserved for that other Jordan fellow out in Chicago.

With an inning left, announcer Richie Ashburn leaned out of the WOGL radio booth, pointed to his watch, and waved his arms to lead the fans in cheers. They responded gleefully to the old Whiz Kid in the trademark golfing cap and powder-blue sweater.

"I've never seen anything like this," said Ashburn. "I would like to think that this sets a record that is never broken. This is not my best time of the night."

But baseball is his game, and this doubleheader was baseball at its essence. A summer sun never really sets on the game.

Mickey Morandini, dragging himself through the clubhouse and past his weary teammates, seemed to understand the continuum. "See you today," he said. And he was right.

Gwen Knapp, Pam Belluck, and Frank Fitzpatrick

Maybe it was the postgame line that formed around the two beer taps in the locker room.

Maybe it was the liberal appointment of mini-sandboxes stuffed with spent cigarette butts and brown plugs of chewed tobacco.

Maybe it was the plates piled high with greasy fried chicken proffered gingerly around the room by red-shirted clubhouse boys, ample lads all.

A quick peek behind the curtain of the 1993 juggernaut first-place Philadelphia Phillies is enough to make one thing clear: The new darlings of this sports-mad city do not exactly conform to the fitness-craze, bionic-athlete, "Just Do It" mold of the '90s.

They're hairy and lumpy and unshaven. They wear bright red shoes. They dribble tobacco down their shirtfronts, and they don't exactly run—they waddle. And . . . oh, yeah, they win, and win, and win.

"I'm not an athlete, I'm a ballplayer," pugnacious first baseman–philosopher John Kruk once declared, he of the Babe Ruth belly and team-leading batting average.

Call it retro, call it grunge, call it beer gut chic: When it comes to style, the arriviste Phillies are the Jurassic Park contingent of Major League Baseball.

And boy, does this city love them! Fickle Philadelphia has always, of course, been as quick to embrace a winner as to boo a loser, but when you sell out a simple afternoon midseason home game at midweek, tying up traffic in every direction for miles before game time, and when you average crowds (35,000 per game) at a rate that threatens to approach a club attendance record, something more than bandwagon-hopping is going on.

And what will the rest of America and the world learn about Philadelphia from this collection of wide-bodied wonder boys who like to slide headfirst? And what is it about the Phillies that has so captured the hearts of this determined northeastern metropolis?

Style!

That's right, the graceless, downright, in-your-face Middle America ordinariness of this team is its secret weapon. In a tobacco-free workplace world of cholesterol-counting, fat-free, aerobically fit, vice-disdaining robots, consider the Phillies as the vanguard of a pop-culture assault on the Cult of Human Perfection.

Consider Kruk, the true genius of gut chic. Round face unshaven, a tangle of hair cascading from the back end of his cap to his shoulders, belly distending the red pinstripes of his jersey, chaw bulging in his lower lip. (Actually, in deference to teammate Terry Mulholland's nationwide crusade against chewing tobacco, Kruk has recently been experimenting with sunflower seeds, which he hasn't quite got the hang of yet, which is why pigeons tend to congregate around first base between innings, looking for the ones Kruk dribbles without breaking open.)

Kruk tried to lose weight once. He slimmed down considerably. Cut a handsome figure in his San Diego Padres uniform. One problem, though—he stopped hitting. The Padres traded him to the Phillies. Kruk wisely left the diet on the West Coast, started hitting at a .300 clip, and hasn't turned down a fried drumstick yet.

There's Lenny Dykstra, mouth so jammed with chaw that mangled wet strings of it dangle from his lips. With his uniform off, Dykstra is smaller than he seems on the field, but he does have what looks like a well-chiseled (albeit hairy) weight lifter's physique. He disguises it well on the field, however, yanking on his jersey so that the tails often hang out over his belt, wrapping his arms with sweat bands, and stuffing his back pants pockets with batting gloves and tobacco tins and God knows what all else.

Phils manager Jim Fregosi is a health-conscious guy. He even tried to quit cigarettes in 1992. It lasted until Dykstra broke his wrist—game one, first inning. Fregosi endured that long losing season guzzling vegetable juice, popping ginseng tablets, and chain-smoking Kool Lights.

Truth is, it's hard to be a fitness buff in a world in which there are beer taps in the locker room and late-night fast food is the rule.

"I have a good diet in the winter, but during the season it just goes to pot," all-star catcher Darren Daulton says. "Late-night schedule, sometimes burgers are all you can get."

Daulton is one of the few Phillies who doesn't fit the lumpy, gut chic mold. He's got the wide shoulders, narrow hips, and chiseled features of a screen idol, and, amid this bunch, seems almost apologetic about it.

"During the off-season, I work hard at staying fit," Daulton says. "I have to. I've had a lot of knee surgeries, and I have to lift weights and bike and swim as, like, maintenance. During the season, catching every day keeps me in shape. It's a long season. People talk about Kruk not being in shape. He's in shape—baseball shape. He's not going to win any body contests, but he hits."

Daulton finished stripping off his layers of gear and made straight for the beer tap.

Two hours after game time, Kruk hadn't moved. Feet up, two new beers on the table, and the boys were still passing around chicken.

"Hey, don't knock it," Tommy Greene says. "If that's the way John needs to look to hit, then that's the right way for him to look. No doubt about it."

Amen.

Mark Bowden

This was a test for Tommy Greene. This was only a test. It might have been an actual emergency. But then the Phillies pitcher probably would have slinked off the mound with his head held low against a wall of boos.

Instead, on his long seventh-inning walk to the Philadelphia dugout on July 5, a departing Greene raised his head high to acknowledge a Veterans Stadium ovation born in relief.

In his most encouraging start in a month, Greene limited the Dodgers to a single run through six innings before tiring in the seventh as the reawakening Phillies clubbed the Dodgers, 9-5.

"Personally, I've been going through a tough time," said Greene, who was criticized the week before by catcher Darren Daulton after a poor outing in St. Louis.

Greene (now 10-2) didn't entirely erase the concerns that dogged him during a stretch of five sloppy starts in which his ERA was 9.15. In this game, he allowed six hits, two walks, and four runs in $6\frac{1}{3}$ innings. He was, however, throwing hard and easily and with a confidence that had vanished suddenly after an 8-0 start.

"He was relaxed tonight," said Phils manager Jim Fregosi. "And he was aggressive. Very aggressive."

John Kruk and Dave Hollins each had three hits and two RBIs. Lenny Dykstra scored three more runs, pushing his major-league-leading total to 79, and Wes Chamberlain and Kim Batiste chipped in run-scoring doubles.

The Phillies' second straight victory, their third in four games and their sixth in seven tries against the Dodgers this season, left them with a seven-game lead over the St. Louis Cardinals in the National League East.

"You take any criticism you get in a constructive way," Greene said after becoming the Phils' first 10-game winner. "You try to learn from it. You don't want to put any pressure on yourself."

He said he and Daulton had "talked to each other to see if we could make any corrections, mentally and physically." The remedy apparently was lots of fastballs. Greene was beating the Dodgers with his money pitch.

"I was getting ahead of the hitters, making them swing the bats," he said. "I was saying, 'Here's my pitch. Hit it.'"

Frank Fitzpatrick

The blue eyes were a little bloodshot when Kevin Stocker showed up in South Philadelphia on July 7. The night before had been a long one for the 23-year-old rookie the Phillies have designated as their shortstop savant.

The first phone call came late, just after 11 P.M. the night before. His minor-league manager, George Culver, joked that he was making a curfew check, then got down to business: The Phillies had promoted Stocker and wanted him to start the very next night against the Dodgers.

Stocker said nothing.

"I was shocked," he said as he dressed for the first time as a major-leaguer. Then he did what any other young professional would do when promoted. He called his girlfriend, his parents, and some friends.

He tried to sleep but didn't have much luck. At 6 A.M. he was at the Scranton/Wilkes-Barre ballpark to pick up his equipment. But the equipment was at the airport, loaded on a plane for Scranton's road trip to Columbus, Ohio. Stocker raced to the airport, got his stuff, and made it to Veterans Stadium at about 2:15 P.M.

"I only got lost twice," he said.

Ready or not, Stocker is in the big leagues. He had impressed manager Jim Fregosi in spring training, and Fregosi gave Stocker a rousing welcome when he saw him in the dressing room.

What did he say? "Hello, welcome, good luck," Fregosi deadpanned. Fregosi also said he'd quit smoking.

Larry Bowa, the third-base coach and former Phillies shortstop, spent time talking to Stocker. To say Bowa likes what he sees in the young shortstop is an understatement. Who does Stocker remind him of? "Me," Bowa said.

Bowa said Stocker had even passed the ultimate test during spring training—the Bowa test. In this exercise, the rookie makes a mistake and Bowa gets in his face, screaming all kinds of things, some of which you can understand. The point, though, is to humiliate and intimidate and generally see if you have what it takes to play in the big leagues, particularly in Philadelphia.

"I don't like a player who, after you get on him, goes and sits at the end of the bench, hangs his head, and sulks," Bowa said. "He came back at me. I liked that. But what's he going to do in front of 55,000 people? I don't know. There's only one way to find out."

Bowa said a player needs thick skin to be successful in Philadelphia. Stocker agreed. When asked what he needed to work on most to stay in the big leagues, he said his hitting and developing thick skin. "One thing I can't worry about is what people think about me."

"Awoo, Awoo," pitcher Tommy Greene barked at Stocker and a small group of reporters surrounding him. Stocker smiled and said hello.

Where were we? Thick skin. Yes. Stocker is working on that.

His skin-thickening began shortly after his arrival when he was assigned a locker just a short spit away from veterans row. When Pete Incaviglia saw that, he let out a howl. "Stuck him right in the ghetto, right where he belongs," Inky said as he walked to his own locker.

"Hey, how ya doing, Inky?" Stocker said.

"How you doing, buddy?" Inky said. "Welcome."

"Thanks."

That's as mushy as baseball players get. Especially toward untested rookies. But if Stocker's skin can survive the dressing room, 55,000 booing fans are not going to bother him.

With Triple A Scranton, he was hitting .233 and had 56 strikeouts in 313 at bats, along with 15 errors. He said most of his errors were the result of mental mistakes—he'd dive for the ball, get up, and instead of holding onto it, throw it away. "The glove has come along," he said.

Bowa said Stocker's job here will be "to catch the ball" and not worry about hitting. "Anyone who expects him to come up here and hit .280 is stupid," Bowa said.

It was 4:56 P.M. and Stocker trotted out to shortstop for the first time as a Phillie, to take some ground balls. Bowa smacked one after another, to Stocker's left, to his right, right at him hard, right at him bouncing high off the turf. Bowa hit one after the other and said nothing, just watched as the kid handled everything with the soft movements of a juggler.

Stocker said he couldn't wait for the game to start, he was so nervous. He scratched at his closely cropped blond hair, eyes bloodshot, skin still rookie-thin, and, ready or not, he just couldn't wait for his first major-league game to begin.

Timothy Dwyer

That night was hot. The game was long. Everyone was uncomfortable. This was no time for Mitch Williams.

The Phillies' hot-and-cold closer lost the plate in the ninth inning. And by the time he left the field, screaming at home-plate umpire Jim Quick, a two-run Philadelphia lead was nearing its eventual destination: Gone.

But Larry Andersen, with help from newcomer Kevin Stocker, escaped a none-out, bases-loaded mess in the ninth.

And then the game crawled on for 11 more innings before the Phillies finally beat the Dodgers, 7-6, on Lenny Dykstra's two-run double in the 20th inning of another post-midnight mess at Veterans Stadium.

The 6-hour, 10-minute victory, which tied a 1973 Phils-Braves game for the longest ever at the Vet, gave the first-place Phillies a 2-1 edge in the three-game series against the Dodgers.

Jim Eisenreich and Mickey Morandini got the Phils' first hits in $12^2/_3$ innings to start the 20th, after the Dodgers had taken a 6-5 lead in the top of the inning.

One out after Stocker's sacrifice bunt loaded the bases when reliever Rod Nichols threw late to third, Dykstra slapped a ground-rule double that created another post-midnight celebration outside the Phils dugout.

The game, which ended at 1:47 in the morning on July 8, came five days after the Phils finished a game at 4:40 A.M., the latest finish in baseball history.

Stocker, the newly installed Phillies shortstop, played his first big-league game, going 0 for 6 with two walks.

In the ninth, the Dodgers loaded the bases off Williams on a single by Brett Butler and walks to Mitch Webster and José Offerman. They scored their first run when Williams walked Cory Snyder on a 3-2 pitch the reliever thought was a strike.

With Phils manager Jim Fregosi walking onto the field, Williams moved toward Quick, screamed at him, and was thrown out.

Andersen came in, and Eric Karros's single off the pitcher's leg tied the score at 5-5. With the infield in, Mike Piazza bounced the ball to Stocker—just the second chance of the rookie's first big-league day. Stocker charged it and threw home off-balance to force Butler.

Andersen struck out Eric Davis on an outside pitch that left the Dodgers batter furious with Quick.

Unless you believe the Phillies are planning a major trade—and there is no indication of that—their decision to call up Stocker seemed to imply a peculiar sense of urgency for a team leading its division by six games.

But the Phils' lack of infield range certainly contributed to several earlier defeats. Stocker was put in the lineup to turn some of those dribbling singles into outs.

If the rookie wasn't feeling the heat, he was alone. When the game began, the temperature was 94. And a reading of 131 had been recorded on the searing artificial turf earlier in the day.

Frank Fitzpatrick

He watched a third strike with a befuddled expression, as if it were some algebraic equation. A feeble swing then produced a bouncer that died softly in the pitcher's glove.

This same Mickey Morandini, overmatched in his first two at bats, would drive in five runs with a single and a grand slam in his final two. And those runs provided the difference in the Phillies' 8-3 victory over the San Francisco Giants in a rare Saturday afternoon game on July 10 at Veterans Stadium.

His sixth-inning single had given the Phils a 4-3 lead and, after David West came in to retire Will Clark and Barry Bonds, Morandini's eighth-inning slam—the first of his career—made an 11-game winner out of starter Tommy Greene (now 11-2). The win kept the Phils five games ahead of the St. Louis Cardinals, who beat Colorado.

With the All-Star break approaching and their National League East lead shrinking, the victory was important. The Giants had collected 28 runs and 43 hits in winning the first two games of this series. In the previous three meetings between these first-place clubs, the Phils had been outscored, 39-12.

Frank Fitzpatrick

The Dog Days

The possibility of another late Phillies collapse haunted the ninth-inning moment as John Kruk plodded toward the mound. Mitch Williams, about to confront the potential tying run, awaited him.

Clearly, given the participants, this was not going to be an analytical discussion. No modest talk of mechanics or motions. This was going to be as raw and gritty as the two players involved. A meeting not of minds but of attitudes. Bad attitudes born of three straight defeats.

"That," Williams said later of Kruk's advice, "was a beautiful message."

What Kruk said was this: "I don't give a fuck what happens. Get them motherfuckers out." So Williams did. Archi Cianfrocco bounced immediately into a game-ending double play, and both Curt Schilling and the Phillies had a desperately needed victory, 6-3, over the Padres on July 18 at Jack Murphy Stadium.

"I felt fine," said Williams, who had allowed a one-out Bob Geren double and had walked Ricky Gutierrez before the final-inning confab. "I just got a little funky there to Gutierrez."

A riding fastball jammed Cianfrocco, who bounced a slow roller to Dave Hollins. The third baseman stepped on the bag and threw to first for the final out in what was just the reeling Phils' third win in 10 games and their initial victory after the All-Star break.

"We had to have this one," said Williams, who recorded his 24th save, his first since June 25. "For peace of mind if nothing else."

Indeed, with the St. Louis Cardinals on their tails like relentless bloodhounds, the Phils earned a day of relief with their sweep-averting victory, which followed three nasty defeats to the Padres.

"We were losing ugly," Lenny Dykstra said of the three come-from-ahead losses to San Diego. "But you're going to go through ups and downs. I don't care if you're an English teacher or a major-league ball-player—it's going to happen."

The victory ended a season-high four-game losing streak and, more important, maintained the Phillies' diminishing National League East lead over the Cards at three games.

"We just hit a stretch where we didn't play very well," manager Jim Fregosi said. "Sometimes to get over the hump you need a few breaks."

And they got plenty in a four-run second inning that was a tension-buster for Curt Schilling and his teammates. Pete Incaviglia ended an

0-for-23 slump with a double to start the second. Todd Pratt singled him to third. Kevin Stocker's single made it 1-0 and left runners at first and second. Schilling set down a bad bunt that Padres starter Doug Brocail (now 2-5) pounced on, but the throw sailed past Gutierrez at third, and Pratt scurried home on the error. Dykstra's walk filled the bases, and second baseman Jeff Gardner booted Mariano Duncan's grounder for another run-scoring error. The inning's fourth run scored on Kruk's double-play groundball.

Schilling couldn't wait to throw his first pitch. When the Phillies took the field for the first time, he did not walk casually from the dugout to the mound. He sprinted. When he got to the third-base line, he did not take his usual little hop over the foul line. He vaulted the whole dirt base path and then continued his sprint to the back of the mound, where he picked up the game ball and hurriedly began his warm-up tosses.

No, Schilling could not wait to get started. He was feeling good, and he was feeling confident—and with good reason. For when he warmed up in the bullpen, he had nothing. No fastball, no slider, no curve.

"I left the bullpen with the worst stuff I've had all year," he said.

And he was elated. Because all the while he was going through his month-long slump, he always had Hall of Fame stuff in the bullpen.

"Today," he said, "I didn't have anything but I didn't care. I felt loose. I felt good."

In this game, Curt Schilling won for the first time since late June. And it came at a good time for him and his Phils, who had dropped the first three games of their West Coast Character Test and watched their once mighty lock on first place shrivel.

Schilling said the slump had changed him a little, made him appreciate the nuances of pitching a little more, the importance of pitching rather than trying to overpower every hitter with hard stuff.

"For the last five or six starts, [pitching coach Johnny Podres] has been telling me that I had to pitch inside," Schilling said. "I'm not the kind of guy that is going to bean anyone, but today I was throwing inside and I was not trying to throw strikes. I wanted guys to get their feet moving."

He wanted them to feel what he had been feeling. Uncomfortable and unconfident.

Frank Fitzpatrick and Timothy Dwyer

It was late on that afternoon, July 18, when the music returned. After losing four in a row, the Phillies finally had won a game and were headed for the dressing room of Jack Murphy Stadium in San Diego when Pete Incaviglia's voice pierced the dusk: "Turn on the [big-leaguer's adjective] music," he screamed, "I haven't heard it in a week."

Inky's cry of joy was answered without haste. The music boomed. Walk into the Phillies dressing room after a game and the only way you can tell if they have won or lost is the music. When there is music, there is victory. Not dancing and whooping. Just music. Silence greets defeat.

This may come as a surprise, given the Phillies' lunatic-fringe reputation, but so far in this very surprising season, they have ushered in each victory and defeat in pretty much the same low-key way.

It doesn't seem possible that any ship carrying these players could ever stay on an even keel, but that's exactly what they've managed to do, even through their recent, prolonged slump.

When they win, most of the stars retreat to the off-limits training room to get treatment for their various ailments, drink beer, eat food from the buffet, smoke cigarettes, and chew the fat as well as other various tobacco products. Most do not make themselves available to reporters.

Losing is greeted exactly the same way. But no music.

Every baseball player who has been through a pennant race will tell you that it is important for a team to learn how to lose as well as how to win. Most of this team has never been through a pennant race before, and so when these Phillies got off to a fast start, they learned how to win. That was the easy part.

Now, facing a big series with the NL West-leading Giants, some veteran players think they might have learned their most important lesson of the season: how to lose.

Phillies coach Larry Bowa, who played in five league championship series and one World Series, had been waiting for a month such as this one, a stretch of several weeks in which pitchers struggle and hitters stop hitting and mitts suddenly develop massive holes.

"Most of these guys have never been through a pennant race, and the only way to learn about it is to go through one," he said. "Hell, what team comes out and goes wire to wire without a down time? The season's too long for that. And when you get into a little slump, it's important to see how guys are going to react. The important thing is not to get too high and not to get too low."

Emotional stability and your Phillies. Start printing the playoff tickets.

All while they were losing 14 of 20 games in July, Bowa was there telling players to just forget each loss and not get upset. He was not, however, preaching the even-keel gospel.

"Even keel? I don't know about that," said Bowa, who was known to yell and scream a little during his playing and managing days. "I think you should have some emotion. You should get mad when you give games away, like we did down in San Diego when we gave away two games. And when you win a game it's important to celebrate a little, but not get overconfident."

One of the things that might have sparked the Phillies' July slump was overconfidence by some of the young players, according to Larry Andersen, who has played in three league championship series and one World Series.

"You want to stay off the roller coaster," Andersen said. "You get too high and you set yourself up for a big fall. I think we have had some examples of that happening with this team. But it's hard to do that when you're on top of the world. You feel so good about yourself and you think you can get anyone out and that all you have to do is show up at the ballpark to win."

And then the music stops.

Andersen said the recent slump taught the young players something. He said the leadership emerged on the team. "Bubba [Darren Daulton] is really good about talking to guys when they're down, and we try not to let anyone get too high, either. Kruk's good and Lenny, but Lenny mostly does it by just going out and playing."

So now they've won and now they've lost, and they begin a four-game series with the NL West-leading Giants, a team that won three of four from them in Philadelphia.

Listen for the music.

Timothy Dwyer

Barry Bonds savored the two-run homer that clinched the Giants' 5-2 victory of July 25 like a bird-watcher getting his first glimpse of a blue-tailed finch. His lengthy observation completed, Bonds then jogged the bases as leisurely as an octogenarian with arthritis.

On the mound, Phillies reliever Larry Andersen, who threw the seventh- inning "helicopter" pitch to Bonds, did not appreciate the slow show.

"He's got a lot more money than me," Andersen said, "and a lot more talent. But he doesn't have more time. I don't appreciate that. It's not necessary."

So, did Andersen say anything to Bonds as he cruised the bases? "No," he said, "but if I had, we could have had a pretty lengthy conversation." Andersen and Bonds did exchange words later, as the reliever headed to the clubhouse and the San Francisco superstar walked toward the dugout.

"We just exchanged phone numbers and addresses for Christmas cards," Andersen said.

Bonds's homer assured the powerful Giants of their third victory in this four-game series—the second time they've accomplished that against Philadelphia in two weeks. The loss meant the Phillies concluded their longest road trip of the year with a 5-6 record and a four-game National League East lead that is one game smaller than when the journey began July 15.

And the team that has been pursuing the Phillies this entire season, the St. Louis Cardinals, is up next for the Phillies for three games.

Frank Fitzpatrick

In the 9 ½ years since they last appeared in the postseason, the Phillies have committed baseball 1,556 times. All of those games have shared one common trait: They haven't meant a thing.

But now that rarest of attractions is billed for the Vet—a series of baseball games pregnant with significance.

The Phillies, wobbling and unsteady to be sure, cling nonetheless to first place in the National League East as they entertain their nearest pursuers, the St. Louis Cardinals, whose gait, while somewhat more certain than that of the Phillies, also resembles a drunk trying to negotiate a darkened room.

The math, as it always does in these circumstances, favors the team with the lead. The Phils could lose two of the three games yet lose only one off their lead. This, of course, would lead to panic in the streets anyway. Phillies fans, nurtured by decades of defeat and haunted still by the Collapse of '64, live to expect the worst. That way, they reason, they will never be disappointed.

In their minds, the Phillies will survive now and save the folding for September, when it will hurt even more.

Bill Lyon

There is language in how a team leaves the field. On July 29, as the Phillies and Cardinals walked off the searing turf at Veterans Stadium, the words were clear.

Having just beaten St. Louis 6-4, to sweep a three-game series and rebuild their lead in the National League East to a robust seven games, the Phillies bounced away. They smacked hands and backs. They laughed. They tried hard not to swagger.

And the Cardinals? The coaches and players who were still out there when Ozzie Smith's ground ball to second became the game's final out looked as if they might need a tow truck to haul them back to the clubhouse. At second base, Luis Alicea stuck his hands on his hips, glanced at the celebrating pack of Phils, and shook his head slowly.

The NL East's top two teams were now separated as much by emotion as games in the standings.

"They came in here with a chance to put us in a really tough spot," said Curt Schilling, who permitted two runs in 6²/₃ innings. "They could have been one back or three back. Instead, they leave here with us out in front by seven games. And I think we're a good enough ball club to hold a seven-game lead."

They certainly looked like one in outscoring St. Louis, 30-17 in what were the three biggest baseball games in this city in a decade. The significance was not lost on Philadelphia fans, 147,613 of whom attended.

"It's a good feeling as a club to experience winning games like these," said Darren Daulton, whose pinch-hit walk with the bases loaded in the eighth inning of the third game scored the winning run.

"But the most important thing is that the town is really into what's happening. I guess that's called home-field advantage."

As Daulton, who had been taking a day off, popped his head out of the dugout in the eighth inning, fans spotted him, and a roar slowly built among the 55,884 there this day. At the plate, Kevin Stocker, at shortstop again after eight days spent rehabilitating his sprained left ankle, was getting a bases-filling intentional walk.

"Walk a fucking rookie to get to me," Daulton joked afterward. "But I'm not going to second-guess Joe Torre," he said of the Cardinals manager. "I'm hitting two-and-change [.207] against lefthanders, and by loading the bases he sets up a double play."

As Daulton awaited the 3-2 pitch from reliever Rob Murphy (1-5) with the score tied at 4-4, the crowd was on its feet screaming.

The pitch arrived, home-plate umpire Terry Tata called it a ball, and Daulton gave it an unusually long look before starting toward first. Pete Incaviglia, whose single had begun the winning rally, came home, and the Phils, having squandered a 4-0 lead, were back in front.

"Nah, it was a ball all the way," Daulton said when asked if he had doubts.

Daulton, weary and weak on the recent West Coast trip, had eight RBIs in this series to bring his total to one less than league-leader Barry Bonds's 79.

And it was also Schilling's second straight start in which he resembled the Schilling of April and May. Hurt in St. Louis in June by hitters sitting on his fastball, the righthander went to a variety of pitches.

"They are a fastball-hitting club," Schilling said. "So I went out there thinking I was going to get my off-speed stuff over early in the count."

Frank Fitzpatrick

The word for the day, and the night, was letdown.

It was a cautionary word and it blinked like neon in the clubhouse whenever you spoke to a Phillie.

And it was hanging heavy in the air, in angry red danger letters, when Ben Rivera threw the game's first pitch at 7:37 on July 30, a fastball strike on the inside corner to Carlos Garcia of the Pirates.

The Phillies, fresh from that tingling three-game sweep of the Cardinals, had to keep reminding themselves that, exhilarating as it was, that sweep had guaranteed them nothing except the promise to play 59 more games and the chance to lose if they aren't careful.

"We haven't clinched anything by any means," general manager Lee Thomas said, 15 minutes before Rivera's first pitch. "I like our position now a lot better than I did a week ago, but . . . you have to be careful now because the natural tendency is to have a letdown after you've won a big series."

Thomas's prophecy threatened to be fulfilled moments later. Garcia lined Rivera's fifth pitch into right, then stole second. Two more singles, another defensive lapse by the Phillies' uncertain interior defense, and the Pirates had stitched a quick 2-0 lead.

Suddenly, the Phillies' sweep was a fading memory. Reality had rudely intruded. Yesterday's champagne has a way of turning into today's vinegar when the schedule demands that you play virtually every day.

You have the sense that the Phils have weathered the storm. Of course, when you say this out loud to any of them, they clap their hands over their ears and begin to hum loudly. They want to hear none of it. Two months to go, and all that.

It is precisely the attitude they should have. But a slump was inevitable, and you have the distinct feeling that they have endured and survived, and will now prevail.

The bullpen is overworked at the moment and is guaranteed to cause moments of high anxiety during the season's final two months, but the feeling persists that the Phillies have enough. They may scuffle some, but there is enough, both tangibly and intangibly.

Bill Lyon

With the Phillies in a pennant race, the gentle background noise of baseball on the radio is a little louder in the summer of '93. In elevators and taxicabs and subway cars, in pizza parlors and dentists' offices and corner stores, in row houses and traffic jams and backyard tents, the count is within earshot. From stoops and benches and backyards and open windows come the low hum of the score, the inning, the hits, the men left on.

Baseball on the radio does not give you the contract disputes, expletive-deleted quotes, clubhouse rancor. Baseball on the radio, as brought to you by Harry Kalas, Rich Ashburn, Chris Wheeler, and Andy Musser, the voices of the Phillies on 1210 WOGL, is filtered, elemental, old-time.

"Osborne will have to keep an eye on Dykstra."

Those words were spoken on a July afternoon as the Phillies and Cardinals played at Veterans Stadium. Lenny Dykstra had opened the bottom of the first with a single off Donovan Osborne. The voice, grandfatherly and wise, belonged to Ashburn. Among his listeners was Paul Block, an appliance repairman from Northeast Philadelphia, who was sitting in his air-conditioned van in front of the A Plus Mini-Market on Germantown Avenue and Washington Lane in Germantown.

Block was eating a ham sandwich from home, drinking a huge orange soda, reading the Philadelphia Daily News from the back, and listening to the radio, imagining the game.

"I got the idea that Dykstra's got a pretty good lead," Block said. "He's got—what?—18 or 19 straight steals? I figure he's got one foot on the cutout, one foot on the grass."

"Grass?"

"Grass, turf, whatever," the repairman said. "In my mind, it's grass. You watch on TV, it's turf."

Baseball on television has, of course, stolen listeners, and there are people today who think that baseball on the radio is extinct.

In the North Philadelphia neighborhoods in the vicinity of where Connie Mack Stadium once stood, one could go block after block, both in commercial districts and in residential areas, and not find a publicly audible radio tuned into the game. Forty years ago, in those same streets, home-run calls by Gene Kelly and By Saam buzzed through the hot air all summer long.

Still, there is baseball on the radio throughout most of the city these summer days. There was baseball on the radio at Koch's Take Out Shop in West Philadelphia, at Steve's Auto Glass in the Northeast, at Beifeld Jewelers on Eighth Street in Center City, in the cabs waiting for arriving flights at the airport, and at Carey's 19th Hole, a tavern on Henry Avenue in Roxborough.

"Runner goes, 3-2 pitch, hit in the air to right field and hit well. Jordan is back, back some more. It's gone! A two-run home run for Chamberlain, and the Phillies lead the Cardinals, 2-0."

Musser's words wafted through the tavern's air, which was cool and dark and smoky. A dozen men were at the bar, most of them with racing forms and beers in front of them, their eyes on the horses running silently across the TV screen, their ears on the game.

"Chamberlain did what?" a patron asked aloud, to nobody in particular.

"Two-run home run," answered a man at the end of the bar, Paul Denbow of Roxborough.

"Crowd must be goin' nuts," he said, creating in his mind's eye the pandemonium generated by the 56,000 celebrants at the Vet, 10 miles away, in the southernmost reaches of South Philadelphia.

At the stadium, there were scores of radios tuned to 1210 AM, witnesses seeking second opinions, and in the South Philadelphia neighborhoods in the extended shadows of the Vet, the number of radios vibrating with the game must have numbered in the hundreds, if not the thousands.

Radio carried the game at Cosmi's Meat Market and the Leonetti Funeral Home and in front of a row house on the west side of South Eighth Street between Dickson and Greenwich, where an 83-year-old woman named Mildred Collura sat in a beach chair under an awning, wearing a cotton sundress and holding a transistor radio in her left hand, the antenna pointed toward the Vet.

Listening on the radio she inherited from her late husband—Sam the Barber—she raised clasped hands as the Phillies doubled their 2-0 lead. While the Cardinals were tying the game at 4-4, she twisted the flesh of her upper left arm with the fingers of her right hand.

"I'm ashamed I don't have my rosaries out here," she said. She did have an extra battery, however, in case the one in the radio conked out.

Without missing a pitch, she greeted, in Italian, a passerby, 93-year-old Joe Termini, who inquired about the status of the game. When Dykstra singled home the Phillies' sixth run, she raised a fist in the air. When Mitch Williams pitched in the ninth with two out, two on, and the Phillies up by two, the old woman crossed herself.

"Here's the pitch. Swing, and a hard ground ball right at Morandini. Flips to Stocker for a force at second. That'll be the ball game. The Phils win by a score of 6-4 as the Phils sweep the Runnin' Redbirds, and the lead in the National League East is now seven games!"

Collura exhaled at Kalas's words, smiled, looked at the awning above her, and said: "Thank you."

Michael Bamberger

Their season is nearly two-thirds complete and the Phillies have occupied first place for all but one day. More than two million fans have sat in Veterans Stadium's molded plastic seats. The Eagles are suddenly a secondary concern.

In the Phillies clubhouse, the guarded optimism of April and May has become a solid confidence. It is not easy now, on August 3, to recall the uncertainty that hovered above the Phils this off-season.

Jim Fregosi and Lee Thomas, burned by predictions of contention in '92, spoke cautiously all winter. Some players—some very important players—griped about the club's reluctance to pursue big free agents. And ticket sales, if not falling, were certainly stagnant.

What happened?

Well, there are many good explanations. The three new outfielders. The better-than-anticipated bullpen. The worse-than-anticipated division. Here are a few reasons—some obvious, some not so apparent:

Good Eyes, Good Pop. The Phillies walked and homered a lot in 1992, too. Now, however, the Phils lead the National League in both categories. "Everybody always says a walk is as good as a hit," said John Kruk, "but everybody doesn't always believe it. I guess we do." And, with 56 games remaining, the Phils are only 11 homers behind the 1992 total. They are hitting more than one a game (107 in 106)—even though no Phillie is among the NL's top nine in home runs.

Good Vibrations. There still are the occasional spats and sulks, but, perhaps simply because they are winning, the locker room is a much friendlier place these days. In 1992, there was a feeling that the pitchers were letting the hitters down, and that caused resentment. In 1992, there was a constant parade of rookies through the locker-room doors, and baseball is not a sport in which first-year players are accepted graciously. And in 1992, Wally Backman, never reluctant to contribute a postgame gripe or two, was around.

Good Health. They have avoided the long-term injury and, for the most part, have kept their nucleus of everyday players fit. Only Dave Hollins among their core regulars has gone on the DL, and the Phillies went 10-6 in his absence. Lenny Dykstra has started every game but one and played in all 106. With him in the lineup, the Phils are 33 games over .500 since the 1991 season (143-110).

Good Neighbors. The Phils have battered the league's three weakest clubs—New York, Colorado, and Florida. "That's what a first-place club has got to do," said Darren Daulton, "beat up on the teams you're supposed to and play everyone else pretty even."

Frank Fitzpatrick

This is what was going through Jim Fregosi's mind in the eighth inning on the night of August 4: We're ahead, 8-6. David West is one strike away from concluding the inning. Mitch Williams is ready for the ninth. God is in his heaven. My Phillies are in first place.

Somewhere toward the end of that reverie, Fregosi heard a sharp crack and an ensuing roar. What went through the manager's mind at that moment cannot be repeated.

Greg Olson's three-run homer off West gave the Braves a stunning, 9-8 comeback victory over the Phillies at Atlanta–Fulton County Stadium.

"We can't run out the clock in this game," Fregosi said of the 8-5 lead his team squandered in the eighth. "If we could have stalled and run out the clock, we would have. But . . ."

But for one of the few occasions this season, West was rocked. He gave up Fred McGriff's leadoff single, a David Justice walk, and Mark Lemke's run-scoring single. That made the score 8-6. After Lemke's third consecutive single, Olson was down in the count, 1-2, on a couple of nasty breaking balls from West. One was grounded down the third-base line. Kim Batiste gloved it and stepped on the bag for what appeared to be the inning's final out. But umpire Larry Vanover called it foul.

Then West fired a fastball to Olson. It was down the heart of the plate—and up in the leftfield seats in no time.

"Yeah, you know when you make a bad pitch sometimes," West said, "and this time I knew."

The loss, just the Phillies' second in eight games, left them with a 6 1/2-game lead over St. Louis in the National League East.

Frank Fitzpatrick

A t 9:41 P.M. on August 5, two banks of lights at Atlanta–Fulton County Stadium fell dark. A chanting crowd was silenced. A Braves rally was stilled. Fifteen freaky minutes later, the lights and the crowd had juice again. The Braves did not.

Just two pitches after the sixth-inning delay, with the bases filled, with the tying and winning runs in scoring position, with fans bellowing his name, Sid Bream bounced into a rally-killing double play, and the Phillies went on to drub Atlanta, 10-4.

"If that delay had gone on much longer," said Phillies manager Jim Fregosi, "I probably wouldn't have let him continue."

"Him" was Ben Rivera, who pumped a fist in ecstasy when he saw John Kruk dig out Kevin Stocker's low throw to complete the vital double play.

"I was just very happy," said Rivera (now 10-6), who became the third Phillies starter to reach double figures in victories.

Dave Hollins was 3 for 4 with four RBIs in this game, including a two-out, go-ahead single in the fifth and a three-run double, again with two outs, in the eighth. "I think you can see that Hollins's hand is feeling better," Fregosi said. "He's throwing the ball better. And any time you can get four RBIs in a game, that says something."

The Phillies took two of three in this series from the Braves. Their National League East lead over the Cardinals now stands at 6 1/2 games, while Atlanta has descended to 8 1/2 games beneath the Giants in the West.

Frank Fitzpatrick

Darren Daulton smashed 800 feet of home runs, walked three times, knocked in five runs, and scrambled after wayward pitches in the gray dirt near home plate for much of the 4 hours and 12 minutes. It was no surprise that as he stretched out in the trainer's room afterward, he was weary. He was fortunate that he was not disappointed, too.

The Phillies defeated the Marlins 8-7 in 10 innings on August 7, despite blowing leads of 3-0 and 7-5, despite three errors, and despite generally dreadful pitching. In addition to Daulton's 19th and 20th homers, Phils hitters walked a season-high 12 times in the slow and sloppy game before a season-best crowd of 44,689 at Joe Robbie Stadium.

"I'm tired," Phils manager Jim Fregosi said. "We didn't pitch well. We didn't run the bases well. We didn't play defense well. We caught a break."

The biggest break came in the 10th, and it helped winner Mitch Williams (now 3-3) preserve the Phillies' 10th victory in 12 extra-inning games to this point of this strange and so-far successful season. Gary Sheffield, the tying run, was at second base with one out in the 10th. He had stolen second and he took off for third. With Dave Hollins breaking to the bag, Rich Renteria's bouncer plunked Sheffield for the second out. Williams then got pinch-hitter Bob Natal on an infield pop-up to end the dreadful game.

"Sometimes it's better to be lucky than good," Williams said. "Him stealing there saved the game for me."

Frank Fitzpatrick

Curt Schilling's body was pointed toward home plate. His left eye, though, was wrapped around the side of his head. Discreetly, if awkwardly, he peeked at the dugout.

The bases were loaded with Expos in the ninth inning on August 10, and Schilling, perhaps having heard a ball ricocheting wildly around the bullpen, knew that Mitch Williams was up. Schilling was searching for Jim Fregosi.

"I was kind of glancing at Jimmy sideways, making sure he wasn't coming up the steps," he said.

The Phillies manager and Schilling both stayed put, the right-hander worked clear of the final-inning mess, and the Phils defeated Montreal 5-2 before 43,104 at Veterans Stadium.

"Mitch was ready," Fregosi said of his closer. "But I thought Schilling was still throwing the ball good."

Pitching the way he had before tumbling into an emotional funk in June, Schilling (now 10-6) limited the Expos to five hits and struck out seven in winning his 10th game two months after he'd won his eighth.

Frank Fitzpatrick

There were 50 players at Veterans Stadium on August 12, a dozen or so coaches and managers, and 45,002 fans. Joe West annoyed most of them.

But in the lulls that fell between the pugnacious umpire's argumentative moments, the Phillies defeated the Expos 7-4 to sweep their three-game series and shove third-place Montreal 13 games to their rear.

Kevin Stocker, whose two early errors contributed to a 3-0 Montreal lead, singled in the tie-breaking run with two outs in the seventh inning. The Phillies added two more in the eighth before Mitch Williams came in to notch his 31st save, a club record for lefthanders.

The 3-hour, 6-minute game was played in fits and spurts as hitters and pitchers disagreed with West's strike zone and occasionally reacted to the in-your-face, confrontational style of the umpire who likes to wear cowboy boots and a smirk.

But not even West seems able to mess up the Phillies at home these days. Since the All-Star break they have won eight of nine at the Vet, sweeping big series with the Cardinals and the Expos. They have 11 victories in their last 15 games, have swept 10 series this season, and lead St. Louis by eight games in the fading National League East race.

But Stocker, the hero of the game, had his worst day in the big leagues.

Despite hitting the winning single, after the game was over, he talked about all the things he had done wrong. About the errors he had made on the first two ground balls hit to him. About the second-inning strikeout with the bases loaded and nobody out.

No hiding. No alibis. No holds barred. Just a frank admission that he hadn't been mentally ready to play in an early-afternoon game that came hard on the heels of a long, hard night game.

Don't worry about this rookie shortstop. The kid belongs. He's mature beyond his 23 years. If all the terrific days and nights he's had since arriving in the big leagues didn't prove it, the way he handled this bad day did.

"He was not ready to play, and I told him," said coach Larry Bowa, who set a standard for shortstop play at the Vet that his successors will be striving to attain for years. "When I say he was not ready, I mean he should've come in here, got loose, taken [batting practice]. He didn't do that. So, mentally, he wasn't ready. He admitted it, too. He said, 'I was in a fog today.' That's half the battle."

The other half was the way Stocker turned his bad day into a triumphant day. He did it with the clutch hit that broke a personal 0-for-14 slump.

Frank Fitzpatrick and Frank Dolson

There is no other explanation. The Phillies must have a direct line to Miracle Control. They came roaring from behind again to beat the Mets 5-4 in an improbable shocker of a ball game on August 15. Divine intervention is about the only feasible way to account for this team's comeback ways.

Well, there might be one other plausible explanation:

"There's something special going on here this year," Curt Schilling said after he put the Phillies in a 4-0 first-inning hole and then put the Mets offense out of business the rest of the day. "We just know that somehow we're going to find a way. That's how it's been all year. We find a way."

With the score 4-1, Lenny Dykstra launched the eighth inning with one of his inimitable 97-pitch at bats, eventually drawing the walk that would begin to turn this game around. Mets starter Eric Hillman came back and struck out Mariano Duncan. But then John Kruk limped on up there, whaled at the first pitch, and sent it soaring into the lap of one of the 58,103 people in attendance. So it was suddenly a 4-3 contest. And it was about at that moment that everyone in the ballpark seemed to realize they were about to witness another one of those games.

"Once Kruk hit that home run, you knew," Schilling said. "One run—that's like a tie game to us."

There was a brief intermission for Pete Incaviglia to make an out and then for Mets manager Dallas Green to get himself ejected by erratic plate ump Phil Cuzzi. Then the comeback resumed.

Darren Daulton took a late hack at a fire-breathing 3-2 fastball and ripped it down the third-base line for a double. Wes Chamberlain finished a sensational at bat with an electrifying game-tying smash through the shortstop hole. And it was 4-4.

Chamberlain took second on the throw to the plate. Then Kim Batiste—filling in for injured Dave Hollins at third again—marched up for his first meeting with relief pitcher Anthony Young since they combined for Batiste's memorable grand slam two nights before (that, too, a late-inning comeback). Batiste plunked an 0-1 slider into left-center for the game-winning single, of course. And the Phillies had won two games of the three-game series with Mets and had themselves another one for the archives.

"Hey, they give you nine innings to play," said Mitch Williams, who danced through another harrowing ninth for save No. 32. "And we play all nine of 'em."

Jayson Stark

Someday he might look back on these remarkable days and wonder just how he did it. He might ask himself how a rookie could have walked into a pennant race's fires and never felt the heat. For the moment, though, in his first-year innocence, Kevin Stocker will keep imagining this is how it is supposed to be.

Stocker fouled off four straight 3-2 pitches before lining a game-winning, bases-loaded triple to centerfield with two outs in the eighth inning on August 20, and the Phillies defeated the Astros, 6-4, at the Astrodome.

Stocker, besides cementing the infield defense, has hit .365 and driven in 21 runs in his first 31 games.

"All I ever heard about this kid was that he can't hit," said Mitch Williams, who picked up his 35th save with a typically scary ninth. "Well, he's hitting .360 after 100 ABs. If he can't hit, send us a couple more just like him.

"If Mike Piazza's not in the league, he could be Rookie of the Year," said Williams. "That was a veteran at bat right there."

What made Stocker's eighth-inning at bat, and in a way his entire first 31 games, so impressive is that he seems to be dealing so easily with the pressure of playing a vital position for a first-place team.

Frank Fitzpatrick

The team on a pace to win 101 games had lost three straight. The team on a pace to lose 100 games had won five straight. But thanks to a pitching gem by Phillies lefthander Danny Jackson, the little game of Reversal of Fortune came to an end on August 24.

Jackson pitched one of the club's strongest games of the season as the Phillies snapped their losing streak by defeating the Colorado Rockies 4-2 before 43,419 fans at Veterans Stadium. Jackson (now 10-9) became the fifth Phillies starter to record 10 or more victories, joining Tommy Greene, Terry Mulholland, Ben Rivera, and Curt Schilling.

This is the first time a Phillies rotation has had five double-figure winners since 1932, when Ray Benge, Phil Collins, Snipe Hansen, Ed Holley, and the immortal Flint Rhem achieved that distinction.

Sam Carchidi

For all Phillies fans convinced that the summer held nothing but magical moments, we submit the two bracing defeats of August 27 and 28. Starters permitted big leads. Relievers couldn't hold little ones. The two best hitters in the lineup struck out four times against no-name pitchers. Anonymous opposing players pounded out hits. Fans booed.

It was vintage Phillies baseball. Circa 1985-1992.

Two nights in a row, the Phils overcame a 4-0 Cincinnati lead only to watch their bullpen give it back.

With the second of these games coming so soon after an ugly Mitch Williams-induced loss in the first of them, the Phils' fifth loss in seven games made you want to check the National League East standings. Sure enough, there were the Phillies, still holding a comfortable nine-game margin over the second-place Cardinals. Has the Phils' large lead left them lethargic heading into September? "I don't think we're flat," Milt Thompson said. "We're just in one of those ruts where things are going against us."

But in the third game, if any Cincinnati hitter reached the batter's box unconvinced that Danny Jackson was his enemy, one quick, 60-foot, 6-inch glance should have changed his mind. What he saw on the mound was a 205-pound snarl. Jackson planted himself on redwood-sized legs and waited impatiently. His eyes were narrow, his demeanor nasty. And there was a slight bend to his upper lip that suggested disdain.

The Phillies lefthander shut out Cincinnati for seven innings, striking out eight, as the Phils closed a homestand with a revitalizing 12-0 thrashing of the Reds before 58,363.

"Danny Jackson was really spectacular," Phils manager Jim Fregosi said in a moment of rare postgame hyperbole. "He's in a fine groove right now."

And with the help of the Phillies' sunshine supermen—those part-time players who see lots of action in day games after night games—the Phils avoided being swept for the first time this season. Mickey Morandini collected two triples and four RBIs. Wes Chamberlain hit a single and a bases-loaded double and drove in four runs. Ricky Jordan hit a double and two singles.

Frank Fitzpatrick

The Stretch Drive

There is little of the Atlanta Braves' sweet-swinging elegance. The heart of San Francisco's lineup is more fearsome. But what makes the Phillies the National League's highest-scoring team is simple: Their hitters are more annoying.

"Free passes," said Lenny Dykstra, with a smirk that suggested he relishes all those time-chewing at bats that always seem to conclude with a walk. "Walks are such an underrated stat. They can drive the other team crazy. Sometimes they're even more effective than a hit.

"If I go up there and hit a line drive to rightfield for a single, that's just one pitch," he said. "But if I go up there and foul off a lot of balls and make the pitcher work that much harder, make him throw seven or eight pitches, that's very frustrating for him. And not just for the pitcher, but for his manager and for the players in the field behind him."

It is why opponents' pitch counts climb into triple figures so rapidly night after night. It is why, as the season's final month approaches, just one pitcher (the Pirates' Steve Cooke) has thrown a complete game against them this season. It is why their total of bases on balls (550) is 79 more than any other NL club has managed.

And it is why, if the Phillies can score at least one run through the September 4 game against Cincinnati, they officially become the most difficult team to shut out in modern National League history. That would give them a streak of 151 games in which no one has held them scoreless.

The Phillies' fondness for the pitcher-annoying walk is about to land them in the record book in another category as well. When John Kruk walks four more times, he will join Dykstra (110) and Darren Daulton (101) with triple digits in bases on balls. No National League team has ever had three players do that.

"Let's face it, all of our guys like to swing the bats," said dugout coach John Vukovich. "We lead the league in strikeouts, too. But at the same time, and this probably sounds a little funny, we are very patient.

"That's why we haven't been getting shut out," he said. "If you can hit and you're patient, there aren't going to be many one-two-three innings. There are always going to be people on base. And when there are people on base, anything can happen."

Still, the reasons why no one has shut out the Phillies since Doug Drabek, then with the Pirates, did so on September 19, 1992, go beyond walks.

"It's not that hard to figure out, really," Mariano Duncan said. "Just look at the numbers. We lead the league in runs. We lead the league in doubles. We lead the league in triples. We lead the league in home runs. We lead the league in slugging percentage."

Yet, except for Dykstra's phenomenal run total, no single Phillie is really putting together eye-popping individual statistics.

"That's because Jimmy has used a lot of different people in our lineups this season," Vukovich said. "I think it's helped keep everyone fresh. Everyone has been playing so well that he has been able to pick and choose depending on how certain players have done against certain pitchers."

Frank Fitzpatrick

On September 4, the Cincinnati Reds' José Rijo limited the Phillies to a single record-breaking run in seven innings and drove in four himself, and the Reds managed to hold off Philadelphia, 6-5, at Riverfront Stadium.

That one run off Rijo, John Kruk coming home on Darren Daulton's fourth-inning sacrifice fly, gave the Phillies the modern-day National League record for consecutive games without being shut out. They have scored in 151 straight games, eclipsing the mark of 150 by the Pittsburgh Pirates of 1924-25.

"What record?" asked Mariano Duncan, in what was a pretty fair indication of the Phillies' reaction to it. "That doesn't mean anything to me," he said, "because we lost."

The Phillies' first loss in four games left them with an 8½-game lead in the NL East over scorching Montreal, which won its ninth straight.

Frank Fitzpatrick

Like a pudgy snake that suddenly decides to try flying, Pete Incaviglia went airborne 15 feet from first base, diving headfirst, his arms extending in a frantic effort to beat the throw from second, a throw that would have converted an inning-ending double play.

And he made it, gobbling up a big mouthful of dirt as he touched the bag.

The dive allowed the Phils to score one more run in a 5-3 victory over the Cincinnati Reds on September 6 at Riverfront Stadium. Just one more dirty, measly little run in a long game in a long season.

Ah, but dirt is beautiful for the 1993 Phils. Incaviglia's dive helps explain how a team without an easily recognizable pitching ace or a power-hitting superstar can run away with a division.

"That's this team," said winner Curt Schilling. "That's how we've played all year. That's how we've done what we've done. This is a team that reflects the personality of the city we play in. We're blue-collar, hard-working."

Frank Fitzpatrick

September 6 was not a good night for the Phillies. They lost their starting pitcher, Terry Mulholland, after 10 pitches. They fell into a 7-2 hole. They watched their struggling middle reliever, Roger Mason, allow back-to-back-to-back homers in the sixth to a Cubs trio that didn't remind anyone of the legends on Murderers' Row. The Chicago Cubs defeated the Phils, 7-6, at Veterans Stadium. The loss, coupled with Montreal's win, trimmed the Phils' first-place lead to 8½ games over Montreal.

Mulholland suffered a strained left hip flexor and left the game after facing three batters (single, walk, walk).

Sam Carchidi

Except for a cleaning crew in distant centerfield, the dimly lit Veterans Stadium stands were empty 30 minutes after the Phillies' stunning 8-5 loss to the Cubs on September 9. Then, from someplace unseen, a disembodied voice, like that of some long-dormant ghost, hoarsely bellowed the most dreaded words in this city's sports history.

"Nineteen sixty-four," it screamed.

In an ending as swift as it was eerie, the Cubs' fatal rally evoked not only the dismal reminder of 1964 but the second-most haunting event in modern Phillies history as well.

Just like Greg Luzinski in that 1977 Black Friday playoff game, Pete Incaviglia retreated awkwardly toward the leftfield wall for a long fly ball. Like Luzinski, the burly outfielder slammed into the fence. Like Luzinski, he missed it, and a game was lost.

With Kevin Roberson's bases-loaded triple giving the Cubs seven two-out runs in the eighth, the stunned Phillies had lost a third straight game. Their divisional lead over dogged Montreal, 11 games on August 25, was at 6½ as the Expos won their 12th game in 13.

Frank Fitzpatrick

Coming off their worst homestand of the season and with their National League East lead down to 5½ games, the Phillies, on September 14, faced the prospect that their No. 1 starter, Terry Mulholland, might not be able to pitch for the remainder of the regular season.

In uncharacteristically blunt terms, Jim Fregosi said that he was not sure what the immediate future held for the lefthander. The manager said Mulholland, who pulled a hip muscle the week before, was not responding well to treatment.

"I can't give you a definite answer about whether he'll be able to make another start this season," Fregosi said. "That's a serious type of injury for a pitcher," he said. "There's really no telling at this time." Mulholland is 12-9 with a 3.34 ERA.

Frank Fitzpatrick

There is a lot of opera in this Phillies season. All through its first few acts there was little but high spirits and merry song. The inevitable trouble entered near intermission, and voices were raised in mild concern. In mid-September, as this drama builds, the spear carriers and fat ladies are gathering for a conclusion. Whether it is tragic or magic is all that must be decided.

And with a 6-3 comeback win over the New York Mets on September 15 at Shea Stadium, the Phillies took a big step toward a happy ending.

"We had to win that game," said Mariano Duncan. "There was no question about that." They had to win because the Phillies, after a disheartening loss to these woeful Mets the day before, were a team in need of some breathing space as a weekend series with the second-place Expos neared.

After just their fourth victory in 10 games and after a rare Montreal loss, the Phillies find themselves with a revitalized National League East lead of 5 games. So, even with a sweep, the Expos can be no closer than two games. By then, only 13 games will remain.

Frank Fitzpatrick

The Olympic Stadium crowd in Montreal on September 17 was frequently loud enough to rouse the dead. But the game's real hero could barely hear a murmur. Pinch-hitter Curtis Pride, 95 percent deaf, laced a two-run pinch-double to spark an Expos comeback, and Montreal went on to beat the Phillies 8-7 in the 12th inning as this important three-game series began with a long and occasionally entertaining game.

Their win set 45,757 Olympic Stadium fans to writhing and roaring ecstatically. More important, it moved the fast-charging Expos to four games behind the Phillies in the National League East with 15 to play.

The deciding run came off Mitch Williams (now 3-5), the Phils' seventh pitcher. Marquis Grissom doubled inside the rightfield line to start the 12th. "It was a fastball about a foot outside," said Williams. "He's a pull hitter, and I tried to stay away from him. There's nothing I can do about that."

There wasn't anything he could do about what happened next, either. With Dave Hollins playing in front of the bag to guard against a bunt from the speedy Delino DeShields, Grissom stole. It must have stunned Hollins, who stood frozen in front of the bag. Darren Daulton could only hold the ball.

"I knew that he was going to try that," said Williams. "My job is to stop him and get the ball to the plate. That's what I did. There just was no play on him."

DeShields then fled to Lenny Dykstra in mid-center to send Grissom scurrying home with the run that gave charging Montreal its 21st win in 24 games.

Frank Fitzpatrick

Tommy Greene's slider snapped. His fastball was as quick as the Expos' innings. The Phillies were merrily in front, 5-1. Until the eighth inning of the second game of a crucial three between the division-leading Phillies and the second-place Montreal Expos.

"I thought with the way Tommy Greene was throwing, they had no chance," said Mariano Duncan. Two broken-bat singles and Wil Cordero's three-run homer gave Montreal a chance and roused the Olympic Stadium crowd to a furious ecstasy.

But in the kind of pressurized environment they should expect to see if they reach the postseason, the Phillies withstood the tumult and the relentless Expos to post a gutsy 5-4 victory that left them with a five-game National League East lead and just 14 games to play.

"If you can't get it pumping in a situation like that," said Mitch Williams, who picked up his 39th save in a typically scary manner, "then there's nothing pumping inside you." As usual, Williams got considerably more hearts pumping than his own. "We had to have that game," said Williams, "and we got it."

Frank Fitzpatrick

They spent three days in the world's noisiest classroom. And once Mitch Williams's tantrum concluded, once a few players were willing to talk about their disheartening 6-5 loss to the Montreal Expos on September 19, once they realized that their divisional lead remained solid if not yet secure, the Phillies discovered the painful lesson that a weekend in raucous Olympic Stadium had taught them.

"If there's any positive from this," said Darren Daulton, "it's that these games showed everyone in here what the [postseason] atmosphere is going to be like. It was a good game to be involved in, a good experience."

On the negative side, the Phillies did see their National League East lead dip to four games by losing two of three to second-place Montreal. On the positive side, the lead could have been down to two games. And the series did shrink the season by three precious games. Now only 13 remain.

"We're in a good position," said Daulton, "but I wouldn't say it's comfortable." There's no way they could make that mistake. Not when, long after the day's loss, the only sign left hanging in this domed stadium was one in distant leftfield—"1964" was all it said.

The final Expos game, like the two that preceded it in this intriguing divisional showdown, was decided by one run and possessed a potent postseason flavor right down to the riotous ninth, an inning that concluded with Wil Cordero's game-winning, two-run single.

A controversial umpire's call helped decide it. The stands were filled with loud and taunting fans. And, for two teams without much postseason experience, there was plenty of pressure.

"Sure it was a tough loss," said Lenny Dykstra, "but there's no need to dwell on the negatives when we're still four games up and we're going home. This was a very intense series. Every game came down to the last pitch. This was fun baseball."

But not for Williams. The Phillies closer, who lost both games here and saved the Phils' lone victory, couldn't hold a 5-4 lead in the ninth—although he felt he would have had first-base umpire Charlie Williams not missed a call.

"There's no way in the world he was safe," said Williams (now 3-6). "If he's doing his job, there's no way he can miss that call. Impact umpiring. That was brutal."

With one out, Montreal runners at first and second, and the Phils still ahead, Larry Walker hit a chopper that John Kruk bobbled. Williams grabbed Kruk's hurried toss several feet from the bag and arrived almost simultaneously with a headfirst-sliding Walker.

The umpire signaled safe (televised replays were inconclusive) and the bases were filled. "I saw him safe in the position I was in," said Charlie Williams. "We just do the best we can." The call was made particularly bitter for Mitch Williams and his teammates when the next hitter, Sean Berry, popped up to Kruk for what would have been the game's final out.

"I was going to get a force at second, but I just dropped it," said Kruk of his eighth error. "I still thought we had him at first, though. They don't pay me to umpire. I kind of wish they did, though."

Cordero then slapped his deciding hit inside the third-base bag, a place where third basemen often play late in close games. But since a single was all the Expos needed to tie, defensive replacement Kim Batiste was at his normal spot. "I just play where they tell me," he said.

"You're trying to cut off the hole in that situation," said Phils manager Jim Fregosi.

As significant as the umpire's call seemed, it couldn't overshadow these troubling facts. The Phils had a 5-2 lead entering the bottom of the fifth and starter Danny Jackson promptly allowed two Expos runs. And this team that hopes to reach the postseason and prosper there will have to do it with the Mitch Williams's Thrill Machine closing games.

Frank Fitzpatrick

The final score of the September 22 Montreal-Atlanta game had long since been posted, and the Phillies knew the Expos had won to continue their late-season surge.

Inning after inning, the Phils and Florida Marlins went at each other—each able to manage only a single run. Each team went deeper and deeper into its bullpen and deeper and deeper into its bench.

It wasn't supposed to be this kind of struggle. After all, this was the sixth-place, expansion Marlins. But with the Phillies looking to shave another game off their magic number, the Marlins just refused to go quietly into the South Philadelphia night.

Four hours after it began, it finally ended: The Phils had won it,

2-1. Pete Incaviglia, making his first appearance since injuring his leg, drew a four-pitch walk off Marlins ace reliever Bryan Harvey to lead off the bottom of the 12th. Harvey then threw one pitch to Lenny Dykstra before leaving with an apparent groin injury. He was replaced by Richie Lewis, the Marlins' seventh pitcher of the night.

Dykstra, who scored the Phillies' first run way, way back in the first inning, bounced his third hit of the game, a single to right, sending pinch-runner Tony Longmire to third base. Lewis hit Mickey Morandini with a pitch to load the bases with no one out.

Mighty John Kruk struck out, bringing up Dave Hollins, who smacked an 0-1 pitch down the rightfield line to bring in Longmire from third and send 31,556 Veterans Stadium fans—or what was left of them, anyway—home happy.

The Phillies had won and swept the three-game series with the Marlins. Their lead over the Expos remained at 5$^{1}/_{2}$ games. The magic number to clinch the pennant was down to six.

Sam Carchidi

Who will ever forget 1991, when the Braves came stampeding back from 9$^{1}/_{2}$ games behind in the second half to overtake the Dodgers?

And who will ever forget 1992, when they roared from six games back to blow away the Reds?

As it turned out, those two wild charges were just the warm-up act. In 1993, the Braves were having a second half that makes 1991 and '92 look like a little game of catch on the beach.

"I know we were hot last year and the year before at the end of the year," leftfielder Ron Gant said. "But I don't think we were this hot." That, of course, is because no team since division play began has ever been this hot.

It's September 24, and the Braves come rolling into Philadelphia for a playoff-preview series against the Phillies, trailing a stream of numbers that could send your eyeballs to the laser surgeon. So get out the dark glasses. Here goes:

The Braves were 48-16 since the All-Star break. And 46-14 since that noted fire-starter, Fred McGriff, joined the fun July 20. And 33-8 since August 8. And 24-6 since August 20. And 27-5 on the road since July 23.

So what has fueled this sizzling streak? Here are five big factors:

McGriff. When McGriff arrived from San Diego, the Braves were just 12 games over .500 (53-41) and nine games out of first.

They needed help. So in strolled McGriff. He waited until the Braves got behind 5-0 that night. Then he whomped a game-tying three-run homer, fueling the Braves' biggest comeback win of the year. And the pennant race hasn't been the same since.

Gant and Justice. Two guys around McGriff—Ron Gant and Dave Justice—have had seasons practically out of the Eddie Mathews–Henry Aaron scrapbook. Coming into Philadelphia, Gant and Justice were tied for the league lead in RBIs, with 113. Only Barry Bonds had more home runs than Justice's 37. And Gant was right behind, with 35. They were taking turns carrying this team down the stretch.

Greg McMichael. Six months ago, he was the least-known Atlanta Brave on earth. But now, on a team full of marquee names, Greg McMichael is as vital to the Braves as anyone. It wasn't by design that this semi-anonymous 26-year-old righthander became the closer. But it's hard to argue with his record. He inherited the role, practically by accident, on July 28, after Mike Stanton started struggling. It wasn't supposed to be permanent. But McMichael converted one save. And then another. And another. And he wound up saving 15 in a row before finally blowing two in mid-September.

Greg Maddux. He was supposed to be the final piece of the puzzle. He was the defending Cy Young Award winner, joining a rotation that was being compared with the '72 Orioles, even before Greg Maddux got there. But on July 7, Maddux's record was only 7-8. That wasn't all his fault, as evidenced by his 2.84 ERA. But since then, Maddux had reminded everybody what the spring-training furor was all about. Coming into Philadelphia, he was 11-1, with a 1.96 ERA, in his previous 14 starts.

Inevitability. There were other factors in this great Braves run, of course: Jeff Blauser's brilliant year at shortstop. Terry Pendleton's steady climb from a .148 hitter in May to a .270 hitter in September. Tom Glavine's annual surge to 20 wins. Steve Avery's consistent invincibility. Otis Nixon's return to the leadoff hole. But, when you get right down to it, wasn't it all just a matter of time?

Jayson Stark

There was so much adrenaline on Tommy Greene's first pitch of September 24, an umpire should have examined the ball. And, though the overthrown fastball soared way high and wide, it signified the emotion the pitcher and the Phillies brought to a game that they had tried to pass off as ordinary.

A hyped-up Greene overpowered the fearsome Braves, walking eight, but permitting only three singles in $8\frac{1}{3}$, as the Phillies beat Atlanta 3-0 in the first game of a weekend series between division leaders.

"You have to feel something extra in a game like that," said Mitch Williams, who struck out the two Braves he faced and earned a team-record 41st save. "Not just because we're facing the Braves, but because we're getting so close to the end."

With just nine games left, the Phillies maintained their National League East lead at six games over Montreal and reduced their magic number to four. Atlanta's advantage atop the NL West shrank to $1\frac{1}{2}$ games over San Francisco, after the Giants beat San Diego 4-3 later in the night.

It was a game that could easily be duplicated in the National League Championship Series. Two starters with gaudy records and in peak form, a sellout Veterans Stadium crowd, and two teams well matched if not very similar in other ways. The ballet Braves, graceful, elegant, sweet-swinging, versus the bump-and-grind Phillies.

Frank Fitzpatrick

If the Phillies dream of playoff success against the Atlanta Braves or anyone else, they must first catch and throw the ball better than they did in their September 25 loss to Atlanta at Veterans Stadium, 9-7.

"Pitching-wise we just didn't do a good job," said Phils manager Jim Fregosi. (Danny Jackson started, and Roger Mason took the loss.) "And defensively, we didn't play very well." Which is not what you like to hear about a team on the verge of venturing into the pressurized, magnified world of baseball's postseason. "It seems like every time you make a mistake against a team like that, it costs you a run," Darren Daulton said.

The loss in this second game of three with the talented National League West leaders reduced the Phillies' NL East lead to five games over the Montreal Expos, who defeated the Mets in New York. "We'll come back in the series finale," Daulton said after the loss. "We've got Schilling going, and they've got Steve Avery going on three days' rest, which is something new for him."

For the Braves, meanwhile, the victory before 57,176 fans was essential. It allowed them to maintain their $1\frac{1}{2}$-game edge over the reborn Giants.

Frank Fitzpatrick

Maybe that big, shiny divisional lead they wore like a medal all season did them no good. Perhaps a nasty six-month scrap would have served these Phillies better.

In six important and nerve-testing late-September games against the Expos and the Braves over two weekends, the Phillies, unchallenged for so much of '93, looked not quite ready for postseason prime time. Their pitchers were nibbling, their fielders a little bit back on their heels.

Not surprisingly, they lost four of those games against Montreal and Atlanta. In the final defeat, they bowed to the Braves 7-2 to close out the regular season at Veterans Stadium.

Fortunately for them, their National League East lead remained at five games as they embarked on their final seven games—four in Pittsburgh and three in St. Louis.

Frank Fitzpatrick

It no longer matters that they were scruffy and ill-kempt. No one will ask them again about 1964 or backing into a title. There is nothing attached to these '93 Phillies anymore but the title of National League East champions.

All their affected cool, all those swaggering steps and cautious public facades dissolved on September 28 in a moment of unhinged joy. When reliever Donn Pall squeezed first baseman John Kruk's toss to end a 10-7 victory over the Pirates at Three Rivers Stadium, it flicked on some unseen emotional switch. Suddenly, dozens of leaping, hugging, fist-thrusting Phillies stampeded toward first base for several minutes of hysteria that continued soon afterward in a locker room afloat in California champagne.

"It got sickening, watching everybody else celebrate every year," said Kruk. "You get jealous. You want it to be your turn. Now, finally, it is."

"There's never been anything better than winning," said manager Jim Fregosi. "And it's best the first time."

Mariano Duncan drove in five runs, his seventh-inning grand slam breaking open the game with the stubborn Pirates. Lenny Dykstra, a strong candidate for MVP, collected four hits as the Phils finally eliminated second-place Montreal to win their first division title since 1983.

"It's 1993, baby! It ain't 1964," screamed Wes Chamberlain, giving voice to his teammates' frustration about recurring references to the Phils' memorable collapse 29 years before. "Where are those ghosts now?"

The clinching victory came on a field where, for much of the last long, dark decade, the Phils had been skewered and embarrassed. Two years ago there, many of these same Phillies, another last-place season concluding, watched the Pirates win a division title. Few imagined that their turn would follow so soon.

"We've been down so long," said Phillies president Bill Giles, his raincoat drenched with champagne, his face wearing the choicest segment of a chocolate pie. "I had kind of gotten used to us winning from 1976 to 1983. Now we have been down so long that this one is very rewarding to our fans and particularly to me."

If to every team there is a season, 1993 in the NL East belonged to the surprising Phillies. In last place a year before, this season they led the division every day but one—April 11.

The Phils had constructed a massive 11½-game lead by June 14, watched it shrink to three on July 19, then reconstructed it. So consistent were these Phils that they never lost more than four in a row or won more than six straight.

"I'm so proud of these guys," said Fregosi. "I feel like just going off to a corner somewhere and crying." Eventually, the manager and general manager Lee Thomas, his close friend for so long, retreated from the persistent alcoholic spray to Fregosi's tiny office. Once inside, they closed the door behind them.

Like Kruk, most of Fregosi's players had never experienced this kind of success. Only seven Phillies had ever played on division-winning teams.

"How many times is this going to happen?" said Fregosi. "This may have been the toughest, but it's also been the most gratifying." Even Fregosi, in his long career as player and manager, had won just a single division title. He has never reached the World Series.

"I feel so good for guys like Eisenreich and Daulton and Kruk," said Dave Hollins. "They had played so long and were never close to being on a winning team."

In the clincher, the Pirates had just gone ahead 4-3 with a three-run sixth when the Phils exploded for six runs in the seventh. Remember, they had once come back from being down in a game 8-0 in this magical season. A deficit of a single run wasn't going to deter them.

Darren Daulton and Jim Eisenreich singled to begin the seventh. Reliever Rich Robertson then made a terrible decision on Milt Thompson's sacrifice bunt, throwing to third far too late to get Daulton. Kevin Stocker singled in the tying run, and when Pete Incaviglia came out to pinch-hit, Jim Leyland—managing these games as seriously as Montreal could have hoped—brought in Blas Minor. Minor fanned Incaviglia, and Leyland summoned lefthander Denny Neagle to face Dykstra.

Dykstra drew the 127th walk of his remarkable year to put Philadelphia ahead to stay, 5-4. Duncan, watching intently as he neared first base and then breaking into a little skip when he saw the ball clear the leftfield wall, belted a club-record eighth grand slam to break the game open.

"I was glad to see that," said Kruk, on deck at the time. "That meant we weren't going to have to see Mitch [Williams] in the ninth."

Pittsburgh did score twice in the ninth off Pall on Andy Van Slyke's RBI double and Jeff King's single. But it was too little and far too late.

"I'm excited," said Duncan. "But I also know that this is just one step. This team wants to go to the World Series."

In the chaotic clubhouse, Kruk, a green champagne bottle clutched in his hand, walked off toward the trainer's room. "I've got to get me a beer," he said. "This stuff is terrible. Too sweet."

On this night, for these Phillies, there was something far sweeter to taste and, for a few days anyway, to savor.

Frank Fitzpatrick

After 10 frustrating years of day-to-day baseball, the Phillies, with a few days remaining in the regular season, began to plan for a play-off game. And to let that regular season just slide away.

While the September call-ups and bench-riders took on the Pirates on September 30, losing 9-1, the Phils began to grapple with the juicy issues of the postseason, starting with the state of their pitching.

Manager Jim Fregosi said the team would use a four-man rotation in the National League Championship Series even if Terry Mulholland was unable to start.

It had been widely assumed that if the injured Mulholland couldn't rejoin the rotation, the Phils would go with three starters, and that Ben Rivera, who had struggled throughout the season, would be dispatched to the bullpen.

On this night, however, Fregosi said Rivera would join the playoff rotation if Mulholland could not start. So a rotation without Mulholland would likely be Tommy Greene, Curt Schilling, Danny Jackson, and Rivera.

Fregosi said he would determine whether Mulholland could start a playoff game after the lefthander started the last game of the season in St. Louis. Mulholland said it would make no difference if he was used as a starter or a reliever in the playoff series—as long as he was healthy enough to pitch.

Sam Carchidi

The good news from September 30 was that Terry Mulholland, making his first appearance in 24 days, pitched encouragingly in a one-inning relief stint that he hoped would lead to a League Championship Series start.

The bad news was that after a modern-day National League record of 174 games without being shut out, the Phillies couldn't manage to put a run on the scoreboard against the Pittsburgh Pirates, who beat them 5-0.

In the scheme of things, there was no question in the Phillies' minds that the good news far outweighed the bad.

Sam Carchidi

Cement can move. The Atlanta Braves won their 104th baseball game of the season on October 3 and made Atlanta–Fulton County Stadium shake.

It quivered when pitcher Tom Glavine walked off the field, nearly certain of his 22nd victory. It shimmied when David Justice cracked his 40th home run of the year in his final regular-season at bat. It swayed when the Braves posted a 5-3 win over the Colorado Rockies. It just about tumbled three hours later when the Los Angeles Dodgers finished up a 12-1 win over the San Francisco Giants. Then, finally, the scoreboard here could read: "Atlanta Braves, 1993 National League West Champions."

What a doubleheader.

The Braves, two-time defending NL West champions, had finished playing baseball about 4 P.M. They finished and knew nothing. They finished and then had to watch the Giants, the team that had won 103 games, try to force a playoff.

This game was broadcast large and live into the stadium on the Jumbotron screen in the outfield where about 4,000 fans stayed to eat hot dogs, do the tomahawk chop, cheer for Tommy Lasorda, Dodgers manager and "Our Pal," as the scoreboard said. It was broadcast on TVs scattered around the Braves clubhouse, in the training room, in the lobby, everywhere. Around seven, as the Giants huddled in their dugout for the last half-inning of their game, the Braves all came together on the center of the field here to watch the championship become theirs again.

"This is the best one yet," Bobby Cox, Braves manager, said. His cheeks were red with excitement, his eyes red with champagne. "This is the best because we had to win 104 games. One hundred and four games. One hundred and four."

The Braves immediately began planning for the opener three days hence against the Phillies, announcing that lefthander Steve Avery would start.

Diane Pucin

N ow they know whom to loathe. Who to visualize at the bottom of the coming National League brawl. They know the enemy now.

It's the Braves.

With one eye on the scoreboard and another on the serious business of playoff planning, the Phillies slipped sedately into the postseason on October 3 in a state of high readiness.

Though it was nice to know finally whom they would be hosting three days later in Game 1 of the National League Championship Series, that was far from the best development of the day for the Phils.

Terry Mulholland showed he was ready for a playoff start by pitching four superb innings as the Phils dropped a 2-0 decision to the St. Louis Cardinals at Busch Stadium in their final regular-season game. Mulholland, making his first start since he injured his left hip on September 6, allowed just one hit and was razor-sharp, throwing 45 pitches—33 for strikes.

Afterward, manager Jim Fregosi said he was "thrilled" and said Mulholland would pitch Game 3 and, if necessary, Game 7 of the series against Atlanta.

Mulholland's outing clearly boosted the spirits of the Phils, who could now begin the postseason with their starting rotation intact. "We just wanted to make sure he was all right, and there's no doubt in my mind he could go nine innings," Fregosi said.

"It's a big lift, a big lift," catcher Darren Daulton said. "We need him. He's our No. 1 guy."

"Any time you get your ace back, it's an uplifting thing," leftfielder Pete Incaviglia said.

Mulholland's outing confirmed that his one scoreless relief inning three days earlier in Pittsburgh was no fluke. "We told him he needed to go out there twice if he was going to start" in the playoffs, Fregosi said.

"I was getting ahead of the hitters. I felt like myself," said Mulholland, who finished the regular season with a solid 3.25 ERA—the best among the Phils starters. "Physically, I have no problems. For the most part, I'm pain-free."

As for the postseason job ahead, the team was looking forward to tangling with the Atlanta Braves, who were favored even though the Phillies and Atlanta split their 12 regular-season games this year.

"I think this team plays its best when it's backed to the wall," said reliever Mitch Williams. "There's two things to do when you're back to the wall—shrivel up and die, or fight your way out. And I think this team likes to fight."

Sam Carchidi

4

THE POSTSEASON

The Phillies' postseason was one of the more improbable the game has seen. The National League Championship Series was looking bad for the Phils, but they won it. And the World Series was looking good, but they lost it. Here are some of the highlights of both series.

The Playoffs

Sometimes you make a costly ninth-inning error in a postseason game and you feel the pain forever. For Kim Batiste, it hurt for only an inning.

Batiste, a defensive replacement whose ninth-inning throwing error allowed the Atlanta Braves to tie the game, won redemption and the game in the 10th with an RBI single. It gave the Phillies a 4-3 victory as the National League Championship Series opened in entertaining fashion at Veterans Stadium on October 6.

"One of the toughest jobs there is is to go in for defense," said Phils manager Jim Fregosi. "All you can do is screw up."

Which is what Batiste did after fielding Mark Lemke's ground ball. When his throw to second sailed into right, Batiste knew he was in danger of becoming another Fred Merkle or Bill Buckner.

"Oh, my God," he said.

Batiste sagged a little after the error and a lot after Otis Nixon's grounder tied the game off eventual winner Mitch Williams. But when he strolled to the plate, with one out in the 10th and John Kruk at second, something had lifted him up again.

"It was my teammates," he said. "I couldn't have felt better going to the plate. These guys were encouraging me and telling me to put it behind me."

Until Batiste's error, it had all been going so smoothly for the Phillies. Curt Schilling had 10 strikeouts through eight innings. The Phils led, 3-2. But Fregosi felt that his righthander—who insisted his manager was wrong—was tired, so he summoned Williams.

When Williams strutted in from right with those high-bouncing steps and that big red defensive end's number 99 on his back, you knew it was all about to change.

"He had thrown 140-some pitches by then," Fregosi said of Schilling. "He is such a competitor that he wanted to stay in there. I thought he was just outstanding tonight."

Pitching in the biggest game of his life, the emotionally charged Phillies righthander, who played before one empty seat, which he left in his father's memory, fanned 10 and permitted seven hits as the starter in the Phillies' first postseason game since 1983.

Pete Incaviglia homered for the Phils and Kruk drove in a first-inning run with a ground ball. Kruk, who missed the final two regular-season games with back spasms, scored the run that put the Phils ahead 3-2 on Steve Avery's bases-loaded wild pitch in the sixth.

"It's definitely an advantage to open the series at home," said Fregosi. "The early games usually set the tone for the series." If so, Game 1 suggested a well-pitched, closely played series with large and raucous crowds and an occasional poignant sidelight.

"I think that if my Dad were here he would have told me to enjoy myself, to remember that this is only a game," Schilling said before the game.

The 26-year-old righthander seemed not to heed that advice, pitching instead with a visible passion—and an overwhelming fastball.

The Braves led 2-1 in the fourth after Nixon's run-scoring double in the third and David Justice's sacrifice fly in the fourth. But Incaviglia tied the game with a 423-foot bomb to straightaway center.

"It's not always the big home run or the great defensive plays that decide these games," Fregosi said. "Sometimes it's something very small."

Until the ninth, it appeared as though that tiny moment had come after a walk to Kruk, Dave Hollins's double, and a semi-intentional walk to Darren Daulton in the sixth. With Incaviglia at the plate and a count of 2-1, Steve Avery bounced a wild pitch past Damon Berryhill, and Kruk scored.

A pumped-up Schilling, obviously elated to be making this Game 1 start, threw the first postseason pitch seen in Philadelphia since late on the afternoon of October 16, 1983. His pitch wasn't hit. And it would be quite a while before one was.

"I know I'm going to be excited," Schilling said on the day before his start. "But after I throw that first strike, everything should be back to normal."

Not hardly. He struck out a championship series-record five straight hitters (the previous mark was four) to start the game—Nixon, Jeff Blauser, and Ron Gant swinging in the top of the first, Fred McGriff and Justice looking in the second—before Terry Pendleton bounced out to short on a two-strike pitch.

By that time, the only two Phils position players with championship-series experience had given the Phillies a 1-0 lead.

Lenny Dykstra ('86 and '88 Mets) belted a double to the left-center gap on a 1-2 pitch and Mariano Duncan ('85 Dodgers, '90 Reds) singled him to third in the first inning. Dykstra, who led the NL with a remarkable 143 runs in the season, scored the night's first run on an RBI grounder to second by Kruk.

In the third inning, two two-out doubles, both over the head of the shallow Incaviglia in left, evened the game at 1-1. Avery hit the first double and Nixon then lifted the game-tying one just beyond the awkwardly retreating Incaviglia.

The emotion seemed to be subsiding for the Phillies and the crowd as the game progressed. The post-seasoned Braves got to Schilling for another run in the fourth to take a 2-1 advantage.

Schilling walked Gant to begin that inning, and McGriff's single to right pushed him to third. Justice's sacrifice fly to medium left put Atlanta ahead.

Avery, meanwhile, at age 23 making his ninth playoff start, was in one of his smooth grooves, retiring six in a row by the time there were two outs in the bottom of the fourth.

As he had done with Daulton earlier in the inning, he then tried to sneak a 3-2 fastball past Incaviglia. The burly outfielder anticipated it and clubbed the ill-advised pitch beyond the wall in center, 423 feet in all, to tie the score at 2-2.

"Those guys come out to play every night," Pendleton had said of the Phillies. "And they don't care if there's a rainstorm out there, they're still going to come after you."

Frank Fitzpatrick

He could have gone down in Phillies history with Art Mahaffey, throwing that ball off the screen as Chico Ruiz stole home in 1964.

He could have gone down in Phillies history with Greg Luzinski, leaping in vain after Manny Mota's fly ball on Black Friday, 1977.

Yes, Kim Batiste could have gone down with some of the all-time goats in Philadelphia baseball history. Except he wouldn't let himself.

"I wanted to make sure they didn't have anything negative to say," Batiste said after making the big roller-coaster ride from playoff goat to playoff hero faster than you can say "Mitch Williams."

"I've had some bad moments in my years in baseball," Batiste said after Game 1 of the playoffs. "But after tonight, I can honestly say it's great to get the opportunity to come back in this game."

Yes, one minute, he was the defensive replacement who threw a double-play ball into rightfield in the ninth inning.

The next minute, he was the guy who smoked the game-winning single into the leftfield corner that gave the Phillies a 4-3 win over the Braves in 10 heart-stopping innings.

It can be a great game, this baseball. And it can be an awful game. Sometimes all in the same night.

For eight innings, Kim Batiste wasn't a hero or a goat, or even an entry in the box score. But then came the ninth inning. That is his time.

For three months now, he had been trotting into ball games in the ninth as Dave Hollins's defensive replacement. Incredibly, he hadn't made one error in that role in all those months.

But in this game, he slurped up Mark Lemke's sure-fire double-play ball—a double play that would have all but wrapped up a hard-earned 3-2 victory. And then . . .

Then he sidearmed the ball off into the Bermuda Triangle or someplace—for an error that quickly turned into a blown save and a blown win and a ballpark full of unhappy people, people who wouldn't forget.

"After that error, I definitely felt bad," Batiste said. "I said, 'What have I done now?' I was just sitting there, basically talking to myself, saying: 'What are you doing? Where were you throwing that ball?' There were so many things going through my mind."

But then, as he sat there blaming himself for what looked like a certifiable Philadelphia postseason disaster, he began to hear voices— the voices of friends, reassuring him that he wasn't a goat yet, reassuring him that there was still time to make those people cheer again.

"He was taking it real hard in the dugout," said his friend Milt Thompson. "I went up to him and just told him, 'Hey, it's over with. Let's go. You're coming up. It's in our hands. Let's win it.'"

But it wasn't just him. It was "20 guys," Batiste said. "They were telling me, 'Don't worry. You'll get a chance to win this.'"

And then there he was in the 10th. One out. John Kruk had just doubled. And whose turn was it to hit? The guy looking for a shot to redeem himself.

He got behind reliever Greg McMichael, 1-2. McMichael threw him a change-up. Batiste smacked it into the leftfield corner. Kruk came roaring home. And, all of a sudden, out there at second base, there was a mob scene of Phillies, all pounding Kim Batiste on the back—and then lifting him into the electrified night and carrying him off the field.

"It was just an emotional thing," said Thompson, who was in charge of half the heavy lifting. "We all felt so good for him, coming back after the error the way he did. I just looked over, and Danny Jackson was holding him up there, trying to carry him by himself. And I said, 'I better give him a hand. He's got to pitch in this series.'"

So Thompson grabbed a leg. And then the Phillies engaged in a scene you don't often see in this game—professional athletes staging an impromptu parade for the hero of the moment. It was a scene that epitomized exactly why the Phillies had gotten to that point.

Kim Batiste stood at his locker later, unable to wipe the smile off his face. He was asked if he had ever been carried off a field before in his life.

"Not like that," Batiste said. "Maybe I was carried off with a sprained ankle or something like that. But not for getting congratulated."

This was the first run he had driven in since way back on August 15. But there was a certain air of déjà vu to this game, because in that game, against the Mets, he had made an error, too—and then came back to stroke a game-winning single.

In the nearly two months since, he had no errors—and no RBIs. And then he wrapped up both of them in one amazing night.

"That's the way we do things on this team," said Thompson. "We rally around each other. And we find a way."

In Game 1, Kim Batiste found a way. But he couldn't have done it without a little help from his friends.

Jayson Stark

Billy Penn's wearing a Phillies cap. Does he have anything left on his fastball?

The Phils need help. Suddenly, their starting pitching looks as ragged as John Kruk's wardrobe.

In a Game 2 that was as unappealing as Game 1 was enjoyable, Atlanta clubbed starter Tommy Greene for seven runs in $2\frac{1}{3}$ innings and the Braves evened the National League Championship Series at one game apiece with a 14-3 victory.

"It was just one of those games," said Phils manager Jim Fregosi.

"When you have good pitching in your starting rotation, you're going to be able to bounce back after a tough loss a lot of the time," said Braves manager Bobby Cox.

Greg Maddux was the easy winner. The only runs he allowed in seven innings came on Dave Hollins's two-run homer in the fourth. Lenny Dykstra's ninth-inning homer gave the Phils their final run.

."Greg Maddux is as close to No. 1 on the list as you're going to see," said Cox. "He's dynamite. He can really pitch."

All the emotion that Curt Schilling, the Phillies, and their fans had brought to Game 1 fled quickly from Game 2 when it became clear that Greene had nothing.

"There's no carryover effect from one game to the next in the playoffs," said Fregosi. "Each game is separate."

But hardly equal. Fly balls, like the Braves, found little resistance at Veterans Stadium in Game 2. Their 14 runs set a League Championship Series record, and their four home runs tied an NL Championship Series mark.

Greene, who was 10-0 at the Vet in the regular season, could never find a groove. The same could not be said for his fastballs.

"It comes down to making the pitches and I just did not do that tonight," said Greene. "The last time I faced them"—a 3-0 Phils victory on September 24—"I was down in the zone. Tonight I was up, up, up."

Which is where Fred McGriff's towering, first-inning, two-run homer went, as well as far, far, far. It came on another down-the-middle pitch, and it put the Braves in front quickly, 2-0.

"That was the key hit of the night," Cox said. "It got us out in front early."

The home run, only the seventh into the rightfield upper deck in the Vet's 22-year history, had its journey cut short by the façade after traveling an estimated 438 feet.

Homers by Jeff Blauser and Damon Berryhill in a six-run third ended what little enjoyment a crowd of 62,436 could milk from the dismal night. Terry Pendleton, who was 3 for 5 with three RBIs, also homered for the Braves.

"We just did not pitch very well," said Fregosi. "When you give them balls out over the plate, they're going to knock them out of the ballpark. That's a very powerful lineup."

"If you're going to lose the first game like we did, you'd better get a split," Cox said as his team prepared to head home for Games 3, 4, and 5. "It's always great to be going home, but you had better get home with at least one victory."

Greene, the crowd's interest, and the game's competitiveness all vanished in the punishing six-run Atlanta third. Blauser's home run and Pendleton's two-run single made it 5-0.

Fregosi lifted Greene, but with the pitcher due to lead off the bottom of the inning, the manager brought in Bobby Thigpen instead of Ben Rivera, hoping to get two outs and then use a pinch-hitter.

But Thigpen surrendered a three-run homer to the first hitter, Berryhill, and the Phillies found the score an unappetizing 8-0. Hollins's two-run homer in the fourth cut the Atlanta lead to 8-2. A homer by Pendleton in the fifth partially offset Hollins's and left the score 9-2.

In the eighth, the Braves scored four more times, off reliever David West, another Phillies pitcher whose effectiveness must now be questioned after an outstanding season. Ron Gant's bases-loaded double, knocking in three runs, was the inning's big hit. Their final run came on Otis Nixon's RBI double off Larry Andersen in the ninth. And sent the Braves back to Atlanta with solid starting pitching and an all-important victory.

Frank Fitzpatrick

I f you could play every game before a whipped-up crowd in a success-starved city, if you could always start a wildly excited pitcher with a deadly focus, and keep finding heroes at the end of your bench and fresh young arms in your bullpen, then maybe you could beat these Atlanta Braves in a seven-game series.

Otherwise, as the Phillies are learning in big painful doses, you're going to need something else. Something like magic.

Trailing by 2-0 in the sixth, the scary Braves exploded for nine sudden runs in only two innings and thrashed the Phillies again, this time by 9-4, in Game 3 of an increasingly one-sided National League Championship Series.

"We're just not clicking on all cylinders," said John Kruk, whose triple, homer, and three RBIs provided most of the Phils offense against Tom Glavine. "We're not in synch. And you've got to have it all going against these guys."

There are no soft spots in the lineup of these two-time NL champs. And, as a struggling Darren Daulton pointed out, they have no "kid they just brought up from Triple A" in their rotation.

"We were ahead 2-0 and then it was like the Braves just turned on a switch or something," said shortstop Kevin Stocker.

Actually, they found that switch on July 20, when Fred McGriff transformed their lineup and their season.

The Braves, who have won a remarkable 53 of 70 games since acquiring McGriff, now lead this best-of-seven series, 2-1.

Phils starter Terry Mulholland, who had pitched just five innings since September 6 because of a pulled hip muscle, was superb for the first five of Game 3. He hit a wall in the sixth, when the Braves drove him from the game with five runs.

Frank Fitzpatrick

So the Phillies spent all season stomping on home plate, and all of a sudden they can't find it.

The greatest run-scoring machine in the National League has thrown a rod at the worst possible moment.

The only way the Phils have any sort of chance in the National League playoffs is to outscore the Atlanta Braves. Instead, it's happening the other way around.

If the Phils are going to win, it is going to have to be by 11-8 or 10-5. But in the first three games of the National League playoffs, they have scored only 11 runs—total. The Braves had more than that in one night, and have hit the Phils with three touchdowns and a safety in just two games.

When the Phils are scoring in torrents, it washes away the sins of commission and omission by their slow and uncertain defense. And it doesn't matter that their bullpen goes up like flash paper, as long as they can pour out runs from a steady spigot.

But the spigot delivers runs now in sporadic drips and drops. A big inning is a deuce. No one can remember the last bat-around. Lenny Dykstra, the best leadoff man in baseball, is 3 for 13. The Phils engine room is mute and impotent. Dave Hollins is 2 for 10. Darren Daulton is 1 for 11. Pete Incaviglia is 2 for 8 and Milt Thompson 0 for 5. The four, five, and six hitters have batted in all of three runs. Together.

The only marquee bat that hasn't turned totally to mush is John Kruk's. He came into the playoffs with a batting average that had been in steady decline, but in the postseason, his first after a long, long wait, he is 5 for 11 and leads the team in runs and RBIs.

The Phils are parched for runs, and unless they can end the drought, instantly, they are cooked.

Obviously, there is a reason for their sudden offensive swoon, and that reason is the arms of Atlanta, all those clever Cy Youngs with their circle change-ups and their back-off buzz-bombs.

Certainly the hoariest saw in baseball is that good pitching always beats good hitting, but it's not as though the Phillies have been regularly paralyzed by Atlanta's pitching. They did, after all, score 64 runs in a dozen games against the Braves, and won half of them, in the regular season.

In the postseason, though, the Braves have made a subtle change in how they pitch the Phillies. A little less finesse. A little more hard stuff.

The unanimous scouting report on the Phillies is that they feast on heat and that they are patient to the point of exasperation. So the Braves had not thrown as many fastballs, instead trying to lure the Phillies into offering at change-ups. But subconsciously this approach tended to make the Braves pitchers less aggressive and less effective.

"We told them to go ahead and challenge them more," said Leo Mazzone, the Braves pitching coach. "Sometimes you can give hitters too much credit. Those guys have a great eye. We told our guys to concentrate on getting ahead in the count. And let's not back off. Let's go after them."

The Phils got exactly one walk in Game 3's 9-4 hammering, and that not until the eighth inning. They were hitting from behind in the count most of the time.

Half their runs came off the Braves bullpen, which is soft and inviting. The problem is, by the time the Phils get to that pen, the game is out of reach.

The Phils, true to their persona, deny that their confidence has waned or that they have become defensive hitters. They can deny all they want, but at bat they look tentative. Instead of attacking the ball, they seem to be feeling for it.

Dykstra has gotten on base five times in the three games, and that is acceptable. But acceptable is a couple of floors below what the Phils need at this point. And the big boppers aren't doing their job. Hollins hit nothing hard in Game 3. Daulton didn't get the ball out of the infield until his fourth at bat. Incaviglia was hitless in four trips. Mariano Duncan, Kruk, and Kevin Stocker provided 70 percent of the hits and 75 percent of the runs.

Ironically, their only win so far was exactly the sort of game they were supposed to lose—low-scoring, one-run difference, extra innings. That night, they were able to survive defensive leaks and bullpen palpitations. But they cannot survive them every game. Not unless they are burying their mistakes under an avalanche of runs.

Now, the only thing getting buried is them.

Bill Lyon

There were many complex twists, intriguing subplots, and moments of fascinating drama in Game 4. But the whole story of the Phillies' nerve-testing victory in this one could be found in Danny Jackson's eyes.

His eyes burned with an unmoving purpose as the Phillies left-hander stood on the same mound where the Braves embarrassed him in the 1992 playoffs, when he was a Pittsburgh pitcher. They stared long and hard at every Atlanta hitter, in each of the gutsiest $7^2/_3$ innings he'd ever pitched.

Jackson limited the Braves to just one run, and the Phillies held on for a 2-1 victory over Atlanta that was equal parts fright and delight.

"He gave us all he had," Phils manager Jim Fregosi said.

The Phillies victory evened at 2-2 this National League Championship Series that had seemed so much in the Braves' favor a little more than 24 hours before.

"That was the best game I've seen him pitch since he was with Kansas City," Braves manager Bobby Cox said of Jackson. "He had a good fastball and a good slider."

Mitch Williams came in to get the final out of the eighth, then worked his way through a typically harrowing ninth inning for a save.

"DJ gave us a huge lift," Williams said. "Any time you can go seven and two-thirds innings against that lineup and only give up one run, everybody on the team notices it. [Curt] Schilling noticed it, and it has to help him when he pitches" Game 5.

The Braves may yet win this League Championship Series, but if they do, no one will ever accuse these Phillies of meek surrender. They battled the Braves for almost every out in one of those tautly played games you just don't see in June.

"They never give up," John Smoltz said. "I thought I had good enough stuff to win that game 1-0, but it didn't work out that way."

His stuff was good enough to strike out 10 Phillies, and when reliever Mark Wohlers fanned five more, Philadelphia had tied a National League Championship Series record with 15 strikeouts. They also stranded 15 baserunners.

"Smoltz was showing us a split-finger pitch tonight that we hadn't seen before," Milt Thompson said. "That made him extra-tough."

It was a game filled with such oddities and at least one moment of controversy—when first-base umpire Jerry Crawford called out Otis Nixon on a seventh-inning sacrifice bunt and infuriated the 52,032 fans at Atlanta–Fulton County Stadium.

John Kruk became the first player in National League Championship Series history to fan four times in a game, Darren Daulton the first to walk four times.

Thompson, permitted to remain in the game and bat against left-handed reliever Kent Mercker in the seventh, saved the game in the eighth when, with two runners on and two outs, his leaping grab of Mark Lemke's long liner to left ended the inning.

"I never take my defense out when we're ahead in a ball game," said Fregosi, in explaining why he didn't pinch-hit Pete Incaviglia with the Phils clutching that tiny 2-1 lead they had held since the fourth inning.

In the two-run fourth, it was Thompson who scored the game-winning run, which came on Jackson's two-out single off loser Smoltz. Kevin Stocker's sacrifice fly just before that hit brought home the Phillies' first run. Both scored after second baseman Lemke committed the Braves' first error of the series on Daulton's inning-opening ground ball.

The Braves run came in the second on Lemke's RBI double.

But the Braves got their first two runners on in the ninth on pinch-hitter Bill Pecota's bloop single and Williams's error on another Nixon sacrifice bunt.

That crisis precipitated a rare Fregosi trip to the mound.

"I just went out to Mitch and told him to get an out and that I didn't care what base he got it at," Fregosi said. "Mitch told [defensive replacement Kim Batiste] that if the bunt came that way, he'd get the out at third."

Williams hungrily gobbled up Jeff Blauser's bunt and, before he could get a firm grip on the ball, threw to third.

"I thought that throw was going up the line," Williams said. "I didn't really have a good grip on it and I ended throwing Batty a palm ball. He made a great play on it."

Batiste stretched as far as he could, snatching the throw away from eternal infamy and holding the bag. Ron Gant then bounced to Mickey Morandini, who stepped on second and fired to first for the game's final out.

"That was a great game to watch," Smoltz said. "They made the pitches and the plays when they had to in this one."

After two games in which their bullpen and defense contributed to hefty Braves wins, the Phillies got several outstanding plays. And Williams, however frighteningly, did the job.

"I thought our defense played well," Fregosi said. "Mickey Morandini did a great job and Milt [Thompson] made the play on Lemke that saved the game."

It was saved on other occasions as well.

Fred McGriff began the sixth with a double to the gap in right-center, but a combination of Jackson's grit and good fortune prevented McGriff from scoring.

Terry Pendleton smoked a liner the other way, but right at Kruk. Jackson jammed David Justice and he flew to deep right. Greg Olson was then hit by an 0-2 pitch to bring up Lemke. The second baseman with the great postseason record lined a ball to left, foul by several feet. He then popped up softly to right to end the inning.

Francisco Cabrera's pinch-single started the seventh. Nixon sacrificed him to second. Kruk looked at second and, in taking his eye off the ball, briefly bobbled the bunt. He grasped it hurriedly and fired to first, apparently too late to get the speedy Nixon.

Crawford, however, emphatically signaled him out and thus became a Shermanesque villain in this city. The crowd screamed at him, and after each subsequent pitch booed loudly or shouted, "Safe, safe, safe," in unison.

"That play didn't beat us," Cox said. "We had a million chances to score and win the game. We could have easily won that game."

Jackson then retired Jeff Blauser on a sharply hit ground ball to short and, as he did to end a threat in the fifth, fanned Gant.

"Any time you win a playoff game, it's a big thrill," Williams said. "It will be fun going home and playing before our home crowd. But we can't really think about that, we still have one game here and we have to concentrate on that."

Frank Fitzpatrick

The Phillies won Game 4 on smoke and mirrors and Milt Thompson's brilliant play.

The catch that Thompson made in the eighth inning off a shot drilled by Mark Lemke to the leftfield wall may have Phillies fans singing his praises through the winter.

With runners on first and second and two outs in the one-run game, Mitch Williams was on the mound for the Phillies. Thompson was playing shallow, so he'd have a chance to make a play at the plate on a single. When Lemke first hit the ball, it looked very catchable, but the ball kept flying and flying, with Thompson sprinting after it.

He reached the warning track, took another step or two, launched himself into the air, grabbed the ball out of the night, and smashed against the wall. Then he held onto the ball.

An inning earlier, with the Phillies batting, the Braves brought in Kent Mercker, a lefthander, and it was wholly feasible that Fregosi would have pinch-hit for Thompson, who came up with two on and one out. Thompson, after all, is a left-handed hitter. And Pete Incaviglia was available.

Fregosi allowed Thompson to bat. He hit into a fielder's choice. That was not very useful. But a few minutes later, he made a catch that was more than useful. It was game-saving.

Michael Bamberger

Game 5, and there was chaos in all the usual places. The ninth inning. The pitcher's mound. Third base. The turmoil had swallowed another Phillies lead, had turned a nice drawing-room baseball game into an insane asylum.

Now, hustling toward the batter's box in the 10th inning of a 3-3 tie, like a man in a hurry to meet his destiny, went Lenny Dykstra. The feisty centerfielder smacked a 3-2 fastball beyond the blue wall in right centerfield in the Atlanta ballpark, giving the Phillies an astounding 4-3 victory over the Atlanta Braves—and changing the entire mood of the National League playoffs.

It gave the underdog Phillies the advantage, three games to two, in the best-of-seven series.

Dykstra's one-out homer came after the Phillies had blown a 3-0 lead and very nearly the game with another unnerving ninth inning.

Nonetheless, said the Phillies starting pitcher, Curt Schilling, "there's nobody in this room who thinks we have anything won. We're going home, but we're going to face maybe the two best pitchers in the league, [Greg] Maddux and Tom Glavine." But if his two league series starts were an accurate indication, Schilling might soon be mentioned in that lofty company. Again, he overpowered the Braves for eight innings only to watch a lead vanish in a harrowing ninth.

The Phillies righthander struck out nine and allowed four hits and two runs, both in the ninth.

Schilling sailed into the bottom of the ninth with a 3-0 lead, thanks to two early runs and Darren Daulton's first postseason homer, in the top of the ninth.

"They had the top of their lineup coming up and I walked [Jeff Blauser] to start the inning," Schilling said. "That was a mistake."

Ron Gant smacked a ground ball to Kim Batiste, who is becoming in this series what Richard Nixon was to the nation's political scene—vilified one moment, reborn the next. The defensive replacement looked at second and, in trying to extract the ball from his glove, dropped it for a huge error—as he had in Schilling's first-game start.

Daulton walked out to the mound for a talk with Schilling.

"I saw Jimmy [Fregosi] starting to come out of the dugout and I told Darren, 'He can't take me out of this game,'" Schilling said. "Darren said, 'I think he can.'"

In came Mitch Williams—along with everything that simple act implies.

Fred McGriff singled in a run. David Justice's sacrifice fly made it 3-2. Terry Pendleton then singled to put runners at first and second. Pinch-hitter Francisco Cabrera, familiar with postseason heroics, bounced a ball that somehow hopped over Kevin Stocker's glove behind second.

The single not only tied the game, but left the winning run at third with one out.

"I can't tell you what I was thinking on the bench," said Schilling. "There were too many things going through my head at the time."

The Braves needed only a well-positioned ground ball through the drawn-in Phillies infield or a medium-deep outfield fly to win. Mark Lemke laced one pitch down the leftfield line that fell frightfully close to fair territory.

Before it landed foul, Fregosi, watching from his distant dugout post, had a one-word reaction. It won't be repeated here.

Williams then struck out Lemke on a nasty breaking ball and got pinch-hitter Bill Pecota on a fly to shallow center to force extra innings. Williams had thus blown two saves—games he would go on to win—in this entertaining series.

"Mitch finally got out of it and kept us in the ball game," said Schilling. "He's one of the reasons we're here. You've got to stick with him. And then Lenny . . ."

His voice trailed off, as though even in the reliving, the moment was still a little too unreal.

Frank Fitzpatrick

The Phils had taken a 1-0 lead off starter Steve Avery in the first inning on Mariano Duncan's single and John Kruk's RBI double to the right-field corner. The lead became 2-0 in the fourth when Ron Gant misplayed Pete Incaviglia's long fly to left for a three-base error and Wes Chamberlain drove him home with a sacrifice fly.

Chamberlain, pulled from Game 5, as in so many others this year, for defense, actually permitted the struggling Curt Schilling to find himself in the early innings with three outstanding plays.

"I didn't feel good about my stuff coming out of the pen," said Schilling. "I don't think we would have won the game without those plays."

Chamberlain held Jeff Blauser to a single in the first, cutting off a ball bound for the corner. Later in that inning, Fred McGriff rocketed a ball that seemed destined to land beyond the wall. Instead, it slammed into the top of the fence. Chamberlain turned immediately, picked off the carom, and hit Kevin Stocker. The shortstop's throw home nabbed Blauser for the final out.

"When he hit it, I thought it was out," said Chamberlain. "So I just turned and positioned myself to get it off the wall in case it hit. It bounced right to me and I hit the cutoff man."

In the second, Chamberlain threw out Damon Berryhill, who was trying to stretch his two-out single into a double. On the play before that, Incaviglia's fine sliding catch robbed Terry Pendleton of extra bases.

Frank Fitzpatrick

But back to the 10th inning. A game, maybe a series, maybe a season, had slithered out of the Phillies' hands just minutes earlier. It was a time when heroes step forward. It was a time Lenny Dykstra lives for. As dusk descended, Lenny Dykstra walked to the plate to meet the moment he'd waited for all day.

"I told my wife this morning before the game, 'I just hope I can get a situation where I can do something big,'" Dykstra would recall later. "I said, ' hope that situation comes up, because I want to do that. I want to be that player. I want to be that guy.'"

And in the 10th inning of an amazing baseball game, Lenny Dykstra's time arrived. Only moments after the 3-0 Phillies lead in the ninth had dissolved into the shock of a 3-3 tie, the decisive moment of a pivotal game came down to one matchup:

Lenny Dykstra versus Mark Wohlers.

Dykstra ran the count to 3 and 2, exactly as he has done so many times. He programmed the personal computer in his brain, the Mac-Dude, to jump on the full-count fastball he knew was coming.

The fingers stopped wiggling. The swing uncoiled. The baseball flew off into the shadows and crashed off the folded-up football seats just below the rightfield scoreboard.

Dykstra floated around the bases, furnishing his own applause in a stunned stadium. His home run had put the Phils back ahead to stay in Game 5. He had gotten his moment, and he had made it his forever.

"I just like to play in these types of situations," Dykstra said afterward. "To want to be out there in those games, you can't teach that. Some people want to be out there. Some people are scared to be out there."

He made it very clear in which group he placed himself. It would be tough to argue with him. It was the sixth home run in his postseason career. Mike Schmidt hit half that many. Willie Mays never hit even one. But Lenny Dykstra, leadoff man, had hit six. (More would come in the World Series.)

As Dykstra stepped in, he was well aware that the Braves had just changed catchers, inserting Francisco Cabrera after Cabrera's regularly scheduled game-tying pinch hit in the ninth inning. There probably weren't many players in the park who knew that Cabrera hadn't gotten behind the plate since July 25 and had caught just twice all season. But Lenny Dykstra knew. Of course.

So his game plan when he got up there, he said, was to outwait Wohlers if he could, maybe draw a walk "and then turn it into a double—steal second and maybe third."

"That was my thinking early," he said, then laughed. "I liked my thinking later better."

But he almost never got a chance to unveil that portion of his thinking. The count got to 2 and 2. Wohlers—who struck out five Phillies in two innings Sunday night—came back with a 2-2 flameball that spit fire as it whooshed just by the outside corner.

Dykstra never flinched. Umpire Jerry Crawford called it ball three. The Braves dugout exploded. Lenny Dykstra wondered what the big deal was.

"The pitch was way outside, man," he said. "When it's outside, you don't swing. Just 'cause the catcher sets up out there and the pitch goes out there doesn't mean it's a strike."

Even his teammates got a chuckle out of that line.

"Way outside?" gulped Dave Hollins. "Maybe it was outside. But it was outside by a little bit, not way outside."

Whatever, it was 3 and 2. And that was fastball time. And that was Lenny Dykstra's time. He is one of baseball's most theatrical players. And he crashed a theatrical home run to win a baseball game his team absolutely, positively had to win.

Which is, of course, exactly how he planned it.

"I expect myself to do what I did today," said Lenny Dykstra, the right man for the right moment on a team that feeds off every move he makes.

Jayson Stark

With their fans whooping the cry of the long-suffering, with baseball's most talented team reduced to stunned observers, the unkempt, unshaven, underdog Phillies won the championship of the National League in Game 6 of the playoffs against the Atlanta Braves.

After a season of scrappy, passionate victories that took them from worst to first in their division, the Phils played with a cold, unwavering confidence in beating the Braves 6-3 to win the series, four games to two.

Mitch Williams even threw strikes.

If not for the ninth-inning appearance of Williams, John Kruk's torn uniform pants flapping on national television, and manager Jim Fregosi smoking cigarettes in the dugout, you might not have known that the supremely confident machine that beat the mighty Braves was the ragtag Phils.

Their country-boy fireballer Tommy Greene held baseball's best lineup in check for seven innings, and the victory before 62,502 raucous and chilled fans at Veterans Stadium gave the Phillies only their fifth pennant in 110 years.

"We had one goal," said Williams, who threw one of his rare one-two-three ninths to cap the victory and trigger a rowdy celebration on the field and in the clubhouse.

Curt Schilling, who started Games 1 and 5 and recorded 19 strike-outs but not a victory, was named the NL Championship Series most valuable player. "I can't think about that now," a hoarse Schilling said. "I'll think about it in the morning. I've got to go drink now."

The celebration that began with Darren Daulton leaping into the air lasted far into the night in the Phillies' buoyant clubhouse.

"I've never been that excited on the field," the normally reserved Daulton said of his leaping and diving after Williams's strikeout of pinch-hitter Bill Pecota ended the ninth. "I don't know what came over me," Daulton said. "I've just never been this happy. It's unbelievable. It probably won't hit me until tomorrow when I wake up with a hangover. I hope it's a good one."

Three two-run hits—a homer by Dave Hollins, a Mickey Moran-dini triple, and Daulton's double—built the Phillies a 6-1 lead against the two-time NL champion Braves.

The pennant culminated a long quest by these Phillies, an us-against-them crusade that almost all of them said was the driving force in their unexpected run to the league championship.

And just who was the "them" mentioned by nearly every Phillie in the champagne-drenched locker room?

"All the people who called us rejects, who doubted us, who called us tramps, gypsies, and thieves, who said we were fat and out of shape," Terry Mulholland said. "And I don't care if we changed anyone's mind or not. All I know is that we believed in ourselves and we proved to the world what we are capable of doing."

What they did in Game 6 was score all of their runs off Game 2 winner Greg Maddux, perhaps the league's toughest pitcher. The six runs were the most the Braves righthander had allowed in 91 starts.

Greene, the winner, threw seven solid innings, permitting all three Braves runs. But fittingly, this 25th National League Championship Series ended with Williams on the mound and Kim Batiste at third.

A wildly enthusiastic Vet crowd roared loud and often through the first few innings when, really, very little worthy of the noise occurred. Except for Morandini's stab of Dave Justice's one-out liner in the second inning of the still-scoreless game.

"To me, their defense was the key to this series," Braves manager Bobby Cox said. "That ball Morandini caught could have gone all the way to the wall."

Maddux uncharacteristically walked Greene to open the third.

When Lenny Dykstra followed with a single, Maddux and the fans turned their controls up from medium to high.

The Braves righthander, and likely winner of a second consecutive Cy Young Award, got Morandini on a foul pop-up and forced Kruk to bounce softly to first.

But Maddux, who had been hit on the right calf by a Morandini ground ball in the first, seemed to battle his control. Now he walked Dave Hollins to fill the bases and drive the 62,502 fans closer to pure frenzy.

They got there when Daulton smacked a 2-1 pitch just inside the rightfield foul line. Two runs scored on the ground-rule double to give the Phillies the early lead, 2-0.

"I think that took some pressure off," Morandini said. "We had the lead off Maddux, and that was important."

Frank Fitzpatrick

After 110 years, Philadelphia at long last has the perfect baseball team.

Oh, this isn't the best team the city has ever had. The 1980 world champions were more elegant. The 1983 Phillies had more pedigrees. Those war wagons of the late 1970s had more talent. But this team is the most beloved. Beloved in the way that you want to hug it one moment, slap it silly the next. Beloved because it has warts and splotches and failings and faults, and rises above them anyway.

They're just so damn human.

This team is what Philadelphia has wanted, and the team that it deserves.

The Phillies have a personality for just about everyone's tastes, and at Veterans Stadium, before a parka-bundled house of shrieking believers watching Game 6, the Phillies threw their whole zoo crew at the Braves.

There was the Tasmanian Devil, Lenny Dykstra, hitting safely in every game of the series and, of course, doing what he does best, which is boot-scooting on home plate. Twice. The Phillies are practically immortal when Dude gets home more than once in a game.

There was the cover-boy catcher, Darren Daulton, coming through again in the situation in which he thrives most—bases loaded. Of his 105 RBIs this season, 30 were with jammed sacks. And in this clincher of a game, in just such a situation, one in which the natural temptation is to over-try, he lashed a two-run double. You want a name for this team? Try The Daulton Gang.

There was the Boy Scout who's trying so hard to be one of the biker boys, Mickey Morandini, starting double plays and climbing invisible ladders to flag down scorching liners. Morandini doesn't fit the Phillies scruffy image but he has grown the best scraggles of mesquite around his chin that he can. He still can't bring himself to spit and scratch. But you forget he can play the hell out of second base. Tough isn't how you look, it's how you play. Oh yes, he also tripled into the rightfield corner, driving in a pair.

There was Dave Hollins, whose ankles are always wrapped, clubbing a 422-foot moon-shot to center, with Morandini on. Hollins is straight off the Marine recruiting poster, with a jaw on which you can strike a match. He runs the bases like a high school linebacker.

There was Tommy Greene, a.k.a. Jethro, the North Carolina backwoods boy who started out throwing stones at rabbits and ended up pegging baseballs past the Braves, old-fashioned heat most of the time, but a nasty breaking ball, too, which was all the more remarkable considering how slick the balls are when it's 40 degrees and how your fingers can stiffen like claws in the cold.

There was Milt Thompson, well traveled and playing left in the shadow of the imposing Pete Incaviglia. He made the most of his chance —he was on base his first three times up, scoring a run, all against Greg Maddux, who is merely the best pitcher in the game right now.

There was John Kruk, whose bat wasn't needed this time around. Kruk still did his part for the team's image, though. Sprawling in the dirt early, he ripped a section of his right pants leg loose, and the flap hung there. It completed his usual pigpen ensemble, which, as always, was topped off with the seven-pack chewing gum lump.

There was David West, in from that wildly erratic bullpen, with that reach-back, cock-and-flame delivery that can be unhittable. The trick, though, is to get the ball somewhere in the vicinity of the plate. In the eighth inning of Game 6, West found the plate, one-two-three.

And that meant, of course, Mitch Williams in the ninth.

Williams and the ninth, in a 6-3 game, is nitro mixed with napalm.

He came in, to universal surprise, throwing strikes. Three of them past the first hitter. A full count on the second, and a fly out to center.

The mounted police readied themselves beyond the outfield fence. The crowd stood, mocking that ubiquitous and annoying tomahawk chop.

To the third hitter, Williams again went full. And struck him out. It was 11:17 P.M.

This is a team harder to kill than a sidewalk weed.

It reflects Philadelphia, from row house grit to Main Line panache.

The players have all the pungency and character of a grease-oozing, onion-slathered cheesesteak, and they routinely furnish all the kettle-drum thunder of a symphony orchestra.

They might not have much culture, but remember that in Philadelphia, the Art Museum is best known not for what hangs inside but for the bent-nosed pug who danced atop its steps. And Rocky could throw batting practice for these Phillies.

Bill Lyon

The World Series

They used it all, the Phillies did, all of their nasty little bullyboy tricks, all of their sly intimidations, all of their messing-with-your-head distractions.

They knew that the Blue Jays knew them mostly by reputation, most of it unsavory, and right from the start the Phillies wanted to see what they might get away with, whether they might be able to unnerve the team that seemed as polite as the Phils are crude.

So the Phillies showed up unshaven and unshorn, menacingly stubbled and swaggering about in their best go-ahead-try-me bluster. They remind you of street pigeons, puffing their chests, blowing out their feathers trying to make themselves bigger, more threatening than they are.

It was Game 1 of the World Series, played under a roof that could cover Rhode Island, but it was more like a schoolyard, with one of those testosterone-turf tests where the new kid whose notoriety has preceded him tries to find out if he can make the locals back down.

Ah, but the Beastie Boys have run into a team that will not be skulking away in disgraced retreat. This may take a while.

The Blue Jays, so proper and trim, may be Team Briefcase, but it turns out they carry a blackjack inside the briefcase. They have starch in more than their shirts. They have seen the Beastie Boys now and they are not daunted.

It began, as it always does, with Lenny Dykstra, mouth agape, dribbling chaw droppings, cock-strutting into the box and sneeringly declining to take his bat off his shoulder. He worked a five-pitch walk.

And stole second.

The Phillies hadn't even bothered trying to run against Atlanta, but here they were, first inning, first batter. They were probing.

John Kruk, caricatured and vilified in the local papers for all the familiar reasons, stepped in, jaws hammering furiously on his celebrated cud, helmet blackened as though he had just emerged from Mine No. 5. He coaxed the count to 2-2, fouled off two, and then singled home Dykstra. It was a masterful at bat by Kruk, and it established a pattern.

They all followed his example. They stood in against Juan Guzman, yielding not an inch, not even when he buzzed them inside, and they dared him and they made him throw a 36-pitch first inning, and they got a second run when their leader, Darren Daulton, the head

Bubba, the one you wanted to be when you were in high school, ripped an RBI single.

In the bottom of the first, the Blue Jays' two swiftest jackrabbits, Rickey Henderson and Devon White, were snuffed in a double play, which ought to be impossible considering their speed, and, in fact, was—replays showed White safe at first, convincingly. The Blue Jays squawked. So did Roberto Alomar when he was called out on strikes.

Only one inning, and the champions seemed disconcerted. They were arguing with umpires, they were down by two, and it looked as if the bullyboys had thrown them off their game.

But the Jays are made of stern stuff, sterner than they look. They spliced four hits together and got those two back.

So the Phillies attacked again in the third. Another hit and yet another steal—the Phils are confident they can run on Pat Borders—and there was Kruk again, back out of Mine No. 5, buried early in the count, working it to 2-2, fouling off two more tough pitches, singling in another run, backing up the image with performance.

And again the Jays had a rebuttal, though it was because of Milt Thompson's three-base error.

So the new kid pushed his chest into the local's one more time, Mariano Duncan tripling and scoring on a wild pitch.

And the local shoved right back—Devon White, home run. Turns out the Jays are not as mild as they look.

On and on they played, the pace maddeningly slow. They were in no hurry. The first game is important; it establishes what will come, shows what will work, what needs to be discarded. And this first game was even more important than usual, for it showed that the Jays will not be intimidated. This, however, does not mean that the Phils will stop trying. Nor should they.

So they postured and pounded on one another, each trying to enforce his will, the Phils pushing, the Jays pushing back.

And then, for the first time, the Jays got the lead, got it when the freshest-faced, most polite Jay of them all swatted a solo homer.

John Olerud has a swing of sweet simplicity. Appearance to match. He had to have been president of the student council. In an earlier generation, he would have worn penny loafers.

But the ball went 373 feet. More evidence that the Jays belie their appearance. They turned four consecutive hits into three runs in their portion of the seventh inning, and that seemed to soften the Beastie Boys.

But the Phils do not willingly submit, of course. Ever. No, they must be beaten.

In Game 1, they were, 8-5.

Bill Lyon

Racing a line drive to the centerfield fence with 52,000 fans screaming for him to lose, forcing a pitching change just by walking toward home plate, puncturing a Blue Jays comeback with a two-strike home run—nobody loves these moments more than Dude.

Lenny Dykstra dominated Game 2 of the World Series with a sensational, wall-pounding catch in the fourth inning and a leadoff homer in the seventh, and the Phillies held on for a 6-4 victory over Toronto that tied the 90th Series at one game apiece.

"I always think I've got to do something out there," Dykstra said. "Right now I'm a happy human."

Even the Phils red-light centerfielder, though, can't tame the kind of late-inning terror that Mitch Williams can generate. The Phillies reliever allowed the inevitable walk and two stolen bases as Toronto added a run in the eighth, then picked off an early-breaking Roberto Alomar at third to end the inning in typical Williams fashion.

Emboldened by the ease with which Paul Molitor had stolen third earlier in the inning, Alomar, who had already stolen second, tried to steal third as well. But he left too soon—Williams turned in the midst of that high kick and fired to Dave Hollins, who tagged out Alomar.

"Roberto is an excellent baserunner," said Jays manager Cito Gaston. "Normally, he wouldn't do that."

"I'm not surprised at anything they try when Mitch is on the mound," Phils manager Jim Fregosi said of the stolen bases, which cost his club one run. "They've been watching us, and they know that with that big leg kick, you can run on Mitch."

Terry Mulholland, bothered by the sticky clay mounds in both the bullpen and on the field, battled his footing and his control for $5^2/_3$ innings and earned his first postseason victory when Roger Mason and Williams held off the Jays.

"I hope in my teammates' minds I'm the kind of guy they want out there when they need a good effort," Mulholland said.

In the ninth, Williams walked the leadoff hitter, then gave up a ground ball to third that allowed Kim Batiste, a magnet for postseason turmoil, to again make things exciting. The defensive replacement's off-target throw turned a potential double play into just one out. Williams, however, got Pat Borders to bounce into a game-ending double play started by shortstop Kevin Stocker.

The Phillies took a 5-0 lead in the third inning off Jays starter Dave Stewart, a loser for just the fourth time in 14 postseason decisions. Jim Eisenreich's three-run homer on an 0-2 pitch was the game's big hit.

"I'll always cherish it," said Eisenreich. "I was seeing the ball good tonight."

But Joe Carter's two-run homer in the Jays fourth made it closer —the Jays inning was cut short by Dykstra's grab of the Alomar shot— and Tony Fernandez's RBI double in the sixth made it downright uncomfortable.

That's when Dykstra's home run off Tony Castillo made things slightly easier for the Phils, giving them a 6-3 lead.

"I really didn't know much about that guy when I went up there," said Dykstra. "But in those situations, when you get a pitch to handle, you have to do something with it. If I didn't, the next pitch might have been on the [edge of the plate] and I'd be walking back to the dugout."

There was an almost visible anticipation among the Phillies to get this game started. They seemed to detect a little premature smugness in the Canadian air after Game 1—a feeling that these Fat Phils from that other league were no match for the sleek and suave Blue Jays. Gaston had said that the Phils offense reminded him of Cleveland's. And a SkyDome banner draped over the rightfield bullpen read: "Phillies? You Can't Be Serious."

"The way they're ripping us up here, you would think this was a one-game series," Williams said before the game. "I believe that was just Game 1, wasn't it?"

Still, as much as they hungered to return to Philadelphia tied at one, the Phils knew it wouldn't be easy. Not with "Steam Vac" Alomar roaming the carpet. Not with a Jays lineup that possessed more danger per square inch than Atlanta's. Not with Duane Ward, a 6-foot-4 threat lurking in the bullpen.

"These are two outstanding offensive clubs," Fregosi said. "I think it's going to be a high-scoring series. But I think we've got to hold them under five runs. You've got to get them before they can go to that big horse [Ward] in the pen."

The only problem with that strategy was that it forced them to do something not many teams have done in postseason—knock Stewart around.

So, with his eyes glowing and that blue cap pulled down far enough to almost obscure them, Stewart tackled the Philadelphia lineup. The Phillies scratched the big righthander in the first two innings. In thc third inning of the scoreless game, they drew blood.

Stewart walked Dykstra and Mariano Duncan (just the second baseman's 13th base on balls in '93) to begin the third. John Kruk followed with a broken-bat flare into center that scored Dykstra (Kruk's third RBI of the Series). Hollins also looped one in front of centerfielder Devon White to make it 2-0 Phils.

Darren Daulton advanced the runners with a right-side ground ball and Stewart got ahead of Eisenreich, 0-2. The pitcher tried to slip a high fastball past Eisenreich, whose bat appeared to have slowed a bit in the last few weeks. It didn't work. The Phils rightfielder smacked it 391 feet, beyond the wall in right center. The three-run homer gave the Phils a 5-0 lead.

Mulholland passed his first test anyway.

"It's important we shut them down after we score," said Fregosi, who watched Game 1 starter Curt Schilling fail to do that three times. "Every time we scored, we let them get right back in the game."

Borders singled with one out in the bottom of the third, but Dykstra ran down White's long, two-out drive to end the inning.

The Jays were beginning to hit some balls hard, though, and one inning later, Molitor's leadoff single and Carter's two-run homer pulled Toronto within 5-2. The inning would have been worse had Dykstra not leaped into the soft centerfield wall to snatch Alomar's shot.

Mulholland, meanwhile, had one big advantage against these Jays. His great pickoff move would keep their speedy runners close. In fact, just six runners tried to steal off the lefthander this season and just one made it. And that one came when Todd Pratt was catching.

Frank Fitzpatrick

As for Eisenreich, he's the one you'd want to surrender to.

After Billy Penn's barbarian baseball team has overrun your village and threatened to put it to the torch, he's the one you'd want to hand over your sword to.

Jim Eisenreich makes the Phillies presentable in public.

Gentleman Jim. Him, the maitre d' will seat; later, he can smuggle the rest of the scruffians in through the back door.

In Planet SkyDome, in Game 2 of the baseball championship of

North America, Daulton caught a hell of a game, Dude ran down tracers and crushed another homer, Krukker cranked more hits, and Inky kept splattering himself all over the leftfield fence. But the biggest bopper of them all on this team of primal screams was the most self-effacing of them all.

Jim Eisenreich doesn't use the Phillies spittoons, their kitty litter boxes, their snuff tins, or their tobacco pouches. Nor does he join them in growing hair that resembles a Chia pet. What he does do that they can all relate to is swing a piece of white ash.

He used it to scald that 391-foot three-run homer when the Phillies finally had their first bust-out inning of the postseason, a five-run third off ol' Penitentiary Face himself, Dave "The Glare" Stewart.

The years have taken Stewart's hair and some precious miles per hour off his fastball, but the trade-off is accumulated pitching knowledge. With two on and the Phillies already having scored two in the third, Stewart worked like a safecracker, turning the tumblers carefully on Eisenreich. He was right to be cautious—Eisenreich has a remarkable .344 lifetime average against Stewart. Plus three homers.

But he was in a quick 0-2 hole against Stewart, who is mostly guts and guile now, sliders and splitters. And then, hoping to catch Eisenreich looking for a splitter low, one of those dirt-kickers that hitters corkscrew themselves into the ground trying to reach, Stewart tried to sneak past what is left of his rising fastball, in on the fists.

But he left too much of it out and up, where Eisenreich could turn with full torque. He almost smiled. Twice. Once, as he took Larry Bowa's congratulatory slap coming round third, and then again in the dugout, when he bent for a drink and maybe thought no one was looking, Jim Eisenreich actually seemed to entertain, for the briefest flash, what could be interpreted only as a grin.

That was as flamboyant as he gets.

Bill Lyon

Ｔhey play a lot of bad games like this in Toronto. They call it hockey.

One team builds a big lead, then freezes the puck when its opponent tries to come to life.

The Blue Jays came into the Phillies' building for Game 3 of this World Series. They put Philadelphia's bats and fans to sleep with a 10-3 triumph that was as uninspired as a SkyDome sellout. Toronto took the Series lead, two games to one.

For this game, Paul Molitor—normally the Blue Jays DH but playing first base instead of batting champ John Olerud for the first of three Series games without a DH—homered, tripled, and drove in three runs in the first three innings.

"It looks like Cito made the right choice," Manager Jim Fregosi said of Gaston's decision to start Molitor over Olerud.

Toronto led 4-0 after Molitor became the second player since July to homer off loser Danny Jackson. Despite the sideburned, 37-year-old Molitor's big night, Gaston indicated that Olerud would start the next two games here against righthanders Tommy Greene and Curt Schilling.

"We talked about this before the game and we all decided that whatever Cito decides, we're going to try to make it work," Molitor said. "I knew going out there tonight that it might be my last game [in Philadelphia], so I wanted to make it count."

Winning pitcher Pat Hentgen faced several tests, but he got the big strikeout or grounder when he needed it.

"I thought the big turning point was when we had second and third in the first inning and didn't score," said Fregosi.

Indeed, after the Jays had taken a 3-0 lead in the top of the first on Molitor's two-run triple and Joe Carter's sacrifice fly, consecutive one-out singles by Mariano Duncan and John Kruk left the Phils with runners at the corners. Dave Hollins and Darren Daulton were coming up.

On the mound, Hentgen recalled what had happened in his previous start, a loss to the White Sox in Game 3 of the AL playoffs. "Against Chicago, we got two runs, and when I went out there I could have given our team a big lift," said Hentgen. "But I let them get a couple of runs back and we lost that game.

"So when Hollins came up I was definitely going for a strikeout," he said. "I got two strikes on him and then made a real good pitch up and in."

Hollins fanned on that one, and Daulton struck out on another high fastball to end the inning.

"I thought he had good command and he had a good rising fastball," Fregosi said of Hentgen. "But we helped him a little by chasing some high pitches."

Toronto was not so accommodating toward Jackson, the lefthander who had struggled in September but pitched brilliantly in the Phils' Game 4 NLCS triumph that turned that series around.

Fregosi said the 72-minute, two-part rain delay could have bothered

Jackson. "It looked to me like he was ready to go after the first delay," said Fregosi. The tarp was off when a reborn rain forced it back on. "Then we had a longer delay," said Fregosi. "He had enough time to warm up, but it might have affected him."

RBI singles by Jim Eisenreich in the sixth and Duncan in the seventh and a home run by Milt Thompson in the ninth gave Philadelphia its only runs.

Robby Alomar was 4 for 5 with two RBIs, the only out he made coming on a first-inning line drive to third. Tony Fernandez drove in two more runs, and Devon White, Ed Sprague, and Joe Carter added the other RBIs for Toronto.

The Jays offense, which didn't look any less threatening without Olerud, dispatched Jackson in five innings, then picked up four runs off reliever Ben Rivera to end the misery for thousands of prematurely departing fans.

A Veterans Stadium crowd of 62,689 arrived at Philadelphia's first World Series game in a decade eager to explode. As the fans left quietly on the damp, chilly, dreary night, they must have wondered what they really had missed in the last 10 years.

Frank Fitzpatrick

It was a World Series game gone mad. And it was a game that, with a six-run Toronto burst in the eighth inning, turned terribly sour for the Phillies.

Curve balls hung in the air like the thick mist that shrouded Veterans Stadium all through the Phils' crippling 15-14 loss in Game 4 of the World Series.

Steve Carlton threw out the ceremonial first pitch, and it was as close as anything got to the plate for most of the evening. A bullpen phone malfunctioned in the fifth inning, the bullpens themselves many innings earlier. Fans exploded in thunderous glee at ball calls.

And, after the Phillies blew two five-run leads, their season, filled with the improbable, was only one loss away from a disappointing conclusion.

"That might go down in the annals as one of the all-time games for the World Series," Phils manager Jim Fregosi said. "It was unbelievable." If Fregosi didn't look particularly stunned by the outcome, it was probably because, in a way, he had seen it coming.

Asked before the game what would happen if starter Tommy Greene couldn't give him many innings, forcing the manager to go to his tired bullpen early, Fregosi said: "We'd be in a lot of trouble."

They were. Greene lasted just $2^1/3$ innings and allowed seven runs. Roger Mason stopped the Jays for a while, but David West, Larry Andersen, and Mitch Williams couldn't.

By winning the highest-scoring game in World Series history, the Blue Jays took a three-games-to-one lead.

"That was a tough loss, no question about it," said Lenny Dykstra, who belted a pair of two-run homers and tied a Series record with four runs scored. "You don't have to be a baseball genius to figure out that we should have won that game."

In addition to Dykstra's homers, Milt Thompson drove in five runs and Darren Daulton homered and knocked in three.

"We just didn't have anyone who threw the ball well," Fregosi said. "I knew we would have to score a lot of runs, and I thought we had. But . . ."

But Tony Fernandez drove in five runs, giving him a shortstop-record nine for the Series, and Devon White added four for Toronto, including two on an eighth-inning triple that was the game's decisive blow.

"I think the pressure is definitely on them now," said Rickey Henderson, who also had a two-run single in the Jays' six-run eighth.

After the Phils had overcome a 3-0 first-inning lead with four runs of their own, the two offenses jabbed at each other and the woeful bullpens for a few innings. But a five-run fifth put the Phils ahead 12-7, and it seemed they would win in a walk.

Which is how all of the trouble started. With walks. Six of the night's 13 came in the first inning, which ended with 62,737 hoarse fans and a 4-3 Phils lead.

"Every time a pitcher threw a pitch over the plate, it seemed like it was going to get hit hard somewhere," said Duane Ward, who picked up his second save in the Series.

By the time the eighth inning began, the Phils led 14-9. But a single, walk, and error by Dave Hollins made it 14-10. Fernandez's fifth RBI, a single off Williams, got the Jays to within 14-11. Henderson drove in two more with a single, and White's two-run triple put Toronto up 15-14.

Mike Timlin and Ward, two of the few effective pitchers on this long night, shut down the Phils in the eighth and ninth.

"I think after tonight a few guys are going to be pretty drained," Ward said. "It was such an emotional rollercoaster. Up and down. Up and down. Up and down." No one was able to control it until Toronto went ahead in the eighth. It was as if someone took the brake off the game early, and it careened downhill from there.

Greene and Todd Stottlemyre started, but both vanished quickly in a nearly unabated barrage of walks and hits. Many of the nine pitchers who followed were not much better.

So much for sunshine, green grass, and the pastoral splendor of baseball. Game 4 of this World Series began in conditions that made the Vet resemble a Scottish moor—a damp gray mist hanging over the jammed stadium, moistening the turf to a treacherous sheen, muddying the mound, and leaving baseballs difficult to grip.

"That's part of the game," Jim Eisenreich said. "I would hate to see all domed stadiums. . . . If you're playing in the north, you're going to have these conditions."

So, amid the pressure and slick conditions came a raucous first inning. Toronto took a 3-0 first-inning lead for a second consecutive night. Henderson's leadoff double, a walk to White, and Joe Carter's infield single (on which Hollins couldn't get to his feet after a diving stop) filled the bases with one out.

Greene got John Olerud, back in the lineup at first base, to pop up to John Kruk. But the Phils righthander walked the night's third baseman, Paul Molitor, to force in the game's first run. Fernandez's line single to right made it 3-0.

Even though the Phils led the NL in runs this season, they hadn't had a bust-out postseason game. "We really haven't swung the bats well, in either the playoffs or the Series," Fregosi said.

Not.

After a Greene single to start the Phils second inning, Dykstra yanked a Stottlemyre fastball inside the rightfield foul screen for his third homer of this postseason and second of the Series. His first two-run shot of the night gave the Phils a 6-3 lead.

The Blue Jays bats don't take many nights off, though, and they drove Greene from the mound and retook the lead in the third.

Frank Fitzpatrick

After the game, Mitch Williams stood at his locker in the clubhouse wearing a black World Series cap and fouling off excuses being offered up to him for his game-blowing eighth-inning appearance.

"I stunk," he said. "I've stunk before except tonight it was on national

TV in front of the whole country instead of just our little cable TV station here in Philadelphia. That was the only difference. But I don't need you offering excuses to me. I don't need any. I just didn't do the job."

Williams was surrounded at the locker. A few feet behind the mob sat third basemen Dave Hollins, who was slumped over and staring into his locker. Someone asked Hollins how tough a loss was it, and he did not answer. He swallowed once, twice, and his eyes watered up.

"Tough," he said.

All season long the Phillies have lived and died with Mitch Williams driving the car at the end of the game. He never takes the shortest route home, but by and large his numbers show that more often than not he is successful.

In the middle of the game, he made his customary walk from the dugout to the bullpen. All along the rightfield line, fans stood up and cheered for him, the Wild Thing strolling to the bullpen in the middle of the wildest game of the wildest season in 10 years. Williams nodded his appreciation and waved his red glove at his adoring fans.

A short time later the fans would rise as one and boo him.

He entered the game with the Phils nursing a 14-10 lead with one out in the eighth inning of a bruisingly ugly game. How comfortable was the lead? The crowd cheered his entrance.

He gave up a single. The crowd groaned. He gave up a walk. They buzzed like the neighbors of someone who had just been robbed. He got a strikeout and there was a sellout sigh of relief. But it was short-lived.

When he finally finished the inning, the Phils were behind,15-14, and you could feel the air in the stadium rushing upward through the mist. The Phils went meekly in the ninth.

Williams had already showered by the time the Phils had made their last out of the game, but beads of sweat were forming under the band of his black baseball cap a full half hour after the game.

He said he would forget this night as soon as he walked out the clubhouse door. Someone asked him if it was his toughest loss ever. He made a sound like air rushing out of a giant balloon. "I've had losses like this before," he said, "but never in the World Series. So I guess you could say it was my toughest loss."

Mitch Williams spoke those words defiantly. He adjusted his black cap and asked: "Am I done?"

Williams was definitely done—and he may have finished the rest of the Phillies, too.

Timothy Dwyer

The clock was ticking toward 1 A.M. But Curt Schilling's brain already was ticking toward 8:12 P.M.

It was the wee hours of the morning. The aftershocks of World Series Game 4, one of the most devastating postseason losses in Phillies history, were still registering on the clubhouse Richter scale. But in Game 5, the '93 Phillies also had Curt Schilling. They weren't asking much of him. Just save the season. And he did.

He went out to face a Blue Jays team that had just scored 25 runs in the previous two games, to face a Blue Jays lineup that had been shut out once all season—94 games before by Fernando Valenzuela, on the final day of June.

And Curt Schilling shut them out for nine remarkable innings, for 148 gut-wrenching pitches. When he was through, the Phillies had beaten the Blue Jays 2-0. And their season wasn't over. Not yet, anyway.

Two weeks before, in Atlanta, Lenny Dykstra gave a little speech about people who rise to the occasion in games like this.

"To want to be out there in these games, you can't teach that," Dykstra said. "Some people want to be out there. Some people are scared to be out there."

By Game 5, it was very clear which one of those groups Curt Schilling belongs in. Lead him out there with every spotlight in North America beaming down on him. Then make him prove himself. You will get no complaints from him.

"I wanted the ball," Schilling said after his first shutout since April 23. "I wanted the responsibility. I've said before, if you don't want the ball in these situations, why show up? You want your teammates to count on you at times like this."

And this night, when his team needed him as it has never needed him before, he proved himself once again.

It was just a few months before, when Schilling was reeling from losing five games in a row, that his catcher, Darren Daulton, questioned his toughness. But nobody is questioning Curt Schilling's insides any-more—not after a postseason in which he threw three starts as brilliant as any Phillie has ever thrown in this setting.

"That guy showed us all," Daulton said after the game. "He's turned into a big-time, big-game pitcher."

Game 5 was the biggest of them all. He gutted his way to a three-hitter through seven innings. But when he reached the eighth, he was running on fumes. "I was really out of gas in the seventh," he said.

"Anytime Darren comes out and says, 'You might have to use mirrors to get a couple outs,' I know I'm losing my stuff."

But on this night, there was no one else but him. He gave up two consecutive hits to start the eighth inning. He turned around and took a quick peek at the bullpen. Not a soul was heating up. That told Curt Schilling all he needed to know.

"That was probably the first time in my career that's ever happened," Schilling said later. "And that got me more pumped up than anything, because I knew this team was either going to end its season or go to Toronto based on what I did."

So he turned around and went to work. The top of the Blue Jays order awaited.

Rickey Henderson was first. Schilling blew on his fingers to combat the effect of the rapidly plunging thermometer. The crowd murmured edgily.

The count went to 2-and-1, then 2-and-2. Then one foul. And another foul. As 62,000 people chanted, "Curt-Curt-Curt," he fired one more fastball. Henderson thumped it back toward the mound. Schilling threw up his glove. The ball hit it and popped out.

For one anxious moment, Schilling couldn't find the ball. Then he looked down at his feet and found it sitting right there. He lunged after it, fired home, and hung up pinch-runner Willie Canate. One big out.

Then it was Devon White's turn. Schilling got the count to 0-and-2 this time. Then two more foul balls. Schilling blew on his fingertips again. Those 62,000 people were on their feet for the 10th consecutive pitch. Schilling reached back for one more backdoor slider—a pitch he hadn't thrown all night until this at bat.

White missed it. Two out. It was the ninth consecutive strike Curt Schilling had thrown. But he wasn't out of this yet.

Finally, up came Roberto Alomar, the guy whose two-run double had knocked Schilling out of his start in Game 1. They would duel for nine nerve-wracking pitches. Alomar fouled off one 2-2 fastball that was clocked at 94 m.p.h. Then he fouled off another fastball. And another. And another. Schilling took a little stroll and took a giant gulp of air.

Then he snapped off his biggest breaking ball of the night. Alomar bounced it to Mariano Duncan for the third out. Veterans Stadium erupted.

"If I had to point to one inning in my career where I gave everything I had for one inning, that was the inning," Schilling said, still clutching the lineup card in his right hand.

When Lenny Dykstra clutched Game 5's final out, Schilling merely walked off the mound, punched a fist halfheartedly into the air, and calmly shook Daulton's hand.

In their remarkable season's final home game, a pitching-rich nine innings that was everything their 15-14 loss in Game 4 was not, the Phillies had scratched out two runs off Juan Guzman in the first two innings and held on.

The Phils scored Game 5's first run on a first-inning walk and stolen base by Dykstra, Toronto catcher Pat Borders's throwing error, and John Kruk's ground out. Their final run came on doubles by Daulton and rookie Kevin Stocker in the second.

Jayson Stark and Frank Fitzpatrick

The Phillies season ended the way you always feared it would—with Mitch Williams surrendering a ninth-inning lead.

On a maddening evening that will haunt Phillies fans for decades, Williams gave up a three-run homer to Joe Carter to give the Blue Jays an 8-6 victory in Game 6 of the World Series. It was the Jays' second straight world championship.

Although the Jays did it in six unforgettable games, the Phils and their fans will most remember the "Wild Thing" walking into an ugly destiny in the ninth inning. Two innings earlier, trailing 5-1, the Phillies had staged another of their wondrous comebacks. Lenny Dykstra slammed a three-run homer off starter Dave Stewart to key a five-run, seventh-inning rally that had moved the Phils into a 6-5 lead.

Then, after the Phils had escaped a bases-loaded jam in a hair-raising eighth inning, in came Williams.

After the game, Williams's teammates said the Phils closer had been under tremendous strain after receiving repeated phone calls threatening his life the previous two days. Williams apparently told manager Jim Fregosi that he got plenty of sleep before the game, but he confided to teammates that he had actually gotten little.

Fregosi's decision to stay with his closer, even though Williams had blown a five-run lead in Game 4, will be debated bitterly by Phils fans. But go with Williams he did. "Mitch Williams has done the job for us all year," said Fregosi, his voice slightly shaken. "I just told him that we wouldn't have gotten this far without him."

When Williams entered the game, he walked Rickey Henderson on four pitches to start the ninth.

One out later, Paul Molitor, who had tripled and homered earlier, singled the tying run to second. Carter then smashed a 2-2 pitch beyond the leftfield wall to make the Jays the first team since the 1977-78 Yankees to win back-to-back titles.

Carter said he sensed that Williams was not throwing the ball well.

"We came into the ninth inning down one run, but with Mitch out there you knew something good would happen," said Carter, "and it did."

"I knew his velocity was not good," said Carter. "Really the only pitch he was throwing for strikes was the slider. I swung through one slider for strike two. If I failed it wouldn't be because I wasn't trying.

"I'm a low-ball hitter, and I got one I could handle. I hit it good, but I wasn't sure it would go out. I didn't know if it was high enough."

This overachieving Phillies team had gotten as far as only four other Phillies teams had. Its quest for the ancient franchise's second championship, though, ended so painfully that it seems destined to live forever in Philadelphia's scarred sports consciousness.

And in the unlikely event that memories of that ninth inning ever fade, Phillies fans will probably recall the five-run, eighth-inning lead that Williams blew in their 15-14 loss in Game 4.

"I was just hoping something would happen," said Jays manager Cito Gaston. "We just have never quit all year, same as the Phillies."

The Blue Jays had taken a 5-1 lead off Terry Mulholland, thanks mainly to Molitor's triple in a three-run first inning and to his fifth-inning homer. But Stewart, the glaring king of active postseason pitchers, was struggling with his control, and he walked Kevin Stocker to begin the seventh. Mickey Morandini, making his first World Series start, singled Stocker to third.

Dykstra worked the count to 3-1 before belting a knee-high Stewart fastball into the rightfield seats. His fourth homer of this Series, and 10th in postseason play, cut the Jays' lead to a tenuous 5-4.

"I'll tell you what," said Carter. "I've always thought Rickey Henderson was the best leadoff man in baseball. But after seeing that little guy [Dykstra] in this Series I might have to change my opinion. He is really something."

The Phillies seemed loose and confident before the game began.

Even though Mulholland hadn't gone more than $5^2/_3$ innings since August, the manager was sure he could do that in Game 6. "There's no doubt in my mind that he's very confident," said Fregosi. "He's had enough outings now that he should be able to go deep into the game."

Instead, it looked like he might not survive the first inning, and he never really found a rhythm.

As Fregosi noted, the erratic Phillies bullpen was rested and ready to be used as it has all season.

"We would like to be three or four runs ahead in the ninth inning," said Phils coach Larry Bowa. "It's going to be up to our starting pitcher to take us deep into the ball game."

Instead, Devon White walked with one out in the first and Molitor followed with a triple off the rightfield wall. When Carter's sacrifice fly was caught near the leftfield wall and Molitor scurried home, it was quickly 2-0 Jays. A John Olerud double and a Roberto Alomar single made it 3-0 before Mulholland could finish the inning.

Meanwhile, the Phils weren't hitting the pitches Stewart was throwing near the plate. They were hitless through three, their only baserunners coming on walks to John Kruk in the first and Dykstra in the third.

Then with two outs in the fourth, Darren Daulton looped a double down the leftfield line on a 3-2 pitch. On another full count, Jim Eisenreich's single to center gave the Phils their first run. Stewart, laboring now, went 3-2 on a third straight hitter, before getting Milt Thompson on a ground ball to second.

The Blue Jays got the run right back in their half of the fourth. The amazing Alomar doubled off the top of the left-field wall, moved to third on Tony Fernandez's ground ball, and scored his club's fourth run on Ed Sprague's fly ball to the wall in right.

Two infield errors—by Alomar on Morandini's bouncer and Sprague on Mariano Duncan's chopper—plus a two-out walk by Kruk left the bases loaded for Dave Hollins. But the Phils' third baseman bounced out to Olerud and a fat chance had been squandered.

This was not the pregame prescription for victory.

"We know that we're going to have to play an almost perfect game to beat them," said Bowa. "They just keep coming at you. From top to bottom, that's an awesome lineup."

And one of its most awesome pieces, Molitor, who would be named the MVP of the series, pushed the Jays lead to 5-1 in the bottom of the inning. Toronto's designated hitter slugged a Mulholland pitch 391 feet to left for his second homer of the Series.

On the very near horizon, you could see the lights of a season's end approaching.

Frank Fitzpatrick

He sat at his locker, his heroic home run all but forgotten, and all he could say was: I tried.

"I tried and tried and tried again," said Lenny Dykstra. "But it wasn't enough." It wasn't enough to save the Phillies. It wasn't enough to save the season. It wasn't enough to keep Mitch Williams from serving up the ninth-inning home run to Joe Carter that ended the Phillies' magic carpet ride.

But even though he couldn't make the SkyDome scoreboard stop reading: "Blue Jays 8, Phillies 6," there was one thing Lenny Dykstra could say after Game 6 of the World Series, and until the day he dies:

He tried. Oh, how he tried.

If it weren't for him, there would have been no Joe Carter home run. There would have been no bottom of the ninth for the Wild Thing to wander into.

There would have been just another baseball game. But Lenny Dykstra turned it into something else, something special, with one swing of the bat, with one three-run homer that was one inning away from going down as one of the most unforgettable games in the history of the Phillies.

It came in the seventh inning, an inning that told you everything you needed to know about the Phillies and about the man who wore No. 4 on his back. His team trailed, 5-1. There were two men on. There was nobody out. And Lenny Dykstra walked to the plate for the 842nd time since the plane headed north from Clearwater, Fla., so many months before.

It was probably going to be the last time, too—unless . . . unless he had one last Mr. October magic act left in him. "When I went up there, one thing occurred to me," Dykstra would say later in a deathly quiet clubhouse. "I looked up and I said, 'Man, it's the seventh inning. I'd better do something before it's too late.'"

So he did, of course. Because that is all he has been doing since the calendar turned to October. He spent the final three weeks rising to almost mythical heights at a time when only the special players in this game find another stairway to climb.

But as you watched him head for the plate in the seventh inning, you couldn't help wondering: What more could he do?

He had hit a game-winning home run in the 10th inning of a play-off game in Atlanta. He had had one of the herculean World Series games of our era in that 15-14 wackathon of Game 4. He had manufactured the game-winning run without a hit in a game of survival in Game 5.

So what more could he do? What more could he have left? Only this:

A three-run home run soaring through the SkyDome haze for his fourth homer of the Series, his sixth of the postseason, and his eighth, ninth, and tenth runs batted in of the Series.

One flick of the bat that suddenly spun this entire World Series in reverse. One majestic swing that sucked every ounce of noise out of a thumping, pumping, space-age ballpark.

In the end, of course, it didn't matter. In the end, none of it changed anything. Joe Carter was the hero. Joe Carter hit the biggest home run. And Dykstra could only watch it.

"It was a weird feeling, watching that ball go out," he whispered. "Helpless, man. I can't really describe it."

But we can all describe this: Lenny Dykstra had himself a World Series, and Lenny Dykstra had himself a sorcerer's season that put a stamp on him that nobody will ever be able to erase.

"I was able to do this year what I always planned on doing," he said. "It was nice because I got to prove to people in baseball what I could do as a player, what I expected myself to do. What I did this year is the way I play, the way I should play."

And the way he played in this World Series is the way only the great ones play.

Had Mitch Williams been the Mitch Williams this team had hoped and prayed he would be, it would have been a very different scene ending Game 6. It would have been Lenny Dykstra who was accepting that MVP trophy, not Paul Molitor. And it would have been Lenny Dykstra's team that was having the party.

But in a way, Dykstra said, if you had to go down, this was the way to go down.

"If you had to pick a way to lose a game, then this was probably the way to lose a game," he said. "We were so close. We lost two heart-breaking ball games in this World Series, and that's the reason they're celebrating over there, and we're not celebrating over here.

"But we've got a lot of things to be proud of. I think we proved to America and everybody in the world that this ball club doesn't quit. This was a typical Phillies game. It just had a tough ending."

Endings don't get any tougher than this one. And this Dude couldn't change it, no matter how much he wanted to. But until that ending, until they told him he couldn't play any more, Lenny Dykstra tried. Like very few baseball players ever have.

Jayson Stark

Jerry Lodriguss

Mitch Williams leaped
with joy as the Phils
won the pennant.

Teammates rushed from the dugout to share in
celebrating the first pennant in 10 years.

Charles Fox

Eric Menche

Visiting Phillies fans at the Series opener at SkyDome expressed their optimism with signs that responded to talk in Toronto about the Phils' scruffy image. They watched Fregosi warmly greet Dykstra as the players were being introduced, but they also saw Kruk strike out in the sixth inning, stranding three runners.

Jerry Lodrigus

Jerry Lodriguss

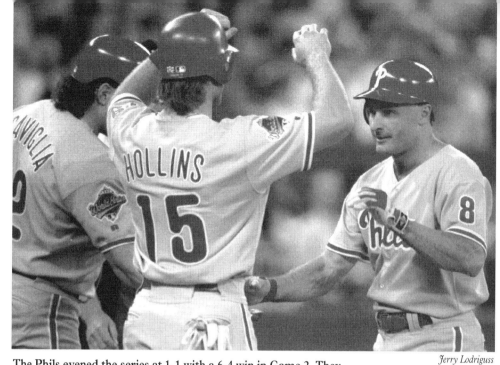

Jerry Lodriguss

The Phils evened the series at 1-1 with a 6-4 win in Game 2. They got crucial help from two home runs, one by Eisenreich (greeted at the plate by Hollins and Incaviglia, who scored ahead of him) and a solo shot by Dykstra in the seventh.

Jerry Lodriguss

Jerry Lodriguss

Daulton tried unsuccessfully to break up
a double play; Roberto Alomar made the
throw first. Earlier, Alomar punched a single
to left beyond the diving reach of Hollins.

Jerry Lodriguss

John Costello

Elizabeth Malby

As the Series moved to the Vet, the crowd was festive even though heavy rain delayed the start of Game 3 for more than one hour. Matt Picariello, 10, of Philadelphia, was attending his first World Series game; it was 10 years ago that the last Series game was played at the Vet.

Eric Mencher

Jerry Lodriguss

Dykstra came up with a sinking liner to end Toronto's half of the seventh, but the Blue Jays scored three times and won, 10-3. The Phils went scoreless in the second inning despite a double by Kruk down the rightfield line that got past Paul Molitor.

Eric Mencher

Jerry Lodriguss

In Game 4, which set a record for runs scored, the
Phils got five in the fifth, two of them on a home
run by Daulton. He was greeted at home by
Hollins, who had scored from first.

	1	2	3	4	5	6	7	8	9	10	R	H	E
BLUE JAYS	3	0	4	0	0	2	0	6	0		15	17	0
PHILLIES	4	2	0	1	5	1	1	0	0		14	14	1

Jerry Lodriguss

Charles Fox

Ed Hille

Eric Mencher

In drizzle and heavy mist, members of the Philadelphia Orchestra waited to play the national anthem. But the game went on—and on and on—for a record four hours and fourteen minutes. Fans saw Dykstra hit a two-run homer in the fifth and watched Devon White try to catch Thompson's triple in the first.

Jerry Lodriguss

Schilling had every reason to be pleased after shutting out the Blue Jays, 2-0, in Game 5, a must-win for the Phillies. Former Phillies manager Nick Leyva, now a Toronto coach, also might have been pleased by a rose given to him by the Phanatic. Leyva then handed it to a young fan.

Eric Mencher

Jerry Lodriguss

Eisenreich stopped the ball on a short hop in
the third, holding Pat Borders to a single.
In the eighth, Hollins tagged Willie Canate
between third and home.

Jerry Lodriguss

Jerry Lodrigus

In Game 6, Dykstra hit his fourth homer of the
Series, a three-run blast that drove in Stocker and
Morandini in the seventh. The Blue Jays jumped to
a three-run lead in the first; Stocker tried in vain to
snag a single by Roberto Alomar.

Eric Mencher

Eric Mencher

Joe Carter's homer with one out in the bottom of the ninth brought the World Series victory and jubilation to the Blue Jays, and it brought questions for a subdued Mitch Williams, who served up the 2-2 pitch.

Ron Cortes

Jerry Lodriguss

Denise Steskal, 14, of Port Richmond, waited at Philadelphia International Airport for the Phils to arrive from Toronto. Like many other fans, she thought they returned as winners.

Myrna Ludwig

5

THE
NUMBERS

Baseball is the perfect sport for the fan who is a statistics buff. As many a baseball writer has noted, the return of box scores and standings to the sports pages is the clearest sign that the long winter—which began with the last out of the World Series—is over.

This chapter is meant for that fan. Here are the numbers, tables, and charts found in most daily sports sections, along with considerable statistical data that are not so easily available. These numbers paint an intricate, not-so-obvious portrait of the 1993 Phillies. They include:

- NL East standings, month by month
- Phillies game by game
- Regular season statistics
- Batting in night games
- Batting in day games
- Batting with men in scoring position
- Batting against left-handed, right-handed pitchers
- Batting at home, away
- Batting order statistics
- Fielding statistics

- Errors by position
- Stealing statistics
- Overall pitching
- Pitching against right-handed, left-handed batters
- Pitching at home, away
- Win-loss records
- Starting pitchers' records
- Relief pitching
- Box scores for each postseason game
- Composite box scores for the NLCS and World Series

NL East Standings

April 30

EAST	W	L	Pct.	GB	Home	Away	Last 10	Streak
PHILLIES	16	5	.762	—	10-3	6-2	8-2	Won 2
St. Louis	13	9	.591	3½	7-5	6-4	6-4	Won 2
Montreal	13	9	.591	3½	8-4	5-5	7-3	Won 1
Pittsburgh	11	10	.524	5	5-6	6-4	4-6	Lost 1
Chicago	10	11	.476	6	6-5	4-6	4-6	Lost 3
Florida	10	12	.455	6½	3-6	7-6	6-4	Won 3
New York	8	12	.400	7½	4-8	4-4	2-8	Lost 5

May 31

EAST	W	L	Pct.	GB	Home	Away	Last 10	Streak
PHILLIES	34	14	.708	—	19-7	15-7	7-3	Won 3
Montreal	27	21	.563	7	17-6	10-15	5-5	Lost 1
Chicago	24	22	.522	8	15-12	9-10	5-5	Won 1
St. Louis	25	23	.521	9	15-11	10-12	6-4	Won 1
Pittsburgh	23	24	.489	10½	12-13	11-11	4-6	Won 1
Florida	21	28	.429	13½	9-14	12-14	5-5	Lost 2
New York	16	31	.340	17½	9-16	7-15	4-6	Lost 1

June 30

EAST	W	L	Pct.	GB	Home	Away	Last 10	Streak
PHILLIES	52	24	.684	—	28-11	24-13	6-4	Won 1
St. Louis	44	31	.587	7½	23-15	21-16	8-2	Lost 1
Montreal	40	36	.526	12	25-13	15-23	4-6	Won 1
Pittsburgh	37	38	.493	14½	21-16	16-22	7-3	Lost 1
Chicago	36	38	.486	15	20-17	16-21	4-6	Won 2
Florida	34	41	.453	17½	17-20	17-21	3-7	Lost 1
New York	22	52	.297	29	11-27	11-25	2-8	Won 1

July 31

EAST	W	L	Pct.	GB	Home	Away	Last 10	Streak
PHILLIES	65	39	.625	—	36-18	29-21	6-4	Lost 1
St. Louis	58	44	.569	6	33-18	25-26	3-7	Won 1
Montreal	55	48	.534	9½	34-17	21-31	6-4	Won 2
Chicago	52	49	.515	11½	29-23	23-26	6-4	Won 2
Pittsburgh	47	56	.456	17½	26-24	21-32	4-6	Won 1
Florida	43	59	.422	21	23-26	20-33	4-6	Lost 1
New York	35	67	.343	29	17-35	18-32	5-5	Lost 2

August 31

EAST	W	L	Pct.	GB	Home	Away	Last 10	Streak
PHILLIES	81	50	.618	—	46-22	35-28	4-6	Lost 1
Montreal	72	60	.545	9½	44-22	28-38	8-2	Won 5
St. Louis	71	60	.542	10	41-26	30-34	2-8	Lost 2
Chicago	64	67	.489	17	36-33	28-34	4-6	Won 1
Pittsburgh	61	70	.466	20	32-32	29-38	4-6	Lost 1
Florida	54	76	.415	26½	30-32	24-44	3-7	Lost 2
New York	46	85	.351	35	22-44	24-41	4-6	Won 1

Final standings

EAST	W	L	Pct.	GB	Home	Away	Last 10	Streak
PHILLIES	97	65	.599	—	52-29	45-36	4-6	Lost 2
Montreal	94	68	.580	3	55-26	39-42	7-3	Won 1
St. Louis	87	75	.537	10	49-32	38-43	5-5	Won 2
Chicago	84	78	.519	13	43-38	41-40	6-4	Won 1
Pittsburgh	75	87	.463	22	40-42	35-45	5-5	Lost 1
Florida	64	98	.395	33	35-46	29-52	2-8	Lost 6
New York	59	103	.364	38	28-53	31-50	7-3	Won 6

Phillies day-by-day

Date	Opponent	Score	Record	Pos.	Lead	WP	LP
4/5	At Houston............	3-1	1-0	T1	½	Mulholland	Drabek
4/6	At Houston............	5-3	2-0	1	1	Schilling	Swindell
4/7	At Houston............	6-3	3-0	1	1	DeLeon	Bell
4/9	Chicago.............	7-11	3-1	2	-½	McElroy	Rivera
4/10	Chicago.............	5-4	4-1	T1	1	Mulholland	Morgan
4/11	Chicago.............	3-0	5-1	1	1	Schilling	Guzman
4/12	Cincinnati...........	5-4	6-1	1	1½	DeLeon	Foster
4/13	Cincinnati...........	4-1	7-1	1	1½	Greene	Belcher
4/14	Cincinnati...........	9-2	8-1	1	1½	Rivera	Browning
4/16	At Chicago...........	1-3	8-2	1	1½	Morgan	Mulholland
4/17	At Chicago...........	3-6	8-3	1	1	Guzman	Schilling
4/18	At Chicago...........	11-10	9-3	1	2	Mt. Williams	Scanlan
4/20	San Diego...........	4-3	10-3	1	2	Ayrault	J. Hernandez
4/21	San Diego (rain).......						
4/22	San Diego...........	1-2	10-4	1	1½	Benes	Mulholland
4/23	Los Angeles.........	2-0	11-4	1	1½	Schilling	R. Martinez
4/24	Los Angeles.........	7-3	12-4	1	1½	Jackson	Gross
4/25	Los Angeles.........	5-2	13-4	1	2½	Greene	Candiotti
4/26	San Francisco........	9-8	14-4	1	3	Andersen	Minutelli
4/27	San Francisco........	3-6	14-5	1	3	Burkett	Mulholland
4/28	At San Diego.........	5-3	15-5	1	3	Schilling	Gr. Harris
4/29	At San Diego.........	5-3	16-5	1	3½	Jackson	Seminara
4/30	At Los Angeles.......	7-6	17-5	1	4½	Ayrault	Daal
5/1	At Los Angeles.......	1-5	17-6	1	3½	Candiotti	Rivera
5/2	At Los Angeles.......	9-1	18-6	1	4½	Mulholland	Hershiser
5/4	At San Francisco......	4-3	19-6	1	4½	Andersen	Righetti
5/5	At San Francisco......	2-11	19-7	1	4½	Swift	Jackson
5/7	St. Louis.............	4-3	20-7	1	4½	Greene	Magrane

Date	Opponent	Score	Record	Pos.	Lead	WP	LP
5/8	St. Louis............	2-1	21-7	1	5½	Mulholland	Perez
5/9	St. Louis............	6-5	22-7	1	6½	Davis	L. Smith
5/10	Pittsburgh	5-1	23-7	1	7	Jackson	Walk
5/11	Pittsburgh	4-8	23-8	1	6	Wagner	Davis
5/12	Pittsburgh	4-1	24-8	1	7	Greene	Tomlin
5/14	At Atlanta...........	7-10	24-9	1	6	Glavine	Mulholland
5/15	At Atlanta	3-5	24-10	1	4½	G. Maddux	West
5/16	At Atlanta...........	5-4	25-10	1	4½	Jackson	McMichael
5/17	At Florida...........	10-3	26-10	1	5½	Rivera	Hough
5/18	At Florida...........	6-0	27-10	1	5½	Greene	Armstrong
5/19	At Florida...........	3-5	27-11	1	5½	R. Lewis	Davis
5/20	Montreal............	9-3	28-11	1	6½	Schilling	Nabholz
5/21	Montreal............	2-6	28-12	1	5½	K. Hill	Jackson
5/22	Montreal............	5-6	28-13	1	4½	Fassero	Mt. Williams
5/23	Montreal............	14-7	29-13	1	5½	Mulholland	Heredia
5/24	New York	6-3	30-13	1	6½	Greene	Tanana
5/25	New York	4-2	31-13	1	6½	Schilling	Schourek
5/26	New York	4-5	31-14	1	5½	Franco	Mt. Williams
5/28	At Colorado	15-9	32-14	1	6	Rivera	B. Henry
5/29	At Colorado	6-0	33-14	1	6	Mulholland	Blair
5/30	At Colorado	18-1	34-14	1	7	Greene	Farmer
5/31	At Cincinnati	4-6	34-15	1	7	Reardon	Andersen
6/1	At Cincinnati	6-3	35-15	1	7	Andersen	Cadaret
6/2	At Cincinnati	5-2	36-15	1	8	Rivera	Smiley
6/4	Colorado	1-2	36-16	1	6½	Blair	Mulholland
6/5	Colorado	6-2	37-16	1	6½	Greene	Reynoso
6/6	Colorado	11-7	38-16	1	7½	Schilling	Ashby
6/7	Houston	7-5	39-16	1	8½	Jackson	Swindell
6/8	Houston	3-6	39-17	1	7½	Kile	Rivera
6/9	Houston	8-0	40-17	1	8½	Mulholland	Harnisch
6/10	At New York.........	7-6	41-17	1	9½	West	Gibson
6/11	At New York.........	5-2	42-17	1	10½	Schilling	Schourek
6/12	At New York.........	3-0	43-17	1	10½	Jackson	Gooden
6/13	At New York.........	5-3	44-17	1	11½	Rivera	A. Young
6/14	At Montreal	10-3	45-17	1	11½	Mulholland	Shaw
6/15	At Montreal	4-8	45-18	1	10½	Barnes	Greene
6/16	At Montreal	3-4	45-19	1	9½	Rojas	West
6/17	Florida	1-4	45-20	1	8½	Hammond	Jackson
6/18	Florida	7-3	46-20	1	9½	Rivera	Bowen
6/19	Florida	5-2	47-20	1	9½	Mulholland	Armstrong
6/20	Florida	4-3	48-20	1	9½	Greene	Hoffman
6/21	Atlanta	1-8	48-21	1	8½	G. Maddux	Schilling
6/22	Atlanta	5-3	49-21	1	9½	Jackson	P. Smith
6/23	Atlanta	8-3	50-21	1	9½	Rivera	Smoltz
6/25	At Pittsburgh	8-6	51-21	1	9½	DeLeon	Candelaria
6/26	At Pittsburgh	2-4	51-22	1	8½	Cooke	Schilling
6/27	At Pittsburgh	3-4	51-23	1	7½	Belinda	Mt. Williams
6/28	At St. Louis	1-3	51-24	1	6½	Cormier	Jackson
6/29	At St. Louis	13-10	52-24	1	7½	Rivera	Urbani
6/30	At St. Louis	3-9	52-25	1	6½	Osbourne	Greene
7/1	At St. Louis	5-14	52-26	1	5½	Tewksbury	Schilling
7/2	San Diego...........	2-5	52-27	1		Ettles	Mulholland
	San Diego...........	6-5	53-27	1	6	Mt. Williams	Hoffman
7/3	San Diego...........	4-6	53-28	1	6	Gr. Harris	Jackson
7/4	San Diego...........	8-4	54-28	1	7	Rivera	Worrell
7/5	Los Angeles..........	9-5	55-28	1	7	Greene	Hershiser
7/6	Los Angeles..........	5-7	55-29	1	6	Astacio	Schilling
7/7	Los Angeles..........	7-6	56-29	1	6	Mk. Williams	Trlicek
7/8	San Francisco	2-13	56-30	1	5	Swift	Jackson
7/9	San Francisco	8-15	56-31	1	5	Black	Rivera
7/10	San Francisco	8-3	57-31	1	5	Greene	Burkett
7/11	San Francisco	2-10	57-32	1	5	Hickerson	Schilling
7/13	**ALL STAR GAME**						
7/15	At San Diego	2-5	57-33	1	4	Gr. Harris	Jackson
7/16	At San Diego	3-5	57-34	1	4	P.A. Martinez	Greene
7/17	At San Diego	2-4	57-35	1	3	Benes	Mulholland
7/18	At San Diego	6-3	58-35	1	3	Schilling	Brocail
7/19	At Los Angeles	7-5	59-35	1	3	Mason	Daal
7/20	At Los Angeles	8-2	60-35	1	4	Jackson	R. Martinez

Date	Opponent	Score	Record	Pos.	Lead	WP	LP
7/21	At Los Angeles	7-0	61-35	1	4	Greene	Hershiser
7/22	At San Francisco	1-4	61-36	1	5	Burkett	Mulholland
7/23	At San Francisco	2-1	62-36	1	5	West	M. Jackson
7/24	At San Francisco	4-5	62-37	1	4½	Burba	Rivera
7/25	At San Francisco	2-5	62-38	1	4	Swift	Jackson
7/27	St. Louis	10-7	63-38	1	5	Mason	Magrane
7/28	St. Louis	14-6	64-38	1	6	Mulholland	Guetterman
7/29	St. Louis	6-4	65-38	1	7	West	Murphy
7/30	Pittsburgh	2-4	65-39	1	6	Walk	Rivera
7/31	Pittsburgh	10-2	66-39	1	7	Jackson	Tomlin
8/1	Pittsburgh	5-4	67-39	1	7	Mason	Cooke
8/2	At Atlanta	5-3	68-39	1	7½	Mulholland	Avery
8/3	At Atlanta	8-9	68-40	1	6½	Howell	West
8/4	At Atlanta	10-4	69-40	1	6½	Rivera	G. Maddux
8/5	At Florida	3-4	69-41	1	6½	Aquino	Mason
8/6	At Florida	8-7	70-41	1	6½	Mt. Williams	Turner
8/7	At Florida	5-6	70-42	1	6½	Hough	Mulholland
8/10	Montreal	5-2	71-42	1	6	Schilling	Nabholz
8/11	Montreal	6-5	72-42	1	7	West	Wetteland
8/12	Montreal	7-4	73-42	1	8	Mason	Scott
8/13	New York	9-5	74-42	1	9	Thigpen	A. Young
8/14	New York	5-9	74-43	1	8	B. Jones	Jackson
8/15	New York	5-4	75-43	1	9	West	A. Young
8/17	At Colorado	10-7	76-43	1	9	Rivera	Reynoso
8/18	At Colorado	7-6	77-43	1	9	Thigpen	B. Ruffin
8/19	At Colorado	5-6	77-44	1	8	M. Moore	Mason
8/20	At Houston	6-4	78-44	1	9	West	T. Jones
8/21	At Houston	2-3	78-45	1	9	D. Jones	Andersen
8/22	At Houston	3-7	78-46	1	9	Kile	Rivera
8/23	Colorado	2-3	78-47	1	9	Wayne	Mason
8/24	Colorado	4-2	79-47	1	10	Jackson	Blair
8/25	Colorado	8-5	80-47	1	11	Schilling	Sanford
8/27	Cincinnati	5-8	80-48	1	10	Ruffin	Mt. Williams
8/28	Cincinnati	5-9	80-49	1	9	Service	Thigpen
8/29	Cincinnati	12-0	81-49	1	10	Jackson	Pugh
8/30	At Chicago	6-10	81-50	1	9½	Pesac	Mason
8/31	At Chicago	7-0	82-50	1	9½	Rivera	Morgan
9/1	At Chicago	4-1	83-50	1	9½	Mulholland	Harkey
9/3	At Cincinnati	14-2	84-50	1	9½	Greene	Ayala
9/4	At Cincinnati	5-6	84-51	1	8½	Rijo	Jackson
9/5	At Cincinnati	5-3	85-51	1	9½	Schilling	Pugh
9/6	Chicago	6-7	85-52	1	8½	Harkey	Mk. Williams
9/7	Chicago	4-5	85-53	1	7½	Guzman	Rivera
9/8	Chicago	5-8	85-54	1	6½	Hibbard	West
9/9	Chicago	10-8	86-54	1	7	Jackson	Bautista
9/10	Houston	6-2	87-54	1	7	Schilling	Swindell
9/11	Houston	1-4	87-55	1	6	Portugal	Mk. Williams
9/12	Houston	2-9	87-56	1	5	Harnisch	Rivera
9/13	At New York	5-0	88-56	1	5½	Greene	B. Jones
9/14	At New York	4-5	88-57	1	4½	Tanana	Jackson
9/15	At New York	6-3	89-57	1	5½	Schilling	Schourek
9/17	At Montreal	7-8	89-58	1	4	Scott	Mt. Williams
9/18	At Montreal	5-4	90-58	1	5	Greene	Boucher
9/19	At Montreal	5-6	90-59	1	4	Scott	Mt. Williams
9/20	Florida	7-1	91-59	1	4½	Schilling	Hough
9/21	Florida	5-3	92-59	1	5½	Pall	Rodriguez
9/22	Florida	2-1	93-59	1	5½	Mason	Harvey
9/24	Atlanta	3-0	94-59	1	6	Greene	Glavine
9/25	Atlanta	7-9	94-60	1	5	Bedrosian	Mason
9/26	Atlanta	2-7	94-61	1	5	Avery	Schilling
9/27	At Pittsburgh	6-4	95-61	1	6	Rivera	Cooke
9/28*	At Pittsburgh	10-7	96-61	1	6	Thigpen	Robertson
9/29	At Pittsburgh	1-9	96-62	1	5	Walk	Foster
9/30	At Pittsburgh	0-5	96-63	1	4	Wakefield	Greene
10/1	At St. Louis	4-2	97-63	1	4	Schilling	Olivares
10/2	At St. Louis	4-5	97-64	1	4	Murphy	Mk. Williams
10/3	At St. Louis	0-2	97-65	1	3	Guetterman	Mt. Williams

* clinched NL East Division title.

Regular season statistics

HITTING	G	AB	R	H	2B	3B	HR	RBI	BB	SO	HBP	GDP	SH	SF	Avg.	OBP	SLG
Williams, Mitch	65	1	0	1	0	0	0	1	0	0	0	0	0	0	1.000	1.000	1.000
Andersen	64	1	0	1	0	0	0	0	0	0	0	0	0	0	1.000	1.000	1.000
Lindsey	2	2	0	1	0	0	0	0	0	1	0	0	0	0	.500	.500	.500
West	76	5	0	2	0	0	0	2	0	2	0	0	0	0	.400	.400	.600
Davis	25	3	1	1	0	0	0	0	0	0	0	0	0	0	.333	.333	.333
Amaro	25	48	7	16	2	2	1	6	6	5	0	1	3	1	.333	.400	.521
Mason	34	3	0	1	0	0	0	0	0	1	0	0	0	0	.333	.333	.333
Stocker	70	259	46	84	12	3	2	31	30	43	8	8	4	1	.324	.409	.417
Eisenreich	153	362	51	115	17	4	7	54	26	36	1	6	3	2	.318	.363	.445
Kruk	150	535	100	169	33	5	14	85	111	87	0	10	0	5	.316	.430	.475
Dykstra	161	637	143	194	44	6	19	66	129	64	2	8	0	5	.305	.420	.482
Jordan	90	159	21	46	4	1	5	18	8	32	1	2	0	2	.289	.324	.421
Pratt	33	87	8	25	6	0	5	13	5	19	1	2	1	1	.287	.330	.529
Duncan	124	496	68	140	26	4	11	73	12	88	4	13	4	2	.282	.304	.417
Batiste	79	156	14	44	7	1	5	29	3	29	1	3	0	1	.282	.298	.436
Chamberlain	96	284	34	80	20	2	12	45	17	51	1	7	0	4	.282	.320	.493
Incaviglia	116	368	60	101	16	3	24	89	21	82	6	9	0	7	.274	.318	.530
Hollins	143	543	104	148	30	4	18	93	85	109	5	15	0	7	.273	.372	.442
Thompson	129	340	42	89	14	2	4	44	40	57	2	8	3	2	.262	.341	.350
Daulton	147	510	90	131	35	4	24	105	117	111	2	2	0	8	.257	.392	.482
Morandini	120	425	57	105	19	9	3	33	34	73	5	6	4	2	.247	.309	.355
Longmire	11	13	1	3	0	0	0	1	0	1	0	0	0	0	.231	.231	.231
Greene	32	72	9	16	2	0	2	10	5	20	1	0	6	1	.222	.269	.333
Bell	24	65	5	13	6	1	0	7	5	12	1	0	2	0	.200	.268	.323
Millette	10	10	3	2	0	0	0	2	1	2	0	1	3	0	.200	.273	.200
Schilling	34	75	3	11	1	0	0	2	2	19	0	1	13	0	.147	.169	.160
Rivera	30	51	3	5	0	0	0	0	3	24	0	0	13	0	.098	.148	.098
Williams, Mike	17	12	1	1	0	0	0	0	0	3	0	1	3	0	.083	.083	.083
Jackson	32	65	3	5	2	0	0	2	3	37	1	0	12	0	.077	.130	.108
Mulholland	29	62	3	4	0	0	0	0	1	27	0	0	8	0	.065	.079	.065
Manto	8	18	0	1	0	0	0	0	0	3	1	0	0	0	.056	.105	.056
DeLeon	24	6	0	0	0	0	0	0	0	5	0	1	1	0	.000	.000	.000
Green	3	2	0	0	0	0	0	0	0	2	0	0	1	0	.000	.000	.000
Ayrault	10	2	0	0	0	0	0	0	0	2	0	0	0	0	.000	.000	.000
Mauser	8	4	0	0	0	0	0	0	1	2	0	0	0	0	.000	.200	.000
Fletcher	1	0	0	0	0	0	0	0	0	0	0	0	0	0	.000	.000	.000
Thigpen	17	1	0	0	0	0	0	0	0	0	0	0	0	0	.000	.000	.000
Pall	8	0	0	0	0	0	0	0	0	0	0	0	0	0	.000	.000	.000
Brink	2	1	0	0	0	0	0	0	0	0	0	0	0	0	.000	.000	.000
Foster	2	2	0	0	0	0	0	0	0	0	0	0	0	0	.000	.000	.000
Phillies	162	5685	877	1555	297	51	156	811	665	1049	42	105	84	51	.274	.351	.426
Opponents	162	5642	740	1419	247	39	129	673	573	1117	37	93	65	42	.252	.322	.378

Batting in night games

HITTING	G	AB	R	H	2B	3B	HR	RBI	BB	SO	HBP	GDP	SH	SF	Avg.	OBP	SLG
Lindsey	1	1	0	1	0	0	0	0	0	0	0	0	0	0	1.000	1.000	1.000
Mason	22	2	0	1	0	0	0	0	0	0	0	0	0	0	.500	.500	.500
Amaro	17	34	7	12	2	1	1	3	3	3	0	1	1	0	.353	.405	.559
Eisenreich	112	274	45	92	14	4	7	41	24	26	1	6	3	1	.336	.390	.493
Davis	17	3	1	1	0	0	0	0	0	0	0	0	0	0	.333	.333	.333
Kruk	110	403	76	126	27	3	8	60	87	64	0	5	0	4	.313	.431	.454
Stocker	49	182	32	55	9	2	2	27	21	30	8	6	2	0	.302	.398	.407
Dykstra	115	461	105	139	30	4	16	52	90	48	2	6	0	5	.302	.414	.488
Batiste	53	112	9	33	6	1	4	22	1	24	0	2	0	0	.295	.301	.473

HITTING	G	AB	R	H	2B	3B	HR	RBI	BB	SO	HBP	GDP	SH	SF	Avg.	OBP	SLG
Incaviglia	82	253	45	72	13	2	17	63	16	52	6	7	0	4	.285	.337	.553
Duncan	90	374	49	104	20	4	7	51	8	65	2	10	3	1	.278	.296	.409
Chamberlain	67	191	23	53	14	2	8	27	12	29	0	7	0	1	.277	.319	.497
Thompson	91	241	28	66	12	2	1	31	31	38	1	8	3	0	.274	.359	.353
Hollins	102	390	72	103	18	4	14	69	57	74	4	13	0	6	.264	.359	.438
Daulton	111	391	65	100	25	3	18	77	88	80	2	2	0	7	.256	.389	.473
West	51	4	0	1	0	0	0	0	0	2	0	0	0	0	.250	.250	.250
Morandini	84	294	36	71	14	5	2	19	21	49	4	4	3	2	.241	.299	.344
Bell	15	40	4	9	4	1	0	3	5	7	1	0	1	0	.225	.326	.375
Jordan	61	89	8	19	2	0	2	11	6	20	0	2	0	2	.213	.258	.303
Pratt	15	34	2	7	2	0	2	7	1	7	0	0	0	1	.206	.222	.441
Greene	25	60	6	12	2	0	1	8	5	16	0	1	4	1	.200	.258	.283
Millette	7	10	2	2	0	0	0	1	0	2	0	1	2	0	.200	.200	.200
Longmire	9	11	1	2	0	0	0	1	0	1	0	0	0	0	.182	.182	.182
Schilling	22	52	2	7	1	0	0	1	1	14	0	1	10	0	.135	.151	.154
Mk. Williams	13	12	1	1	0	0	0	0	0	3	0	1	3	0	.083	.083	.083
Rivera	22	37	2	3	0	0	0	0	1	17	0	0	10	0	.081	.105	.081
Jackson	21	38	2	3	2	0	0	2	3	20	1	0	9	0	.079	.167	.132
Mulholland	20	43	2	3	0	0	0	0	0	21	0	0	4	0	.070	.070	.070
Manto	6	16	0	1	0	0	0	0	0	2	1	0	0	0	.063	.118	.063
Mt. Williams	46	0	0	0	0	0	0	0	0	0	0	0	0	0	.000	.000	.000
Andersen	45	0	0	0	0	0	0	0	0	0	0	0	0	0	.000	.000	.000
DeLeon	18	5	0	0	0	0	0	0	0	4	0	1	1	0	.000	.000	.000
Ayrault	7	2	0	0	0	0	0	0	0	2	0	0	0	0	.000	.000	.000
Mauser	6	3	0	0	0	0	0	0	0	1	0	0	0	0	.000	.000	.000
Green	1	0	0	0	0	0	0	0	0	0	0	1	0	0	.000	.000	.000
Thigpen	14	1	0	0	0	0	0	0	0	0	0	0	0	0	.000	.000	.000
Pall	7	0	0	0	0	0	0	0	0	0	0	0	0	0	.000	.000	.000
Foster	1	2	0	0	0	0	0	0	0	0	0	0	0	0	.000	.000	.000
Brink	1	1	0	0	0	0	0	0	0	0	0	0	0	0	.000	.000	.000
Phillies	162	4066	625	1099	217	38	110	576	481	721	33	84	60	35	.270	.350	.424
Opponents	162	4080	520	1025	175	28	86	472	406	806	18	62	44	34	.251	.319	.371

Batting in day games

HITTING	G	AB	R	H	2B	3B	HR	RBI	BB	SO	HBP	GDP	SH	SF	Avg.	OBP	SLG
West	25	1	0	1	1	0	0	2	0	0	0	0	0	0	1.000	1.000	2.000
Andersen	19	1	0	1	0	0	0	0	0	0	0	0	0	0	1.000	1.000	1.000
Mt. Williams	19	1	0	1	0	0	0	1	0	0	0	0	0	0	1.000	1.000	1.000
Longmire	2	2	0	1	0	0	0	0	0	0	0	0	0	0	.500	.500	.500
Jordan	29	70	13	27	2	1	3	7	2	12	1	0	0	0	.386	.411	.571
Stocker	21	77	14	29	3	1	0	4	9	13	0	2	2	1	.377	.437	.442
Pratt	18	53	6	18	4	0	3	6	4	12	1	2	1	0	.340	.397	.585
Greene	7	12	3	4	0	0	1	2	0	4	0	0	2	0	.333	.333	.583
Kruk	40	132	24	43	6	2	6	25	24	23	0	5	0	1	.326	.427	.538
Dykstra	46	176	38	55	14	2	3	14	39	16	0	2	0	0	.313	.437	.466
Duncan	34	122	19	36	6	0	4	22	4	23	2	3	1	1	.295	.326	.443
Hollins	41	153	32	45	12	0	4	24	28	35	1	2	0	1	.294	.404	.451
Chamberlain	29	93	11	27	6	0	0	18	5	22	1	0	0	3	.290	.324	.484
Amaro	8	14	0	4	0	1	0	3	3	2	0	0	2	1	.286	.389	.429
Eisenreich	41	88	6	23	3	0	0	13	2	10	0	0	0	1	.261	.275	.295
Daulton	36	119	25	31	10	1	6	28	29	31	0	0	0	1	.261	.403	.513
Morandini	36	131	21	34	5	4	1	14	13	24	1	2	1	0	.260	.331	.382
Incaviglia	34	115	15	29	3	1	7	26	5	30	0	2	0	3	.252	.276	.478
Batiste	26	44	5	11	1	0	1	7	2	5	1	1	0	1	.250	.292	.341
Thompson	38	99	14	23	2	0	3	13	9	19	1	0	0	2	.232	.297	.343
Schilling	12	23	1	4	0	0	0	1	1	5	0	0	3	0	.174	.174	.174
Bell	9	25	1	4	2	0	0	4	0	5	0	0	1	0	.160	.160	.240
Rivera	8	14	1	2	0	0	0	0	2	7	0	0	3	0	.143	.250	.143
Jackson	11	27	1	2	0	0	0	0	0	17	0	0	3	0	.074	.074	.074
Mulholland	9	19	1	1	0	0	0	0	1	6	0	0	4	0	.053	.100	.053
DeLeon	6	1	0	0	0	0	0	0	0	1	0	0	0	0	.000	.000	.000
Green	2	2	0	0	0	0	0	0	0	2	0	0	0	0	.000	.000	.000
Davis	8	0	0	0	0	0	0	0	0	0	0	0	0	0	.000	.000	.000
Ayrault	3	0	0	0	0	0	0	0	0	0	0	0	0	0	.000	.000	.000
Lindsey	1	1	0	0	0	0	0	0	0	1	0	0	0	0	.000	.000	.000
Mauser	2	1	0	0	0	0	0	0	1	1	0	0	0	0	.000	.500	.000

HITTING	G	AB	R	H	2B	3B	HR	RBI	BB	SO	HBP	GDP	SH	SF	Avg.	OBP	SLG
Millette	3	0	1	0	0	0	0	1	1	0	0	0	1	0	.000	1.000	.000
Manto	2	2	0	0	0	0	0	0	0	1	0	0	0	0	.000	.000	.000
Fletcher	1	0	0	0	0	0	0	0	0	0	0	0	0	0	.000	.000	.000
Mk. Williams	4	0	0	0	0	0	0	0	0	0	0	0	0	0	.000	.000	.000
Mason	12	1	0	0	0	0	0	0	0	1	0	0	0	0	.000	.000	.000
Thigpen	3	0	0	0	0	0	0	0	0	0	0	0	0	0	.000	.000	.000
Brink	1	0	0	0	0	0	0	0	0	0	0	0	0	0	.000	.000	.000
Foster	1	0	0	0	0	0	0	0	0	0	0	0	0	0	.000	.000	.000
Pall	1	0	0	0	0	0	0	0	0	0	0	0	0	0	.000	.000	.000
Phillies	162	1619	252	456	80	13	46	235	184	328	9	21	24	16	.282	.355	.432
Opponents	162	1562	220	394	72	11	43	201	167	311	19	31	21	8	.252	.330	.395

Scoring Percentage

Percentage of Phils' runs scored

Lenny Dykstra accounted for 16.3 percent of the total number of runs the Phillies scored this season. That means one run every 10 innings.

Barry Bonds, second in the majors in runs scored, scored a run every 11.2 innings.

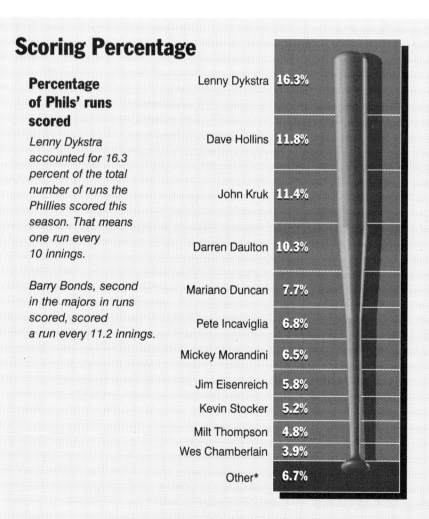

Lenny Dykstra **16.3%**

Dave Hollins **11.8%**

John Kruk **11.4%**

Darren Daulton **10.3%**

Mariano Duncan **7.7%**

Pete Incaviglia **6.8%**

Mickey Morandini **6.5%**

Jim Eisenreich **5.8%**

Kevin Stocker **5.2%**

Milt Thompson **4.8%**

Wes Chamberlain **3.9%**

Other* **6.7%**

* Amaro 0.8%, Batiste 1.6%, Bell 0.6%, Jordan 2.4%, Lindsay 0% Longmire 0.1%, Manto 0%, Milette 0.3%, Pratt 0.9%

Batting with men in scoring position

HITTING	G	AB	R	H	2B	3B	HR	RBI	BB	SO	HBP	GDP	SH	SF	Avg.	OBP	SLG
Mt. Williams . . .	1	1	0	1	0	0	0	1	0	0	0	0	0	0	1.000	1.000	1.000
West	2	2	0	1	1	0	0	2	0	1	0	0	0	0	.500	.500	1.000
Millette	4	3	0	1	0	0	0	2	1	0	0	1	0	0	.333	.500	.333
Amaro	14	12	0	4	0	1	0	4	3	0	0	0	1	1	.333	.438	.500
Longmire	4	3	0	1	0	0	0	1	0	0	0	0	0	0	.333	.333	.333
Pratt	22	22	0	7	3	0	1	8	1	6	1	1	1	1	.318	.360	.591
Duncan	99	152	0	48	9	2	2	60	0	31	1	5	3	2	.316	.316	.441
Batiste	37	45	0	14	2	0	1	21	2	11	0	0	0	1	.311	.333	.422
Incaviglia	92	125	0	38	4	1	7	66	8	35	2	5	0	7	.304	.338	.520
Eisenreich	93	122	0	37	4	1	3	47	14	12	0	1	0	2	.303	.370	.426
Hollins	128	170	0	50	14	1	5	70	37	40	2	7	0	7	.294	.412	.476
Thompson	83	92	0	27	5	0	1	36	23	18	0	1	3	2	.293	.427	.380
Kruk	130	165	0	46	10	2	3	68	50	29	0	8	0	5	.279	.436	.418
Bell	15	18	0	5	2	0	0	7	1	5	0	0	1	0	.278	.316	.389
Chamberlain . .	64	76	0	20	2	1	3	32	9	10	0	3	0	4	.263	.326	.434
Daulton	125	159	0	38	9	2	7	79	56	33	1	1	0	8	.239	.424	.453
Dykstra	136	135	0	31	6	1	3	46	34	17	1	3	0	5	.230	.377	.356
Stocker	63	70	0	16	2	1	1	28	16	13	5	3	1	1	.229	.402	.329
Morandini	93	103	0	23	2	3	1	28	16	17	3	3	3	2	.223	.339	.330
Jordan	51	47	0	10	0	0	2	14	1	9	0	1	0	2	.213	.220	.340
Greene	23	28	0	5	1	0	1	8	3	9	0	1	2	1	.179	.250	.321
Schilling	17	18	0	2	0	0	0	2	0	2	0	1	1	0	.111	.111	.111
Jackson	20	23	0	1	0	0	0	2	1	10	0	0	2	0	.043	.083	.043
Rivera	18	16	0	0	0	0	0	0	2	7	0	0	2	0	.000	.111	.000
Mulholland	13	14	0	0	0	0	0	0	0	5	0	0	1	0	.000	.000	.000
Mk. Williams . . .	4	4	0	0	0	0	0	0	0	1	0	1	1	0	.000	.000	.000
Ayrault	1	1	0	0	0	0	0	0	0	1	0	0	0	0	.000	.000	.000
Manto	3	3	0	0	0	0	0	0	0	1	0	0	0	0	.000	.000	.000
Davis	1	0	0	0	0	0	0	0	0	0	0	0	0	0	.000	.000	.000
Mauser	1	1	0	0	0	0	0	0	0	1	0	0	0	0	.000	.000	.000
Green	1	1	0	0	0	0	0	0	0	1	0	0	0	0	.000	.000	.000
Foster	1	1	0	0	0	0	0	0	0	0	0	0	0	0	.000	.000	.000
Totals	162	1632	0	426	76	16	41	632	278	325	16	46	22	51	.261	.364	.403
Opponents	162	1429	0	367	72	14	36	541	204	300	10	41	23	42	.257	.345	.402

Dykstra vs. Leadoff MVPs

Five leadoff men have won the MVP award. Lenny Dykstra's numbers compare favorably with all of them.

YEAR		AVG.	RUNS	HITS	2B	3B	HR	RBI	BB	SB
1993	Lenny Dykstra	.305	143	194	44	6	19	66	129	37
1990	Rickey Henderson	.325	119	159	33	3	28	61	97	65
1973	Pete Rose	.338	115	230	36	8	5	64	65	10
1965	Zoilo Versalles	.273	126	182	45	12	19	77	41	27
1962	Maury Wills	.299	130	208	13	10	6	48	51	104
1950	Phil Rizzuto	.324	125	200	36	7	7	66	91	12

The Philadelphia Inquirer

Batting against left-handed, right-handed pitchers

RIGHT-HANDED PITCHERS

Name	G	AB	R	H	2B	3B	HR	RBI	BB	SO	HBP	GDP	SH	SF	AVG	OBP	SLG
Mt. Williams	1	1	0	1	0	0	0	1	0	0	0	0	0	0	1.000	1.000	1.000
Lindsey	2	2	0	1	0	0	0	0	0	1	0	0	0	0	.500	.500	.500
West	4	4	0	2	1	0	0	2	0	1	0	0	0	0	.500	.500	.750
Davis	2	2	1	1	0	0	0	0	0	0	0	0	0	0	.500	.500	.500
Millette	4	5	1	2	0	0	0	2	1	2	0	1	3	0	.400	.500	.400
Kruk	130	350	69	115	27	4	9	55	84	48	0	7	0	2	.329	.456	.506
Eisenreich	112	304	44	98	15	3	6	43	20	25	1	4	0	1	.322	.365	.451
Dykstra	142	420	97	133	30	4	17	48	81	35	1	5	0	5	.317	.424	.529
Jordan	54	90	16	27	4	0	3	11	2	19	1	2	0	1	.300	.319	.444
Stocker	65	178	31	52	7	3	2	24	17	34	8	5	2	1	.292	.377	.399
Duncan	104	298	42	86	15	3	5	49	7	59	4	4	2	2	.289	.312	.409
Daulton	127	322	60	91	25	3	16	76	79	66	1	2	0	7	.283	.418	.528
Thompson	114	283	36	79	14	2	4	42	34	48	2	6	2	1	.279	.359	.385
Incaviglia	95	206	32	56	9	1	11	47	12	48	5	6	0	6	.272	.319	.485
Morandini	109	326	45	84	17	7	2	27	25	63	4	5	4	2	.258	.317	.371
Batiste	43	113	7	29	6	0	1	18	2	20	1	3	0	0	.257	.276	.336
Hollins	127	348	61	85	16	1	10	59	72	76	2	10	0	4	.244	.373	.382
Pratt	25	62	3	15	2	0	1	4	3	15	0	1	0	1	.242	.273	.323
Chamberlain	70	150	14	36	11	1	3	20	7	28	0	5	0	2	.240	.270	.387
Longmire	11	13	1	3	0	0	0	1	0	1	0	0	0	0	.231	.231	.231
Bell	18	41	1	8	4	1	0	7	2	8	0	0	1	0	.195	.233	.341
Greene	20	42	4	6	1	0	0	2	4	10	0	1	5	0	.143	.217	.167
Schilling	25	49	3	5	0	0	0	1	0	13	0	0	6	0	.102	.120	.102
Amaro	18	20	4	2	0	0	0	1	2	4	0	1	2	1	.100	.174	.100
Mk. Williams	7	10	1	1	0	0	0	0	0	2	0	1	3	0	.100	.100	.100
Mulholland	22	47	3	4	0	0	0	0	1	21	0	0	6	0	.085	.104	.085
Rivera	26	43	2	3	0	0	0	0	3	21	0	0	7	0	.070	.130	.070
Jackson	23	44	3	2	0	0	0	1	3	28	1	0	7	0	.045	.125	.045
Ayrault	1	1	0	0	0	0	0	0	0	1	0	0	0	0	.000	.000	.000
Mauser	5	4	0	0	0	0	0	0	1	2	0	0	0	0	.000	.200	.000
DeLeon	4	4	0	0	0	0	0	0	0	3	0	1	1	0	.000	.000	.000
Manto	4	10	0	0	0	0	0	0	0	2	1	0	0	0	.000	.091	.000
Green	1	0	0	0	0	0	0	0	0	0	0	0	1	0	.000	.000	.000
Thigpen	1	1	0	0	0	0	0	0	0	0	0	0	0	0	.000	.000	.000
Foster	1	2	0	0	0	0	0	0	0	0	0	0	0	0	.000	.000	.000
Brink	1	1	0	0	0	0	0	0	0	0	0	0	0	0	.000	.000	.000
Phillies	**162**	**3796**	**581**	**1027**	**204**	**33**	**90**	**540**	**463**	**704**	**32**	**70**	**52**	**36**	**.271**	**.352**	**.413**
Opponents	**162**	**3429**	**466**	**877**	**143**	**29**	**84**	**418**	**334**	**706**	**22**	**49**	**33**	**26**	**.256**	**.324**	**.388**

LEFT-HANDED PITCHERS

Name	G	AB	R	H	2B	3B	HR	RBI	BB	SO	HBP	GDP	SH	SF	AVG	OBP	SLG
Andersen	1	1	0	1	0	0	0	0	0	0	0	0	0	0	1.000	1.000	1.000
Amaro	15	28	3	14	2	2	1	5	4	1	0	0	1	0	.500	.563	.821
Pratt	15	25	5	10	4	0	4	9	2	4	1	1	1	0	.400	.464	1.040
Stocker	49	81	15	32	5	0	0	7	13	9	0	3	2	0	.395	.479	.457
Batiste	16	43	7	15	1	1	4	11	1	9	0	0	0	1	.349	.356	.698
Greene	16	30	5	10	1	0	2	8	1	10	0	0	1	1	.333	.344	.567
Mason	2	3	0	1	0	0	0	1	0	0	0	0	0	0	.333	.333	.333
Chamberlain	65	134	20	44	9	1	9	25	10	23	1	2	0	2	.328	.374	.612
Hollins	96	195	43	63	14	3	8	34	13	33	3	5	0	3	.323	.369	.549
Eisenreich	59	58	7	17	2	1	1	11	6	11	0	2	3	1	.293	.354	.414
Kruk	98	185	31	54	6	1	5	30	27	39	0	3	0	3	.292	.377	.416
Dykstra	110	217	46	61	14	2	2	18	48	29	1	3	0	0	.281	.414	.392
Incaviglia	67	162	28	45	7	2	13	42	9	34	1	3	0	1	.278	.318	.586
Jordan	45	69	5	19	0	1	2	7	6	13	0	0	1	0	.275	.329	.391
Duncan	81	198	26	54	11	1	6	24	5	29	0	9	2	0	.273	.291	.429
Rivera	7	8	1	2	0	0	0	0	0	3	0	0	6	0	.250	.250	.250
Schilling	14	26	0	6	1	0	0	2	1	6	0	1	7	0	.231	.259	.269
Daulton	102	188	30	40	10	1	8	29	38	45	1	0	0	1	.213	.346	.404
Morandini	58	99	12	21	2	2	1	6	9	10	1	1	0	0	.212	.284	.303
Bell	13	24	4	5	2	0	0	0	3	4	1	0	1	0	.208	.321	.292
Thompson	58	57	6	10	0	0	0	2	6	9	0	2	1	1	.175	.250	.175
Jackson	13	21	0	3	2	0	0	1	0	9	0	0	5	0	.143	.143	.238
Manto	4	8	0	1	0	0	0	0	0	1	0	0	0	0	.125	.125	.125

Name	G	AB	R	H	2B	3B	HR	RBI	BB	SO	HBP	GDP	SH	SF	AVG.	OBP	SLG
Mulholland	9	15	0	0	0	0	0	0	0	6	0	0	2	0	.000	.000	.000
Mk. Williams	2	2	0	0	0	0	0	0	0	1	0	0	0	0	.000	.000	.000
Ayrault	1	1	0	0	0	0	0	0	0	1	0	0	0	0	.000	.000	.000
DeLeon	1	2	0	0	0	0	0	0	0	2	0	0	0	0	.000	.000	.000
Millette	3	5	2	0	0	0	0	0	0	0	0	0	0	0	.000	.000	.000
West	1	1	0	0	0	0	0	0	0	1	0	0	0	0	.000	.000	.000
Davis	1	1	0	0	0	0	0	0	0	0	0	0	0	0	.000	.000	.000
Green	1	2	0	0	0	0	0	0	0	2	0	0	0	0	.000	.000	.000
Phillies	**162**	**1889**	**296**	**528**	**93**	**18**	**66**	**271**	**202**	**345**	**10**	**35**	**32**	**15**	**.280**	**.350**	**.453**
Opponents	**162**	**2213**	**274**	**542**	**104**	**10**	**45**	**255**	**239**	**411**	**15**	**44**	**32**	**16**	**.245**	**.321**	**.362**

Batting at home, away

HOME

HITTING	G	AB	R	H	2B	3B	HR	RBI	BB	SO	HBP	GDP	SH	SF	Avg.	OBP	SLG
Eisenreich	76	156	26	51	7	2	3	24	10	15	1	2	2	0	.327	.371	.455
Kruk	74	257	50	84	14	4	8	47	54	34	0	4	0	2	.327	.441	.506
Jordan	44	82	11	26	2	1	3	13	5	16	0	2	0	1	.317	.352	.476
Chamberlain	56	168	21	52	13	1	5	30	6	25	1	4	0	1	.310	.335	.488
Stocker	34	126	25	38	4	1	1	10	15	24	5	2	1	1	.302	.395	.373
Batiste	41	80	5	24	5	0	1	15	0	13	0	1	0	0	.300	.300	.400
Dykstra	81	307	71	92	25	3	12	36	69	29	0	4	0	3	.300	.425	.518
Duncan	57	211	32	61	8	3	5	28	5	44	3	6	2	0	.289	.315	.427
Incaviglia	60	205	36	57	7	2	15	47	12	47	3	2	0	2	.278	.324	.551
Hollins	72	262	53	71	13	1	9	39	44	49	4	9	0	5	.271	.378	.431
Morandini	61	225	28	59	10	3	2	19	15	33	2	4	1	2	.262	.311	.360
Daulton	74	262	40	68	16	3	10	55	48	56	1	2	0	1	.260	.375	.458
Pratt	16	43	5	11	3	0	4	8	1	10	1	1	1	0	.256	.289	.605
Bell	17	47	4	12	5	1	0	5	4	9	0	0	1	0	.255	.314	.404
Thompson	64	159	20	40	7	1	2	19	22	25	0	3	0	1	.252	.341	.346
Longmire	6	5	1	1	0	0	0	0	0	0	0	0	0	0	.200	.200	.200
Millette	7	7	1	1	0	0	0	1	1	1	0	1	2	0	.143	.250	.143
Amaro	13	15	2	1	0	0	0	0	1	2	0	0	1	0	.067	.125	.067
Manto	3	4	0	0	0	0	0	0	0	1	0	0	0	0	.000	.000	.000
Phillies	**162**	**2793**	**441**	**771**	**143**	**26**	**80**	**407**	**322**	**499**	**22**	**49**	**33**	**20**	**.276**	**.353**	**.432**
Opponents	**162**	**2920**	**371**	**725**	**140**	**20**	**57**	**335**	**268**	**629**	**20**	**43**	**25**	**16**	**.248**	**.314**	**.368**

AWAY

HITTING	G	AB	R	H	2B	3B	HR	RBI	BB	SO	HBP	GDP	SH	SF	Avg.	OBP	SLG
Lindsey	2	2	0	1	0	0	0	0	0	1	0	0	0	0	.500	.500	.500
Amaro	12	33	5	15	2	2	1	6	5	3	0	1	2	1	.455	.513	.727
Stocker	36	133	21	46	8	2	1	21	15	19	3	6	3	0	.346	.424	.459
Millette	3	3	2	1	0	0	0	1	0	1	0	0	1	0	.333	.333	.333
Pratt	17	44	3	14	3	0	1	5	4	9	0	1	0	1	.318	.367	.455
Eisenreich	77	206	25	64	10	2	4	30	16	21	0	4	1	2	.311	.357	.437
Dykstra	80	330	72	102	19	3	7	30	60	35	2	4	0	2	.309	.416	.448
Kruk	76	278	50	85	19	1	6	38	57	53	0	6	0	3	.306	.420	.446
Duncan	67	285	36	79	18	1	6	45	7	44	1	7	2	2	.277	.295	.411
Hollins	71	281	51	77	17	3	9	54	41	60	1	6	0	2	.274	.366	.452
Thompson	65	181	22	49	7	1	2	25	18	32	2	5	3	1	.271	.342	.354
Incaviglia	56	163	24	44	9	1	9	42	9	35	3	7	0	5	.270	.311	.503
Batiste	38	76	9	20	2	1	4	14	3	16	1	2	0	1	.263	.296	.474
Jordan	46	77	10	20	2	0	2	5	3	16	1	0	0	1	.260	.293	.364
Daulton	73	248	50	63	19	1	14	50	69	55	1	0	0	7	.254	.409	.508
Longmire	5	8	0	2	0	0	0	1	0	1	0	0	0	0	.250	.250	.250
Chamberlain	40	116	13	28	7	1	7	15	11	26	0	3	0	3	.241	.300	.500
Morandini	59	200	29	46	9	6	1	14	19	40	3	2	3	0	.230	.306	.350
Manto	5	14	0	1	0	0	0	0	0	2	1	0	0	0	.071	.133	.071
Bell	7	18	1	1	1	0	0	2	1	3	1	0	1	0	.056	.150	.111
Phillies	**162**	**2892**	**436**	**784**	**154**	**25**	**76**	**404**	**343**	**550**	**20**	**56**	**51**	**31**	**.271**	**.349**	**.420**
Opponents	**162**	**2722**	**369**	**694**	**107**	**19**	**72**	**338**	**305**	**488**	**17**	**50**	**40**	**26**	**.255**	**.331**	**.388**

Batting order statistics

BATTING #1

Name	Avg	AB	R	H	2B	3B	HR	RBI	SB	CS	TBB	HBP	SO	GDP	OBP	SLG
Duncan, M.	1.000	2	0	2	1	0	0	0	0	0	0	0	0	0	1.000	1.500
Dykstra, L.	.305	637	143	194	44	6	19	66	37	12	129	2	64	8	.420	.482
Amaro, R.	.083	12	2	1	0	0	0	1	0	0	2	0	2	0	.200	.083
Eisenreich, J.	.000	1	0	0	0	0	0	0	0	0	0	0	0	0	.000	.000
Thompson, M.	.000	1	0	0	0	0	0	0	0	0	0	0	0	0	.000	.000
Kruk, J.	.000	1	0	0	0	0	0	0	0	0	0	0	0	0	.000	.000
Batiste, K.	.000	1	0	0	0	0	0	0	0	0	0	0	0	0	.000	.000
Team Average	**.301**	**655**	**145**	**197**	**45**	**6**	**19**	**67**	**37**	**12**	**131**	**—**	**66**	**—**	**.416**	**.475**
League Avg.	**.272**	**676**	**103**	**184**	**30**	**7**	**10**	**54**	**36**	**16**	**68**	**—**	**92**	**—**	**.341**	**.382**

BATTING #2

Name	Avg	AB	R	H	2B	3B	HR	RBI	SB	CS	TBB	HBP	SO	GDP	OBP	SLG
Amaro, R.	.643	14	3	9	2	1	1	4	0	0	3	0	1	0	.706	1.143
Stocker, K.	.500	10	1	5	0	1	0	1	0	0	0	0	1	0	.500	.700
Duncan, M.	.279	390	55	109	20	3	8	55	5	4	10	4	68	11	.304	.408
Morandini, M.	.264	265	41	70	17	5	2	23	9	0	19	1	47	3	.316	.389
Thompson, M.	.263	38	7	10	4	1	1	7	0	1	8	0	3	0	.391	.500
Millette, J.	.000	0	1	0	0	0	0	1	0	0	1	0	0	0	1.000	.000
Lindsey, D.	.000	1	0	0	0	0	0	0	0	0	0	0	1	0	.000	.000
Incaviglia, P.	.000	3	0	0	0	0	0	0	0	0	0	0	1	0	.000	.000
Team Average	**.282**	**721**	**108**	**203**	**43**	**11**	**12**	**91**	**14**	**5**	**41**	**—**	**122**	**—**	**.324**	**.422**
League Avg.	**.279**	**660**	**98**	**184**	**30**	**6**	**10**	**64**	**18**	**7**	**59**	**—**	**96**	**—**	**.341**	**.388**

BATTING #3

Name	Avg	AB	R	H	2B	3B	HR	RBI	SB	CS	TBB	HBP	SO	GDP	OBP	SLG
Incaviglia, P.	1.000	1	0	1	1	0	0	0	0	0	0	0	0	0	1.000	2.000
Eisenreich, J.	.750	4	2	3	0	0	0	2	0	0	0	0	0	0	.750	.750
Kruk, J.	.318	529	100	168	33	5	14	84	6	2	109	0	85	10	.431	.478
Jordan, R.	.287	101	14	29	2	1	5	13	0	0	3	1	20	1	.314	.475
Manto, J.	.000	1	0	0	0	0	0	0	0	0	0	0	0	0	.000	.000
Longmire, T.	.000	4	0	0	0	0	0	0	0	0	0	0	1	0	.000	.000
Team Average	**.314**	**640**	**116**	**201**	**36**	**6**	**19**	**99**	**6**	**2**	**112**	**—**	**106**	**—**	**.415**	**.478**
League Avg.	**.291**	**645**	**95**	**188**	**32**	**3**	**19**	**94**	**16**	**6**	**66**	**—**	**91**	**—**	**.357**	**.439**

BATTING #4

Name	Avg	AB	R	H	2B	3B	HR	RBI	SB	CS	TBB	HBP	SO	GDP	OBP	SLG
Jordan, R.	.400	5	1	2	0	0	0	1	0	0	0	0	0	0	.400	.400
Millette, J.	.333	3	2	1	0	0	0	1	0	0	0	0	1	0	.333	.333
Batiste, K.	.333	3	1	1	1	0	0	0	0	0	0	0	0	0	.333	.667
Daulton, D.	.275	51	6	14	4	0	0	7	0	0	9	1	14	0	.393	.353
Hollins, D.	.273	543	104	148	30	4	18	93	2	3	85	5	109	15	.372	.442
Incaviglia, P.	.200	15	2	3	1	0	1	3	0	0	1	0	1	2	.222	.467
Manto, J.	.000	2	0	0	0	0	0	0	0	0	0	0	1	0	.000	.000
Thompson, M.	.000	2	0	0	0	0	0	0	0	0	0	0	2	0	.000	.000
Chamberlain, W.	.000	1	0	0	0	0	0	0	0	0	0	0	1	0	.000	.000
Morandini, M.	.000	3	0	0	0	0	0	0	0	0	0	0	0	0	.000	.000
Team Average	**.268**	**630**	**116**	**169**	**36**	**4**	**19**	**105**	**2**	**3**	**95**	**—**	**131**	**—**	**.365**	**.429**
League Avg.	**.274**	**627**	**99**	**172**	**33**	**3**	**26**	**105**	**9**	**5**	**68**	**—**	**103**	**—**	**.346**	**.461**

BATTING #5

Name	Avg	AB	R	H	2B	3B	HR	RBI	SB	CS	TBB	HBP	SO	GDP	OBP	SLG
Jordan, R.	1.000	1	1	1	1	0	0	0	0	0	0	0	0	0	1.000	2.000
Lindsey, D.	1.000	1	0	1	0	0	0	0	0	0	0	0	0	0	1.000	1.000
Chamberlain, W.	.667	3	0	2	0	0	0	1	0	0	0	0	0	0	.667	.667
Pratt, T.	.375	8	0	3	1	0	0	2	0	0	0	0	2	0	.375	.500
Thompson, M.	.333	6	2	2	0	0	1	1	0	0	2	0	1	0	.500	.500
Duncan, M.	.333	3	1	1	0	0	0	0	0	1	1	0	0	0	.500	.333
Daulton, D.	.254	456	84	116	31	4	24	96	5	0	107	1	95	2	.392	.498
Eisenreich, J.	.233	43	5	10	2	1	1	4	0	0	1	0	4	3	.250	.395
Incaviglia, P.	.227	75	9	17	0	0	2	15	0	0	6	3	21	2	.306	.307
Team Average	**.256**	**597**	**102**	**153**	**36**	**5**	**27**	**119**	**5**	**1**	**117**	**—**	**124**	**—**	**.377**	**.469**
League Avg.	**.270**	**615**	**91**	**166**	**31**	**3**	**23**	**97**	**13**	**6**	**65**	**—**	**108**	**—**	**.340**	**.442**

BATTING #6

Name	Avg	AB	R	H	2B	3B	HR	RBI	SB	CS	TBB	HBP	SO	GDP	OBP	SLG
Eisenreich, J.	.339	248	36	84	12	3	6	43	2	0	22	1	26	2	.392	.484
Incaviglia, P.	.302	182	37	55	10	3	14	52	0	1	7	2	35	5	.330	.621
Chamberlain, W.	.282	124	16	35	10	1	6	26	1	0	6	1	16	3	.313	.524
Pratt, T.	.250	16	0	4	0	0	0	1	0	0	1	0	4	0	.294	.250
Thompson, M.	.209	67	7	14	3	0	1	9	3	0	7	1	13	0	.293	.299
Batiste, K.	.125	8	1	1	0	0	1	2	0	0	1	0	1	1	.222	.500
Duncan, M.	.000	3	0	0	0	0	0	0	0	0	0	0	0	1	.000	.000
Jordan, R.	.000	2	0	0	0	0	0	0	0	0	0	0	0	0	.000	.000
Team Average	**.297**	**650**	**97**	**193**	**35**	**7**	**28**	**133**	**6**	**1**	**44**	**—**	**95**	**—**	**.342**	**.502**
League Avg.	**.272**	**610**	**75**	**166**	**29**	**4**	**20**	**91**	**12**	**5**	**49**	**—**	**109**	**—**	**.329**	**.431**

BATTING #7

Name	Avg	AB	R	H	2B	3B	HR	RBI	SB	CS	TBB	HBP	SO	GDP	OBP	SLG
Daulton, D.	.500	2	0	1	0	0	0	1	0	0	0	0	1	0	.500	.500
Amaro, R.	.429	14	1	6	0	1	0	1	0	0	0	0	1	1	.429	.571
Duncan, M.	.368	19	4	7	2	0	0	3	0	0	0	0	2	0	.368	.474
Batiste, K.	.319	69	5	22	2	1	1	13	0	1	0	0	15	2	.319	.420
Eisenreich, J.	.311	45	6	14	2	0	0	5	3	0	2	0	2	1	.340	.356
Pratt, T.	.294	51	8	15	3	0	5	9	0	0	4	1	12	2	.351	.647
Chamberlain, W.	.290	138	16	40	9	1	6	18	1	1	10	0	28	3	.336	.500
Incaviglia, P.	.288	73	12	21	4	0	7	17	1	0	6	1	17	0	.346	.630
Thompson, M.	.277	195	20	54	4	0	2	24	5	3	20	1	34	6	.346	.328
Morandini, M.	.200	20	3	4	0	0	0	0	1	0	4	1	3	1	.360	.200
Manto, J.	.125	8	0	1	0	0	0	0	0	0	0	0	1	0	.125	.125
Jordan, R.	.000	3	0	0	0	0	0	0	0	0	0	0	2	0	.000	.000
Longmire, T.	.000	1	0	0	0	0	0	0	0	0	0	0	0	0	.000	.000
Team Average	**.290**	**638**	**75**	**185**	**26**	**3**	**21**	**91**	**11**	**5**	**46**	**—**	**118**	**—**	**.340**	**.439**
League Avg.	**.255**	**592**	**60**	**151**	**27**	**3**	**13**	**71**	**8**	**4**	**48**	**—**	**103**	**—**	**.314**	**.377**

BATTING #8

Name	Avg	AB	R	H	2B	3B	HR	RBI	SB	CS	TBB	HBP	SO	GDP	OBP	SLG
Pratt, T.	.400	5	0	2	2	0	0	1	0	0	0	0	0	0	.400	.800
Jordan, R.	.333	3	0	1	0	0	0	0	0	0	0	0	0	1	.333	.333
Stocker, K.	.317	249	45	79	12	2	2	30	5	0	30	8	42	8	.406	.406
Duncan, M.	.292	72	8	21	3	1	3	15	1	0	1	0	16	1	.297	.486
Batiste, K.	.286	63	6	18	4	0	2	10	0	0	2	0	12	0	.303	.444
Morandini, M.	.217	129	10	28	2	4	0	8	3	2	8	3	21	2	.275	.295
Bell, J.	.203	64	4	13	6	1	0	7	0	1	4	1	11	0	.261	.328
Millette, J.	.143	7	0	1	0	0	0	0	0	0	0	0	1	1	.143	.143
Manto, J.	.000	7	0	0	0	0	0	0	0	0	0	1	1	0	.125	.000
Eisenreich, J.	.000	2	0	0	0	0	0	0	0	0	0	0	1	0	.000	.000
Daulton, D.	.000	1	0	0	0	0	0	0	0	0	0	0	1	0	.000	.000
Kruk, J.	.000	0	0	0	0	0	0	0	0	0	0	1	0	0	1.000	.000
Incaviglia, P.	.000	1	0	0	0	0	0	0	0	0	0	0	1	0	.000	.000
Chamberlain, W.	.000	1	0	0	0	0	0	0	0	0	0	0	1	0	.000	.000
Amaro, R.	.000	1	0	0	0	0	0	0	0	0	0	0	0	0	.000	.000
Team Average	**.271**	**606**	**73**	**164**	**29**	**8**	**7**	**72**	**9**	**3**	**46**	**—**	**108**	**—**	**.333**	**.380**
League Avg.	**.256**	**570**	**61**	**146**	**26**	**3**	**10**	**61**	**5**	**2**	**51**	**—**	**94**	**—**	**.319**	**.365**

BATTING #9

Name	Avg	AB	R	H	2B	3B	HR	RBI	SB	CS	TBB	HBP	SO	GDP	OBP	SLG
Longmire, T.	.375	8	1	3	0	0	0	1	0	0	0	0	0	0	.375	.375
Morandini, M.	.375	8	3	3	0	0	1	2	0	0	3	0	2	0	.545	.750
Jordan, R.	.295	44	5	13	1	0	0	4	0	0	5	0	10	0	.353	.318
Thompson, M.	.290	31	6	9	2	1	0	3	1	0	3	0	4	2	.343	.419
Incaviglia, P.	.222	18	0	4	0	0	0	2	0	0	1	0	6	0	.263	.222
Eisenreich, J.	.211	19	2	4	1	0	0	0	0	0	1	0	3	0	.250	.263
Kruk, J.	.200	5	0	1	0	0	0	1	0	0	1	0	2	0	.286	.200
Chamberlain, W.	.176	17	2	3	1	0	0	0	0	0	1	0	5	1	.222	.235
Batiste, K.	.167	12	1	2	0	0	1	4	0	0	0	1	1	0	.231	.417
Pratt, T.	.143	7	0	1	0	0	0	0	0	0	0	0	1	0	.143	.143
Bell, J.	.000	1	1	0	0	0	0	0	0	0	1	0	1	0	.500	.000
Daulton, D.	.000	0	0	0	0	0	0	1	0	0	1	0	0	0	1.000	.000
Duncan, M.	.000	7	0	0	0	0	0	0	0	0	0	0	2	0	.000	.000
Amaro, R.	.000	7	1	0	0	0	0	0	0	0	1	0	1	0	.125	.000
Team Average	**.164**	**548**	**45**	**90**	**11**	**1**	**4**	**34**	**1**	**0**	**33**	**—**	**179**	**—**	**.213**	**.210**
League Avg.	**.181**	**537**	**41**	**97**	**15**	**1**	**4**	**39**	**2**	**1**	**31**	**—**	**155**	**—**	**.226**	**.235**

Fielding statistics

Pos.	Name	G	IP	PO	AS	E	DP	PB	Pct.	Range*
RHP	Schilling	35	243	6	38	0	1	0	1.000	1.630
LHP	Jackson	32	210⅓	7	26	4	3	0	.892	1.412
RHP	Greene	31	200	5	22	1	2	0	.964	1.215
LHP	Mulholland	29	191	5	27	2	2	0	.941	1.508
RHP	Rivera	30	163	8	14	1	1	0	.957	1.215
LHP	West	76	86⅓	2	4	2	1	0	.750	0.625
LHP	Mt. Williams	66	63	2	3	2	0	0	.714	0.714
RHP	Andersen	64	60⅓	3	4	1	1	0	.875	1.044

Errors By Position

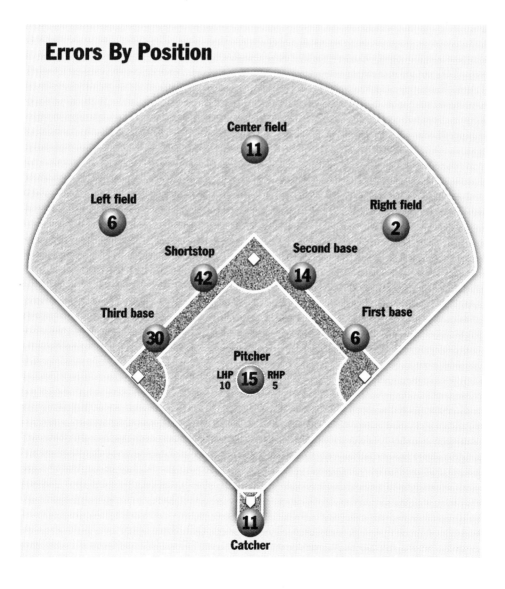

Center field
11

Left field
6

Right field
2

Shortstop
42

Second base
14

Third base
30

First base
6

Pitcher
LHP 10   15   RHP 5

11
Catcher

Pos.	Name	G	IP	PO	AS	E	DP	PB	Pct.	Range*
RHP	Mk. Williams	17	51	2	6	0	1	0	1.000	1.412
RHP	Mason	34	49⅔	0	2	0	0	0	1.000	0.362
RHP	DeLeon	24	47	2	3	0	0	0	1.000	0.957
LHP	Davis	25	31⅓	0	3	0	0	0	1.000	0.862
RHP	Thigpen	17	19⅓	0	3	0	1	0	1.000	1.397
RHP	Pall	8	17⅔	1	2	0	0	0	1.000	1.528
RHP	Mauser	8	16⅓	4	3	0	1	0	1.000	3.857
RHP	Ayrault	10	10⅓	0	1	0	0	0	1.000	0.871
RHP	Green	3	7⅓	0	0	1	0	0	0.000	0.000
RHP	Foster	2	6⅔	1	0	0	0	0	1.000	1.350
RHP	Brink	2	6	0	0	1	0	0	0.000	0.000
RHP	Fletcher	1	0⅓	0	0	0	0	0	0.000	0.000
C	Daulton	147	1287	986	67	9	18	13	.992	7.364
C	Pratt	26	191⅔	169	7	2	3	0	.989	8.264
C	Lindsey	2	3	3	0	0	0	0	1.000	9.000
1B	Kruk	144	1243⅓	1149	69	8	79	0	.993	8.817
1B	Jordan	34	234⅓	212	4	2	23	0	.991	8.296
1B	Eisenreich	1	4	5	0	0	0	0	1.000	11.250
2B	Morandini	111	928	208	287	5	48	0	.990	4.801
2B	Duncan	65	544⅔	109	168	9	29	0	.969	4.577
3B	Hollins	143	1214⅔	73	215	27	8	0	.914	2.134
3B	Batiste	58	210⅔	24	41	3	2	0	.956	2.777
3B	Manto	6	37	2	7	0	0	0	1.000	2.189
3B	Millette	3	10⅓	0	4	0	0	0	1.000	3.484
SS	Stocker	70	639⅔	118	201	14	45	0	.958	4.488
SS	Duncan	59	447⅔	71	136	12	21	0	.945	4.162
SS	Batiste	24	180	48	66	7	13	0	.942	5.700
SS	Bell	22	173⅓	33	57	9	11	0	.909	4.673
SS	Millette	7	31	3	14	0	1	0	1.000	4.935
SS	Manto	1	1	0	1	0	0	0	1.000	9.000
LF	Thompson	102	754	162	6	1	1	0	.994	2.005
LF	Incaviglia	89	690⅔	152	3	5	0	0	.969	2.020
LF	Amaro	3	16	4	0	0	0	0	1.000	2.250
LF	Longmire	2	11	4	0	0	0	0	1.000	3.273
LF	Eisenreich	1	1	0	0	0	0	0	0.000	0.000
CF	Dykstra	160	1422⅓	469	2	10	0	0	.979	2.980
CF	Amaro	8	34⅓	8	1	1	1	0	.900	2.359
CF	Thompson	4	10	0	0	0	0	0	0.000	0.000
CF	Eisenreich	3	6	2	0	0	0	0	1.000	3.000
RF	Eisenreich	133	809	216	6	1	0	0	.996	2.470
RF	Chamberlain	76	559⅔	131	10	1	4	0	.993	2.267
RF	Incaviglia	9	67	14	1	0	1	0	1.000	2.015
RF	Amaro	6	44	13	0	0	0	0	1.000	2.659

* Putouts and assists, multiplied by 9 and divided by innings played.

Stealing

	ATT	SB	CS	PPO	CPO	PCT.
Batiste	1	0	1	0	0	0.000
Bell	1	0	1	0	0	0.000
Chamberlain	3	2	1	0	0	.667
Daulton	5	5	0	0	0	1.000
Duncan	11	6	5	0	0	.545
Dykstra	49	37	12	0	0	.755
Eisenreich	5	5	0	0	0	1.000
Hollins	5	2	3	0	0	.400
Incaviglia	2	1	1	0	0	.500
Jordan	0	0	0	0	0	—
Kruk	8	6	2	0	0	.750
Morandini	15	13	2	0	0	.867
Stocker	5	5	0	1	0	1.000
Thompson	13	9	4	0	0	.692
Totals	**123**	**91**	**32**	**1**	**0**	**.740**

AGAINST CATCHERS

	ATT	SB	CS	PPO	CPO	PCT.
Daulton	134	89	45	4	0	.664
Pratt	16	12	4	0	0	.750
Totals	**150**	**101**	**49**	**4**	**0**	**.673**

AGAINST PITCHERS

	ATT	SB	CS	PPO	CPO	PCT.
Andersen	5	4	1	0	0	.800
Ayrault	4	4	0	0	0	1.000
Davis	1	1	0	0	0	1.000
DeLeon	13	5	8	0	0	.385
Foster	2	2	0	0	0	1.000
Green	1	0	1	0	0	0.000
Greene	23	18	5	1	0	.783
Jackson	22	15	7	0	0	.682
Mason	3	2	1	0	0	.667
Mauser	1	1	0	0	0	1.000
Mulholland	6	1	5	2	0	.167
Rivera	18	15	3	0	0	.833
Schilling	22	11	11	0	0	.500
Thigpen	3	2	1	0	0	.667
West	8	5	3	0	0	.625
Williams, Mk.	9	6	3	1	0	.667
Williams, Mt.	9	9	0	0	0	1.000
Totals	**150**	**101**	**49**	**4**	**0**	**.673**

Overall pitching

Name	G	GS	CG	SHO	INN	H	R	ER	BB	SO	HR	W	L	S	ERA
Fletcher	1	0	0	0	0.1	0	0	0	0	0	0	0	0	0	0.00
Pall	8	0	0	0	17.2	15	7	5	3	11	1	1	0	0	2.55
Andersen	64	0	0	0	61.2	54	22	20	21	67	4	3	2	0	2.92
West	76	0	0	0	86.1	60	37	28	51	87	6	6	4	3	2.92
Brink	2	0	0	0	6.0	3	2	2	3	8	1	0	0	0	3.00
Mulholland	29	28	7	2	191.0	177	80	69	40	116	20	12	9	0	3.25
DeLeon	24	3	0	0	47.0	39	25	17	27	34	5	3	0	0	3.26
Williams, Mitch	65	0	0	0	62.0	56	30	23	44	60	3	3	7	43	3.34
Greene	31	30	7	2	200.0	175	84	76	62	167	12	16	4	0	3.42
Jackson	32	32	2	1	210.1	214	105	88	80	120	12	12	11	0	3.77
Schilling	34	34	7	2	235.1	234	114	105	57	186	23	16	7	0	4.02
Mason	34	0	0	0	49.2	47	28	27	16	32	9	5	5	0	4.89
Mauser	8	0	0	0	16.1	15	9	9	7	14	1	0	0	0	4.96
Rivera	30	28	1	1	163.0	175	99	91	85	123	16	13	9	0	5.02
Davis	25	0	0	0	31.1	35	22	18	24	28	4	1	2	0	5.17
Williams, Mike	17	4	0	0	51.0	50	32	30	22	33	5	1	3	0	5.29
Thigpen	17	0	0	0	19.1	23	13	13	9	10	2	3	1	0	6.05
Green	3	2	0	0	7.1	16	9	6	5	7	1	0	0	0	7.36
Ayrault	10	0	0	0	10.1	18	11	11	10	8	1	2	0	0	9.58
Foster	2	1	0	0	6.2	13	11	11	7	6	3	0	1	0	14.85
Totals	**162**	**162**	**24**	**8**	**1472.2**	**1419**	**740**	**649**	**573**	**1117**	**129**	**97**	**65**	**46**	**3.97**

Pitching against right-handed, left-handed batters

RIGHT-HANDED

Name	G	AB	R	H	2B	3B	HR	RBI	BB	SO	HBP	GDP	SH	SF	AVG.	OBP	SLG
Fletcher	1	1	0	0	0	0	0	0	0	0	0	0	0	0	.000	.000	.000
Brink	2	6	0	1	0	0	1	1	1	3	0	0	0	0	.167	.286	.667
DeLeon	23	85	0	16	1	0	2	9	13	18	3	0	3	1	.188	.314	.271
West	75	226	0	44	9	0	4	33	28	62	2	2	8	2	.195	.287	.288
Andersen	62	146	0	29	4	2	2	12	17	44	0	1	2	0	.199	.282	.295
Foster	2	9	0	2	1	0	0	0	1	2	0	0	0	0	.222	.300	.333
Mason	34	112	0	25	4	1	6	21	9	23	0	1	0	2	.223	.276	.438
Greene	31	394	0	91	20	3	7	36	20	93	2	4	7	5	.231	.268	.350
Pall	8	29	0	7	1	0	1	4	2	5	0	1	0	0	.241	.290	.379
Rivera	30	325	0	80	6	4	9	38	42	71	5	6	5	3	.246	.339	.372
Mulholland	29	601	0	148	31	1	17	57	30	101	3	10	4	4	.246	.284	.386
Williams, Mt.	65	190	0	47	9	0	3	25	39	48	1	6	1	1	.247	.377	.342
Jackson	32	672	0	172	34	6	8	68	64	97	1	14	11	8	.256	.318	.360
Schilling	34	415	0	107	17	2	10	41	20	81	3	8	6	3	.258	.295	.381
Williams, Mk.	17	104	0	28	7	1	1	16	8	21	0	1	1	0	.269	.321	.385
Thigpen	17	40	0	11	1	0	1	5	3	6	0	1	2	0	.275	.326	.375
Davis	25	97	0	27	4	1	4	19	16	21	1	1	1	0	.278	.386	.464
Mauser	8	31	0	11	4	0	1	7	7	8	1	0	0	0	.355	.487	.581
Ayrault	10	31	0	13	0	2	1	11	4	6	1	1	0	0	.419	.500	.645
Green	3	23	0	10	2	0	0	2	3	3	0	2	0	0	.435	.500	.522
Totals	**162**	**3537**	**0**	**869**	**155**	**23**	**78**	**405**	**327**	**713**	**23**	**59**	**51**	**29**	**.246**	**.311**	**.369**

LEFT-HANDED

Name	G	AB	R	H	2B	3B	HR	RBI	BB	SO	HBP	GDP	SH	SF	AVG.	OBP	SLG
Fletcher	1	0	0	0	0	0	0	0	0	0	0	0	0	0	.000	.000	.000
Mauser	8	32	0	4	0	0	0	1	0	6	0	0	0	0	.125	.125	.125
Brink	2	15	0	2	1	0	0	1	2	5	0	0	0	0	.133	.235	.200
West	76	83	0	16	2	1	2	12	23	25	3	5	0	0	.193	.385	.313
Mulholland	29	133	0	29	7	1	3	16	10	15	0	2	1	0	.218	.273	.353
Pall	8	36	0	8	2	0	0	4	1	6	0	1	1	0	.222	.243	.278
Williams, Mt.	65	39	0	9	0	0	0	4	5	12	1	1	3	1	.231	.326	.231
Williams, Mk.	17	94	0	22	5	1	4	13	14	12	0	1	0	0	.234	.333	.436
Greene	31	357	0	84	16	1	5	34	42	74	1	3	2	4	.235	.314	.328
Davis	25	31	0	8	3	0	0	2	8	7	0	2	0	0	.258	.410	.355
Schilling	34	490	0	127	23	4	13	59	37	105	1	5	3	4	.259	.310	.402
DeLeon	24	84	0	23	6	1	3	10	14	16	2	1	0	1	.274	.386	.476
Mason	34	79	0	22	2	0	3	10	7	9	0	0	1	0	.278	.337	.418
Andersen	64	86	0	25	1	1	2	14	4	23	1	4	0	0	.291	.330	.395
Ayrault	10	17	0	5	0	0	0	2	6	2	0	0	0	0	.294	.478	.294
Jackson	32	141	0	42	5	0	4	19	16	23	3	1	3	0	.298	.381	.418
Rivera	30	316	0	95	13	6	7	45	43	52	1	7	0	2	.301	.384	.446
Thigpen	17	35	0	12	4	0	1	8	6	4	1	1	0	1	.343	.442	.543
Foster	2	24	0	11	2	0	3	10	6	4	0	0	0	0	.458	.567	.917
Green	3	13	0	6	0	0	1	4	2	4	0	0	0	0	.462	.533	.692
Totals	**162**	**2105**	**0**	**550**	**92**	**16**	**51**	**268**	**246**	**404**	**14**	**34**	**14**	**13**	**.261**	**.341**	**.393**

Pitching at home, away

AT HOME

Name	G	GS	CG	SHO	IP	H	R	ER	BB	SO	HR	W	L	S	ERA
Fletcher	1	0	0	0	0.1	0	0	0	0	0	0	0	0	0	0.00
Pall	4	0	0	0	9.0	6	2	1	1	7	0	1	0	0	1.00
Andersen	32	0	0	0	31.2	28	6	4	12	33	0	1	0	0	1.14
West	36	0	0	0	43.0	31	18	14	27	52	3	3	1	2	2.93
Greene	17	16	3	0	114.1	87	40	38	37	99	6	10	0	0	2.99
DeLeon	14	1	0	0	28.1	26	17	10	15	20	2	1	0	0	3.18
Davis	11	0	0	0	13.2	12	5	5	10	13	0	1	1	0	3.29
Mulholland	14	14	3	1	92.0	88	44	37	19	73	10	6	4	0	3.62
Jackson	16	16	1	0	109.2	119	56	47	32	67	7	8	5	0	3.86
Schilling	16	16	6	2	113.0	111	52	49	28	100	8	9	4	0	3.90
Williams, Mt.	2	0	0	0	28.0	26	17	13	16	27	1	1	3	19	4.18
Brink	1	0	0	0	2.0	2	1	1	0	3	0	0	0	0	4.50
Williams, Mk.	11	2	0	0	32.0	33	16	16	9	22	3	1	2	0	4.50
Ayrault	5	0	0	0	5.1	4	3	3	5	5	0	1	0	0	5.06
Mason	18	0	0	0	30.2	34	19	18	7	20	5	4	2	0	5.28
Mauser	2	0	0	0	5.0	4	3	3	2	4	1	0	0	0	5.40
Mason	18	0	0	0	30.2	34	19	18	7	20	5	4	2	0	5.28
Green	2	1	0	0	5.2	11	5	5	4	4	1	0	0	0	7.94
Thigpen	8	0	0	0	8.2	9	8	8	3	6	2	1	1	0	8.31
Foster	1	0	0	0	2.2	4	3	3	3	3	0	0	0	0	10.13
Totals	**81**	**81**	**13**	**3**	**755.0**	**725**	**371**	**326**	**268**	**629**	**57**	**52**	**29**	**21**	**3.89**

AWAY

Name	G	GS	CG	SHO	IP	H	R	ER	BB	SO	HR	W	L	S	ERA
Brink	1	0	0	0	4.0	1	1	1	3	5	1	0	0	0	2.25
Williams, Mt.	33	0	0	0	34.0	30	13	10	28	33	2	2	4	24	2.65
West	40	0	0	0	43.1	29	19	14	24	35	3	3	3	1	2.91
Mulholland	15	14	4	1	99.0	89	36	32	21	43	10	6	5	0	2.91
DeLeon	10	2	0	0	18.2	13	8	7	12	14	3	2	0	0	3.38
Jackson	16	16	1	1	100.2	95	49	41	48	53	5	4	6	0	3.67
Greene	14	14	4	2	85.2	88	44	38	25	68	6	6	4	0	3.99
Schilling	18	18	1	0	122.1	123	62	56	29	86	15	7	3	0	4.12
Pall	4	0	0	0	8.2	9	5	4	2	4	1	0	0	0	4.15
Thigpen	9	0	0	0	10.2	14	5	5	6	4	0	2	0	0	4.22
Mason	16	0	0	0	19.0	13	9	9	9	12	4	1	3	0	4.26
Rivera	14	13	1	1	83.0	85	43	40	47	52	8	9	3	0	4.34
Mauser	6	0	0	0	11.1	11	6	6	5	10	0	0	0	0	4.76
Andersen	32	0	0	0	30.0	26	16	16	9	34	4	2	2	0	4.80
Green	1	1	0	0	1.2	5	4	1	1	3	0	0	0	0	5.40
Davis	14	0	0	0	17.2	23	17	13	14	15	4	0	1	0	6.62
Williams, Mk.	6	2	0	0	19.0	17	16	14	13	11	2	0	1	0	6.63
Ayrault	5	0	0	0	5.0	14	8	8	5	3	1	1	0	0	14.40
Foster	1	1	0	0	4.0	9	8	8	4	3	3	0	1	0	18.00
Totals	**81**	**81**	**11**	**5**	**717.2**	**694**	**369**	**323**	**305**	**488**	**72**	**45**	**36**	**25**	**4.05**

Win-loss record

	Win-loss	Pct.
OVERALL	**97-65.**	**.599**
Home.	52-29.	.642
Away.	45-36.	.556
Day	26-20.	.565
Night	71-45.	.612
BY MONTH		
April.	17- 5.	.773
May	17-10.	.630
June.	18-10.	.643
July	14-14.	.500
August.	16-11.	.593
September	14-13.	.519
October.	1- 2.	.333
BY OPPONENT		
Atlanta	6- 6.	.500
Chicago	6- 7.	.462
Cincinnati	8- 4.	.667
Houston.	7- 5.	.583
Los Angeles	10- 2.	.833
Montreal	7- 6.	.538
New York	10- 3.	.769
Pittsburgh	7- 6.	.538
St. Louis	8- 5.	.615
San Diego	6- 6.	.500
San Francisco.	4- 8.	.333
Colorado.	9- 3.	.750
Florida.	9- 4.	.692
RECORD AGAINST PITCHERS		
LH Pitchers	36-19.	.655
RH Pitchers.	61-46.	.570
LH Starters	21-11.	.656
RH Starters	44-31.	.587
Shutouts	11- 2.	.846
1-run games	23-20.	.535
Extra innings.	11- 7.	.611

Starting pitchers' records

	Apr	May	Jun	Jul	Aug	Sep/Oct
Mulholland.	2-3	4-1	3-1	1-3	1-1	1-0
Schilling	4-1	2-0	2-2	1-3	2-0	5-1
Greene.	2-0	5-0	2-2	3-1	0-0	4-1
Jackson	2-0	2-2	3-2	2-4	2-1	3-1
Rivera.	1-1	2-1	5-1	1-3	3-1	1-2

Relief Pitching

				Inherited-runners		
Name	Sv	Opp.	Pct.	Scored	Tot.	Pct.	Holds
Andersen ..	0	4	0	14	48	29	25
Ayrault	0	1	0	3	9	33	0
Brink	0	0	0	0	0	0	0
Davis	0	1	0	3	9	33	3
DeLeon	0	1	0	2	10	20	3
Fletcher	0	0	0	0	1	0	0
Foster	0	0	0	0	0	0	0
Green	0	0	0	0	0	0	0
Greene	0	0	0	0	1	0	0
Mason	0	3	0	6	21	29	5
Mauser	0	0	0	2	9	22	0
Mulholland .	0	0	0	0	0	0	0
Pall	0	0	0	2	8	25	1
Rivera	0	0	0	0	0	0	0
Thigpen	0	2	0	3	4	75	0
West	3	9	33	18	52	35	21
Mk. Williams	0	0	0	5	11	45	0
Mt. Williams	43	49	88	5	9	56	1
Totals	**46**	**70**	**66**	**63**	**192**	**33**	**59**

THE POSTSEASON

League playoffs, Game 1

Atlanta	001	100	001	0—3	9 0
PHILLIES	100	101	000	1—4	9 1

Atlanta	AB	R	H	BI	BB	SO	Avg.
Nixon cf	4	0	2	2	1	1	.500
Blauser ss	4	0	0	0	1	3	.000
Gant lf	4	1	1	0	1	3	.250
McMichael p	0	0	0	0	0	0	.000
McGriff 1b	5	0	1	0	0	2	.200
Justice rf	4	0	0	1	0	1	.000
Pendleton 3b	5	0	1	0	0	0	.200
Berryhill c	3	0	0	0	0	1	.000
b-Pecota ph	0	1	0	0	1	0	.000
Olson c	1	0	1	0	0	0	1.000
Lemke 2b	4	0	1	0	0	0	.250
2-Tarasco pr-lf	1	0	0	0	0	1	.000
Avery p	2	1	2	0	0	1	1.000
a-DSanders ph	1	0	0	0	0	0	.000
Mercker p	0	0	0	0	0	0	.000
c-Belliard ph-2b	0	0	0	0	0	0	.000
Totals	**38**	**3**	**9**	**3**	**4**	**12**	

PHILLIES	AB	R	H	BI	BB	SO	Avg.
Dykstra cf	4	1	1	0	1	1	.250
Duncan 2b	5	0	1	0	0	2	.200
Kruk 1b	4	2	1	1	1	0	.250
DHollins 3b	4	0	1	0	0	0	.250
Batiste 3b	1	0	1	1	0	0	1.000
Daulton c	3	0	0	0	1	1	.000
Incaviglia lf	4	1	2	1	0	1	.500
1-Thompson pr-lf	0	0	0	0	0	0	.000
Chamberlain rf	3	0	2	0	1	1	.667
MtWilliams p	0	0	0	0	0	0	.000
Stocker ss	3	0	0	0	1	0	.000
Schilling p	3	0	0	0	0	1	.000
Eisenreich rf	1	0	0	0	0	0	.000
Totals	**35**	**4**	**9**	**3**	**5**	**7**	

One out when winning run scored.
a-popped out for Avery in the 7th. b-walked for Berryhill in the 9th. c-sacrificed for Mercker in the 9th. 1-ran for Incaviglia in the 8th. 2-ran for Lemke in the 9th.
E—Batiste (1). LOB—Atlanta 11, PHILLIES 8. 2B—Nixon (1), Olson (1), Avery (1), Dykstra (1), Kruk (1), DHollins (1), Chamberlain 2 (2). HR—Incaviglia (1) off Avery. RBIs—Nixon 2 (2), Justice (1), Kruk (1), Batiste (1), Incaviglia (1). S—Belliard. SF—Justice. GIDP—DHollins.
Runners left in scoring position—Atlanta 6 (Blauser 2, Gant 2, Tarasco 2); PHILLIES 3 (Stocker 2, Schilling). Runners moved up—Nixon, Kruk.
DP—Atlanta 1 (Pendleton, Lemke and McGriff).

Atlanta	IP	H	R	ER	BB	SO	NP	ERA
Avery	6	5	3	3	4	5	98	4.50
Mercker	2	2	0	0	1	2	42	0.00
McMichael L, 0-1	1⅓	2	1	1	0	0	22	6.75

PHILLIES	IP	H	R	ER	BB	SO	NP	ERA
Schilling	8	7	2	2	2	10	136	2.25
MtWilliams W, 1-0	2	2	1	0	2	2	43	0.00

IBB—off Avery (Daulton) 1, off Avery (Chamberlain) 1, off Avery (Stocker) 1. WP—Avery.
Umpires—Home, Froemming; First, Pulli; Second, Tata; Third, Quick; Left, Crawford; Right, West.
T—3:33. A—62,012.

How they scored

PHILLIES FIRST (1): Dykstra led off with a double. Duncan singled, Dykstra moved to third. Kruk forced Duncan at second, Dykstra scored.
BRAVES THIRD (1): Avery doubled with two outs. Nixon doubled, Avery scored.
BRAVES FOURTH (1): Gant led off with a walk. McGriff singled, Gant moved to third. Justice flied out, Gant scored.
PHILLIES FOURTH (1): Incaviglia homered with two outs.
PHILLIES SIXTH (1): Kruk walked with one out. Hollins doubled, Kruk moved to third. Daulton walked to load the bases. Kruk scored on a wild pitch.
BRAVES NINTH (1): Pecota batted for Berryhill and led off with a walk. Lemke reached first on an error by Batiste, Pecota moved to third. Tarasco rant for Lemke. Belliard batted for Mercker and sacrificed Tarasco to second. Nixon grounded out, Pecota scored.
PHILLIES TENTH (1): Kruk doubled with one out. Batiste singled, Kruk scored.

League playoffs, Game 2

Atlanta	206	010	041—14	16	0
PHILLIES	000	200	001— 3	7	2

Atlanta	AB	R	H	BI	BB	SO	Avg.
Nixon cf	4	2	3	2	2	0	.625
Wohlers p	0	0	0	0	0	0	.000
Blauser ss	5	1	2	1	0	1	.222
1-Belliard pr-ss	1	1	0	0	0	1	.000
Gant lf	5	1	2	3	0	1	.333
McGriff 1b	5	2	3	2	0	1	.400
Stanton p	0	0	0	0	0	0	.000
Tarasco rf	0	0	0	0	0	0	.000
Justice rf	3	1	0	0	2	0	.000
DSanders cf	0	0	0	0	0	0	.000
Pendleton 3b	5	2	3	3	0	1	.400
Berryhill c	5	1	1	3	0	2	.125
Lemke 2b	5	1	0	0	0	1	.111
GMaddux p	4	1	1	0	0	1	.250
Bream 1b	1	1	1	0	0	0	1.000
Totals	**43**	**14**	**16**	**14**	**4**	**9**	

PHILLIES	AB	R	H	BI	BB	SO	Avg.
Dykstra cf	4	1	1	1	1	2	.250
Morandini 2b	5	0	1	0	0	2	.200
Kruk 1b	3	1	2	0	1	0	.429
DHollins 3b	3	1	1	2	1	0	.286
Daulton c	4	0	1	0	0	1	.143
Andersen p	0	0	0	0	0	0	.000
Eisenreich rf	4	0	0	0	0	1	.000
MThompson lf	4	0	0	0	0	0	.000
Stocker ss	4	0	1	0	0	2	.143
TGreene p	0	0	0	0	0	0	.000
Thigpen p	0	0	0	0	0	0	.000
a-Longmire ph	1	0	0	0	0	1	.000
Rivera p	0	0	0	0	0	0	.000
b-Chamberlain ph	1	0	0	0	0	1	.500
Mason p	0	0	0	0	0	0	.000
c-RJordan ph	1	0	0	0	1	0	.000
West p	0	0	0	0	0	0	.000
Pratt c	1	0	0	0	0	1	.000
Totals	**34**	**3**	**7**	**3**	**4**	**11**	

a-struck out for Thigpen in the 4th. b-struck out for Rivera in the 5th. c-walked for Mason in the 7th. 1-ran for Blauser in the 8th. E—Morandini (1), Stocker (1). LOB—Atlanta 6, PHILLIES 8. 2B—Nixon (2), Gant 2 (2). HR—Dykstra (1) off Wohlers, DHollins (1) off GMaddux, Blauser (1) off TGreene, McGriff (1) off TGreene, Pendleton (1) off Rivera, Berryhill (1) off Thigpen. RBIs—Nixon 2 (4), Blauser (1), Gant 3 (3), McGriff 2 (2), Pendleton 3 (3), Berryhill 3 (3), Dykstra (1), DHollins 2 (2). SB—Morandini (1). CS—Nixon (1).
Runners left in scoring position—Atlanta 4 (Belliard, Pendleton 2, GMaddux); PHILLIES 3 (Morandini, Daulton, MThompson).
Runners moved up—Gant, Justice, Berryhill.

Atlanta	IP	H	R	ER	BB	SO	NP	ERA
GMaddux W, 1-0	7	5	2	2	3	8	97	2.57
Stanton	1	1	0	0	1	0	22	0.00
Wohlers	1	1	1	1	0	3	20	9.00

PHILLIES	IP	H	R	ER	BB	SO	NP	ERA
TGreene L, 0-1	2⅓	7	7	7	2	2	64	27.00
Thigpen	⅔	1	1	1	0	1	13	13.50
Rivera	2	1	1	1	1	2	36	4.50
Mason	2	1	0	0	1	0	26	0.00
West	1	4	4	3	1	2	42	27.00
Andersen	1	2	1	1	0	1	17	9.00

Inherited runners-scored—Thigpen 2-2. PB—Daulton.
Umpires—Home, Pulli; First, Tata; Second, Quick; Third, Crawford; Left, West; Right, Froemming.
T—3:14. A—62,436.

How they scored

BRAVES FIRST (2): Nixon led off with a walk. Blauser struck out. Nixon moved to second on a passed ball. Gant grounded out, Nixon moved to third. McGriff homered, Nixon scored in front of him.
BRAVES THIRD (6): Blauser homered with one out. Gant doubled. McGriff singled, Gant moved to third. Justice walked, McGriff moved to second. Pendleton singled, Gant and McGriff scored, Justice moved to third. Thigpen came in to pitch. Berryhill homered, Justice and Pendleton scored in front of him.
PHILLIES FOURTH (2): Kruk led off with a single. Hollins homered, Kruk scored in front of him.
BRAVES FIFTH (1): Pendleton homered with one out.
BRAVES EIGHTH (4): Lemke reached first on an error by Stocker with one out. Maddux singled, Lemke moved to second. Nixon singled, Lemke scored, Maddux moved to second. Blauser singled, Maddux moved to third, Nixon moved to second. Belliard ran for Blauser. Gant doubled, Maddux, Nixon and Belliard scored.
BRAVES NINTH (1): Bream singled with two outs. Nixon doubled, Bream scored.
PHILLIES NINTH (1): Dykstra homered with two outs.

League playoffs, Game 3

PHILLIES	000	101	011—4	10	1
Atlanta	000	005	40x—9	12	0

PHILLIES	AB	R	H	BI	BB	SO	Avg.
Dykstra cf	5	0	1	0	0	2	.231
Duncan 2b	5	2	2	0	0	1	.300
Kruk 1b	4	1	2	3	0	0	.455
DHollins 3b	3	0	0	0	1	0	.200
Daulton c	4	0	0	0	0	0	.091
Incaviglia lf	4	0	0	0	0	1	.250
Chamberlain rf	4	1	1	0	0	0	.375
Stocker ss	4	0	3	0	0	0	.364
Mulholland p	2	0	0	0	0	1	.000
Mason p	0	0	0	0	0	0	.000
a-MThompson ph	1	0	0	0	0	1	.000
Andersen p	0	0	0	0	0	0	.000
West p	0	0	0	0	0	0	.000
Thigpen p	0	0	0	0	0	0	.000
c-Eisenreich ph	1	0	1	1	0	0	.167
Totals	37	4	10	4	1	6	

Atlanta	AB	R	H	BI	BB	SO	Avg.
Nixon cf	5	0	1	0	0	2	.462
Blauser ss	4	2	2	0	1	0	.308
Gant lf	4	1	1	0	1	1	.308
McGriff 1b	4	2	2	1	1	1	.429
Pendleton 3b	4	2	2	2	0	1	.429
Justice rf	4	1	1	2	0	1	.091
Berryhill c	3	1	1	0	1	0	.182
Lemke 2b	4	0	2	3	0	1	.231
Glavine p	3	0	0	0	0	0	.000
b-Cabrera ph	1	0	0	0	0	1	.000
Mercker p	0	0	0	0	0	0	.000
McMichael p	0	0	0	0	0	0	.000
Totals	36	9	12	8	4	7	

a-struck out for Mason in the 7th. b-struck out for Glavine in the 7th. c-doubled for Thigpen in the 9th. E—Duncan (1). LOB—PHILLIES 7, Atlanta 7. 2B—Chamberlain (3), Stocker (1), Eisenreich (1), Blauser (1), Gant (3), McGriff (1), Justice (1), Lemke (1). 3B—Duncan (2), Kruk (1). HR—Kruk (1) off Glavine. RBIs—Kruk 3 (4), Eisenreich (1), McGriff (3), Pendleton 2 (5), Justice 2 (3), Lemke 3 (3). SB—DHollins (1). CS—Nixon (2).
Runners left in scoring position—PHILLIES 6 (Dykstra, Duncan 3, Daulton, Incaviglia); Atlanta 5 (Nixon, McGriff, Berryhill, Glavine, Cabrera).
Runners moved up—Kruk, Mulholland, Pendleton, Berryhill, Glavine.

PHILLIES	IP	H	R	ER	BB	SO	NP	ERA
Mulholland L, 0-1	5	9	5	4	1	2	70	7.20
Mason	1	0	0	0	0	1	17	0.00
Andersen	⅓	0	0	0	1	0	10	27.00
West	⅔	1	1	1	1	2	19	21.60
Thigpen	1	0	0	0	1	2	14	5.40

Atlanta	IP	H	R	ER	BB	SO	NP	ERA
Glavine W, 1-0	7	6	2	2	0	5	91	2.57
Mercker	1	1	1	1	1	0	15	3.00
McMichael	1	3	1	1	0	1	19	7.71

Mulholland pitched to 5 batters in the 6th.
Inherited runners-scored—Mason 1-1, West 2-2. IBB—off Andersen (McGriff) 1.
Umpires—Home, Tata; First, Quick; Second, Crawford; Third, West; Left, Froemming; Right, Pulli.
T—2:44. A—52,032.

How they scored

PHILLIES FOURTH (1): Duncan led off with a triple. Kruk tripled, Duncan scored.
PHILLIES SIXTH (1): Kruk led off with a home run.
BRAVES SIXTH (5): Blauser led off with a single. Gant walked, Blauser moved to second. McGriff singled, Blauser scored, Gant moved to third. Pendleton singled, Gant scored, McGriff moved to third. Justice doubled, McGriff and Pendleton scored. Mason came in to pitch. Berryhill flied out, Justice moved to third. Lemke reached first on an error by Duncan, Justice scored.
BRAVES SEVENTH (4): Blauser led off with a double. Gant grounded out. McGriff was intentionally walked. Pendleton singled, Blauser scored, McGriff moved to third. West came in to pitch. Justice struck out. Berryhill walked, Pendleton moved to second. Lemke doubled, McGriff, Pendleton and Berryhill scored.
PHILLIES NINTH (1): Chamberlain doubled with one out. Stocker singled, Chamberlain moved to third. Eisenreich batted for Thigpen and doubled, Chamberlain scored.

League playoffs, Game 4

PHILLIES		000	200	000—2	8	1
Atlanta		010	000	000—1	10	1

PHILLIES	AB	R	H	BI	BB	SO	Avg.
Dykstra cf	3	0	2	0	2	1	.313
Morandini 2b	5	0	2	0	0	1	.300
Kruk 1b	5	0	0	0	0	4	.313
DHollins 3b	4	0	1	0	1	3	.214
Batiste 3b	0	0	0	0	0	0	1.000
Daulton c	1	1	0	0	4	0	.083
Eisenreich rf	5	0	1	0	0	1	.182
MThompson lf	4	1	1	0	1	1	.111
Stocker ss	4	0	1	0	1	0	.267
DnJackson p	4	0	1	1	0	3	.250
Williams p	0	0	0	0	0	0	.000
Totals	35	2	8	2	8	15	

Atlanta	AB	R	H	BI	BB	SO	Avg.
Nixon cf	3	0	1	0	0	1	.438
Blauser ss	4	0	0	0	1	0	.235
Gant lf	5	0	0	0	0	2	.222
McGriff 1b	4	1	2	0	0	1	.444
Pendleton 3b	4	0	1	0	0	0	.389
Justice rf	4	0	2	0	0	0	.200
Olson c	2	0	0	0	0	1	.333
Berryhill c	1	0	1	0	0	0	.250
Lemke 2b	4	0	1	1	0	0	.235
Smoltz p	1	0	0	0	1	1	.000
Mercker p	0	0	0	0	0	0	.000
a-Cabrera ph	1	0	1	0	0	0	.500
1-DSanders pr	0	0	0	0	0	0	.000
Wohlers p	0	0	0	0	0	0	.000
b-Pecota ph	1	0	1	0	0	0	1.000
Totals	34	1	10	1	2	6	

a-singled for Mercker in the 7th. b-singled for Wohlers in the 9th.
1-ran for Cabrera in the 7th.
E—Williams (1), Lemke (1). LOB—PHILLIES 15, Atlanta 11. 2B—MThompson (1), McGriff (2), Pendleton (1), Lemke (2). RBIs—Stocker (1), DnJackson (1), Lemke (4). CS—Gant (1). S—Nixon 2. SF—Stocker. GIDP—Gant.
Runners left in scoring position—PHILLIES 8 (Morandini, Kruk, DHollins, Stocker 3); Atlanta 8 (Gant 3, Olson, Lemke 2, Smoltz 2).
Runners moved up—Eisenreich, MThompson, Blauser, Justice.
DP—PHILLIES 1 (Morandini and Kruk).

PHILLIES	IP	H	R	ER	BB	SO	NP	ERA
Jackson W, 1-0	7⅔	9	1	1	2	6	118	1.17
Williams S, 1	1⅓	1	0	0	0	0	16	0.00

Atlanta	IP	H	R	ER	BB	SO	NP	ERA
Smoltz L, 0-1	6⅓	8	2	0	5	10	125	0.00
Mercker	⅔	0	0	0	0	0	6	2.45
Wohlers	2	0	0	0	3	5	41	3.00

Inherited runners-scored—MtWilliams 2-0, Mercker 2-0.
IBB—off Wohlers (MThompson) 1. HBP—by DnJackson (Olson). WP—Wohlers.
Umpires—Home, Quick; First, Crawford; Second, West; Third, Froemming; Left, Pulli; Right, Tata.
T—3:33. A—52,032.

How they scored

BRAVES SECOND (1): McGriff led off with a single. Pendleton flied out. Justice singled, McGriff moved to second. Olson flied out. Lemke doubled, McGriff scored.
PHILLIES FOURTH (2): Daulton led off and reached first on an error by Lemke. Eisenreich flied out. Thompson doubled, Daulton moved to third. Stocker flied out, Daulton scored. Jackson singled, Thompson scored.

League playoffs, Game 5

PHILLIES		100	100	001	1—4	6	1
Atlanta		000	000	003	0—3	7	1

PHILLIES	AB	R	H	BI	BB	SO	Avg.
Dykstra cf	5	1	1	1	0	0	.286
Duncan 2b	5	1	1	0	0	2	.267
Andersen p	0	0	0	0	0	0	.000
Kruk 1b	4	0	1	1	1	1	.300
DHollins 3b	4	0	0	0	0	1	.167
Batiste 3b	0	0	0	0	0	0	1.000
Daulton c	3	1	2	1	1	1	.200
Incaviglia lf	4	1	0	0	0	1	.167
Thompson lf	0	0	0	0	0	0	.111
Chamberlain rf	3	0	1	1	0	1	.364
Eisenreich rf	0	0	0	0	0	0	.182
Stocker ss	4	0	0	0	0	0	.211
Schilling p	2	0	0	0	0	1	.000
Williams p	0	0	0	0	0	0	.000
d-Morandini ph-2b	1	0	0	0	0	0	.273
Totals	35	4	6	4	2	8	

Atlanta	AB	R	H	BI	BB	SO	Avg.
Nixon cf	4	0	0	0	1	1	.350
Blauser ss	4	1	1	0	1	2	.238
Gant lf	5	1	1	0	0	1	.217
McGriff 1b	4	1	2	1	0	1	.455
Justice rf	2	0	0	1	1	1	.176
Pendleton 3b	4	0	1	0	0	1	.364
Berryhill c	3	0	1	0	0	1	.267
b-Cabrera ph-c	1	0	1	1	0	0	.667
Lemke 2b	4	0	0	0	0	3	.190
Avery p	2	0	0	0	0	0	.500
Mercker p	0	0	0	0	0	0	.000
a-Sanders ph	1	0	0	0	0	0	.000
McMichael p	0	0	0	0	0	0	.000
c-Pecota ph	1	0	0	0	0	0	.500
Wohlers p	0	0	0	0	0	0	.000
Totals	35	3	7	3	3	12	

a-fouled out for Mercker in the 8th. b-singled for Berryhill in the 9th. c-flied out for McMichael in the 9th. d-flied out for Mit.Williams in the 10th.
E—Batiste (2), Gant (1). LOB—PHILLIES 5, Atlanta 6. 2B—Kruk (2). HR—Dykstra (2) off Wohlers, Daulton (1) off McMichael. RBIs—Dykstra (2), Kruk (5), Daulton (1), Chamberlain (1), McGriff (4), Justice (4), Cabrera (1). S—Schilling. SF—Chamberlain, Justice.
Runners left in scoring position—PHILLIES 2 (Dykstra, Incaviglia); Atlanta 3 (Pendleton, Pecota 2).

PHILLIES	IP	H	R	ER	BB	SO	NP	ERA
Schilling	8	4	2	1	3	9	131	1.69
Williams W, 2-0	1	3	1	1	0	1	24	2.08
Andersen S, 1	1	0	0	0	0	2	15	15.43

Atlanta	IP	H	R	ER	BB	SO	NP	ERA
Avery	7	4	2	1	2	5	134	2.77
Mercker	1	0	0	0	0	2	13	1.93
McMichael	1	1	1	1	0	0	12	8.10
Wohlers L, 0-1	1	1	1	1	0	1	13	4.50

Schilling pitched to 2 batters in the 9th.
Inherited runners-scored—MtWilliams 2-2.
WP—Avery.
Umpires—Home, Crawford; First, West; Second, Froemming; Third, Pulli; Left, Tata; Right, Quick.
T—3:21. A—52,032.

How they scored

PHILLIES FIRST (1): Duncan singled with one out. Kruk doubled, Duncan scored.
PHILLIES FOURTH (1): Incaviglia reached third on an error by Gant with one out. Chamberlain flied out, Incaviglia scored.
PHILLIES NINTH (1): Daulton led off with a home run.
BRAVES NINTH (3): Blauser led off with a walk. Gant reached first on an error by Batiste, Blauser moved to second. Williams came in to pitch. McGriff singled, Blauser scored, Gant moved to third. Justice flied out, Gant scored. Pendleton singled, McGriff moved to second. Cabrera batted for Berryhill and singled, McGriff scored.
PHILLIES 10TH (1): Dykstra homered with one out.

League playoffs, Game 6

Atlanta			000	010	200—3	5	3
PHILLIES			002	022	00x—6	7	1

Atlanta	AB	R	H	BI	BB	SO	Avg.
Nixon cf	3	1	1	0	1	1	.348
Blauser ss	4	1	2	3	0	1	.280
Gant lf	4	0	0	0	0	1	.185
McGriff 1b	1	0	0	0	3	1	.435
Justice rf	4	0	0	0	0	0	.143
Pendleton 3b	4	0	1	0	0	0	.346
Berryhill c	4	0	0	0	0	1	.211
Lemke 2b	3	1	1	0	1	1	.208
Maddux p	0	0	0	0	0	0	.250
Mercker p	0	0	0	0	0	0	.000
a-Sanders ph	1	0	0	0	0	1	.000
McMichael p	0	0	0	0	0	0	.000
Wohlers p	0	0	0	0	0	0	.000
c-Pecota ph	1	0	0	0	0	1	.333
Totals	29	3	5	3	5	8	

PHILLIES	AB	R	H	BI	BB	SO	Avg.
Dykstra cf	4	2	1	0	1	2	.280
Morandini 2b	5	1	1	2	0	0	.250
Kruk 1b	4	0	0	0	1	0	.250
Hollins 3b	2	1	1	2	2	0	.200
Batiste 3b	0	0	0	0	0	0	1.000
Daulton c	4	0	2	2	0	0	.263
Eisenreich rf	4	0	0	0	0	0	.133
Thompson lf	4	1	2	0	0	0	.231
Stocker ss	3	0	0	0	1	2	.182
Greene p	0	1	0	0	1	0	.000
b-Jordan ph	1	0	0	0	0	0	.000
West p	0	0	0	0	0	0	.000
Williams p	0	0	0	0	0	0	.000
Totals	31	6	7	6	6	4	

a-struck out for Mercker in the 7th. b-grounded out for Greene in the 7th. c-struck out for Wohlers in the 9th.
E—Justice (1), Lemke (2), Maddux (1), Thompson (1).
LOB—Atlanta 6, PHILLIES 9. 2B—Daulton (1). 3B—Morandini (1). HR—Hollins (2) off Maddux, Blauser (2) off Greene. RBIs—Blauser 3 (4), Morandini 2 (2), Hollins 2 (4), Daulton 2 (3). S—Maddux 2, Greene 2. GIDP—Berryhill.
Runners left in scoring position—Atlanta 4 (Blauser, Gant 2, Berryhill); PHILLIES 7 (Dykstra, Kruk, Eisenreich 2, Stocker, Jordan 2).
Runners moved up—Kruk 2, Eisenreich, Thompson.
DP—PHILLIES 1 (Morandini, Stocker and Kruk).

Atlanta	IP	H	R	ER	BB	SO	NP	ERA
Maddux L, 1-1	5⅔	6	6	5	4	3	104	4.97
Mercker	⅓	0	0	0	0	0	4	1.80
McMichael	⅔	1	0	0	2	0	18	6.75
Wohlers	1⅓	0	0	0	0	1	13	3.38

PHILLIES	IP	H	R	ER	BB	SO	NP	ERA
Greene W, 1-1	7	5	3	3	5	5	101	9.64
West	1	0	0	0	0	1	17	13.50
Williams S, 2	1	0	0	0	0	2	16	1.69

Inherited runners-scored—Mercker 1-0, Wohlers 3-0.
IBB—off GMaddux (Dykstra) 1, off McMichael (Stocker) 1. PB—Daulton.
Umpires—Home, West; First, Froemming; Second, Pulli; Third, Tata; Left, Quick; Right, Crawford.
T—3:04. A—62,502.

How they scored

PHILLIES THIRD (2): Greene led off with a walk. Dykstra singled, Greene moved to second. Morandini fouled out. Kruk grounded out, Greene moved to third and Dykstra to second. Hollins walked. Daulton doubled, Greene and Dykstra scored.
BRAVES FIFTH (1): Lemke walked with one out. Maddux sacrificed Lemke to second. Lemke moved to third on a passed ball. Nixon walked. Blauser singled, Lemke scored.
PHILLIES FIFTH (2): Morandini led off and reached first on an error by Lemke. Kruk grounded out, Morandini moved to second. Hollins homered, Morandini scored in front of him.
PHILLIES SIXTH (2): Thompson led off with a single. Stocker struck out. Greene sacrificed Thompson to second. Dykstra was intentionally walked. Morandini tripled, Thompson and Dykstra scored.
BRAVES SEVENTH (2): Nixon singled with two outs. Blauser homered, Nixon scored in front of him.

League championship series composite box score

ATLANTA

Name	G	AB	R	H	2B	3B	HR	RBI	SO	BB	Avg.	PO	A	E	Pct.
Bream 1b	1	1	1	1	0	0	0	0	0	0	1.000	1	0	0	1.000
Cabrera ph-c	3	3	0	2	0	0	0	1	1	0	.667	1	0	0	1.000
Avery p	2	4	1	2	1	0	0	0	1	0	.500	0	2	0	1.000
McGriff 1b	6	23	6	10	2	0	1	4	7	4	.435	50	3	0	1.000
Nixon cf	6	23	3	8	2	0	0	4	6	5	.348	13	0	0	1.000
Pendleton 3b	6	26	4	9	1	0	1	5	2	0	.346	7	5	0	1.000
Olson c	2	3	0	1	1	0	0	0	1	0	.333	10	0	0	1.000
Pecota ph	4	3	1	1	0	0	0	0	1	1	.333	0	0	0	—
Blauser ss	6	25	5	7	1	0	2	4	7	4	.280	6	14	0	1.000
Maddux p	2	4	1	1	0	0	0	0	1	0	.250	3	5	1	.889
Berryhill c	6	19	2	4	0	0	1	3	5	1	.211	42	0	0	1.000
Lemke 2b	6	24	2	5	2	0	0	4	6	1	.208	6	19	2	.926
Gant lf	6	27	4	5	3	0	0	3	9	2	.185	10	1	1	.917
Justice rf	6	21	2	3	1	0	0	4	3	3	.143	14	0	1	.933
Glavine p	1	3	0	0	0	0	0	0	0	0	.000	0	3	0	1.000
Sanders ph-cf-pr	5	3	0	0	0	0	0	0	1	0	.000	0	0	0	—
Belliard ph-2b-ss	2	1	1	0	0	0	0	0	1	0	.000	0	0	0	—
Smoltz p	1	1	0	0	0	0	0	0	1	1	.000	0	0	0	—
Tarasco pr-lf-rf	2	1	0	0	0	0	0	0	1	0	.000	0	0	0	—
McMichael p	4	0	0	0	0	0	0	0	0	0	—	0	1	0	1.000
Mercker p	5	0	0	0	0	0	0	0	0	0	—	0	0	0	—
Stanton p	1	0	0	0	0	0	0	0	0	0	—	0	0	0	—
Wohlers p	4	0	0	0	0	0	0	0	0	0	—	0	0	0	—
Totals	6	215	33	59	14	0	5	32	54	22	.274	163	53	5	.977

PHILADELPHIA

Name	G	AB	R	H	2B	3B	HR	RBI	SO	BB	Avg.	PO	A	E	Pct.
Batiste 3b	4	1	0	1	0	0	0	1	0	0	1.000	2	0	2	.500
Chamberlain rf-ph	4	11	1	4	3	0	0	1	3	1	.364	2	2	0	1.000
Dykstra cf	6	25	5	7	1	0	2	2	8	5	.280	13	0	0	1.000
Duncan 2b	3	15	3	4	0	2	0	0	5	0	.267	5	6	1	.917
Daulton c	6	19	2	5	1	0	1	3	3	6	.263	54	3	0	1.000
Jackson p	1	4	0	1	0	0	0	1	3	0	.250	0	0	0	—
Kruk 1b	6	24	4	6	2	1	1	5	5	4	.250	43	2	0	1.000
Morandini 2b-ph	4	16	1	4	0	1	0	2	3	0	.250	8	9	1	.944
Thompson pr-lf-ph	6	13	2	3	1	0	0	0	2	1	.231	8	0	1	.889
Hollins 3b	6	20	2	4	1	0	2	4	4	5	.200	5	4	0	1.000
Stocker ss	6	22	0	4	1	0	0	1	5	2	.182	10	13	1	.958
Incaviglia lf	3	12	2	2	0	0	1	1	3	0	.167	8	0	0	1.000
Eisenreich rf-ph	6	15	0	2	1	0	0	1	2	0	.133	6	0	0	1.000
Schilling p	2	5	0	0	0	0	0	0	2	0	.000	0	0	0	—
Mulholland p	1	2	0	0	0	0	0	0	1	0	.000	0	2	0	1.000
Jordan ph	2	1	0	0	0	0	0	0	0	1	.000	0	0	0	—
Longmire ph	1	1	0	0	0	0	0	0	1	0	.000	0	0	0	—
Pratt c	1	1	0	0	0	0	0	0	1	0	.000	1	0	0	1.000
Greene p	2	0	1	0	0	0	0	0	0	1	.000	0	3	0	1.000
Andersen p	3	0	0	0	0	0	0	0	0	0	—	0	1	0	1.000
Mason p	2	0	0	0	0	0	0	0	0	0	—	0	0	0	—
Rivera p	1	0	0	0	0	0	0	0	0	0	—	0	0	0	—
Thigpen p	2	0	0	0	0	0	0	0	0	0	—	0	0	0	—
West p	3	0	0	0	0	0	0	0	0	0	—	0	0	0	1.000
Mt. Williams p	4	0	0	0	0	0	0	0	0	0	—	0	1	1	.500
Totals	6	207	23	47	11	4	7	22	51	26	.227	165	47	7	.968

PITCHING SUMMARY

Name	G	CG	IP	H	R	BB	SO	HB	WP	W	L	SV	Pct.	ER	ERA
ATLANTA															
Smoltz	1	0	6⅓	8	2	5	10	0	0	0	1	0	.000	0	0.00
Stanton	1	0	1	1	0	1	0	0	0	0	0	0	—	0	0.00
Mercker	5	0	5	3	1	2	4	0	0	0	0	0	—	1	1.80
Glavine	1	0	7	6	2	0	5	0	0	1	0	0	1.000	2	2.57
Avery	2	0	13	9	5	6	10	0	2	0	0	0	—	4	2.77
Wohlers	4	0	5⅓	2	2	3	10	0	1	0	1	0	.000	2	3.38
Maddux	2	0	12⅔	11	8	7	11	0	0	1	1	0	.500	7	4.97
McMichael	4	0	4	7	3	2	1	0	0	0	1	0	.000	3	6.75
Totals	6	0	54⅓	47	23	26	51	0	3	2	4	0	.333	19	3.15
PHILADELPHIA															
Mason	2	0	3	1	0	0	2	0	0	0	0	0	—	0	0.00
Jackson	1	0	7⅔	9	1	2	6	1	0	1	0	0	1.000	1	1.17
Schilling	2	0	16	11	4	5	19	0	0	0	0	0	—	3	1.67
Mt. Williams	4	0	5⅓	6	2	2	5	0	0	2	0	2	1.000	1	1.69
Rivera	1	0	2	1	1	1	2	0	0	0	0	0	—	1	4.50
Thigpen	2	0	1⅔	1	1	1	3	0	0	0	0	0	—	1	5.40
Mulholland	1	0	5	9	5	1	2	0	0	0	0	1	.000	4	7.20
Greene	2	0	9⅓	12	10	7	7	0	0	1	1	0	.500	10	9.64
West	3	0	2⅔	5	5	2	5	0	0	0	0	0	—	4	13.50
Andersen	3	0	2⅓	4	4	1	3	0	0	0	0	1	—	4	15.43
Totals	6	0	55	59	33	22	54	1	0	4	2	3	.667	29	4.75

SCORE BY INNINGS
Atlanta .... 217 125 645 **0—33**
Philadelphia.............. 202 722 213 **2—23**
DP—Atlanta 1, Philadelphia 2. LOB—Atlanta 47, Philadelphia 52. SB—Morandini, Hollins. CS—Nixon 2, Gant. S—Belliard, Nixon 2, Maddux 2, Schilling, Greene 2. SF—Justice 2, Stocker, Chamberlain.
Mulholland pitched to 5 batters in the 6th (Game 3).
Schilling pitched to 2 batters in the 9th (Game 5).
IBB—off Avery 3 (Stocker, Daulton, Chamberlain); off Wohlers (Thompson); off Maddux (Dykstra); off McMichael (Stocker); off Andersen (McGriff). HBP—by Jackson (Olson). PB—Daulton 2.
Umpires—Froemming, Pulli, Tata, Quick, Crawford, West.
T—Game 1 at Philadelphia, 3:33.
Game 2 at Philadelphia, 3:14.
Game 3 at Atlanta, 2:44.
Game 4 at Atlanta, 3:33.
Game 5 at Atlanta, 3:21.
Game 6 at Philadelphia, 3:04.
A—Game 1 at Philadelphia, 62,012.
Game 2 at Philadelphia, 62,436.
Game 3 at Atlanta, 52,032.
Game 4 at Atlanta, 52,032.
Game 5 at Atlanta, 52,032.
Game 6 at Philadelphia, 63,502.

World Series, Game 1

PHILLIES	201	010	001—5	11	1
Toronto	021	011	30x—8	10	3

PHILLIES	AB	R	H	BI	BB	SO	Avg.
Dykstra cf	4	1	1	0	1	0	.250
Duncan 2b	5	2	3	0	0	2	.600
Kruk 1b	4	2	3	2	1	1	.750
Hollins 3b	4	0	0	0	1	1	.000
Daulton c	4	0	1	1	1	2	.250
Eisenreich rf	5	0	1	1	0	2	.200
Jordan dh	5	0	1	0	0	2	.200
Thompson lf	3	0	0	0	0	1	.000
a-Incaviglia ph-lf	1	0	0	0	0	0	.000
Stocker ss	3	0	1	0	1	0	.333
Totals	**38**	**5**	**11**	**4**	**5**	**11**	

Toronto	AB	R	H	BI	BB	SO	Avg.
Henderson lf	3	1	1	0	1	0	.333
White cf	4	3	2	2	0	0	.500
RAlomar 2b	4	0	1	2	0	1	.250
Carter rf	3	1	1	1	0	1	.333
Olerud 1b	3	2	2	1	1	0	.667
Molitor dh	4	0	1	1	0	0	.250
Fernandez ss	3	0	0	1	1	0	.000
Sprague 3b	4	0	1	0	0	2	.250
Borders c	4	1	1	0	0	1	.250
Totals	**32**	**8**	**10**	**8**	**3**	**5**	

a-fouled out for Thompson in the 8th.
E—Thompson (1), Alomar (1), Carter (1), Sprague (1). LOB—PHILLIES 11, Toronto 4. 2B—White (1), Alomar (1). 3B—Duncan (1). HR—White (1) off Schilling, Olerud (1) off Schilling. RBIs—Kruk 2 (2), Daulton (1), Eisenreich (1), White 2 (2), Alomar 2 (2), Carter (1), Olerud (1), Molitor (1), Fernandez (1). SB—Dykstra (1), Duncan (1), Alomar (1). CS—TFernandez (1). SF—Carter. GIDP—Thompson, White.
Runners left in scoring position—PHILLIES 5 (Duncan, Kruk 2, Eisenreich, Jordan); Toronto 2 (Henderson, Molitor).
Runners moved up—Hollins, Fernandez.
DP—PHILLIES 1 (Stocker, Duncan and Kruk); Toronto 1 (Fernandez and Olerud).

PHILLIES	IP	H	R	ER	BB	SO	NP	ERA
Schilling L, 0-1	6⅓	8	7	6	2	3	99	8.53
West	0	2	1	1	0	0	12	—
Andersen	⅔	0	0	0	1	1	7	0.00
Mason	1	0	0	0	0	1	11	0.00

Toronto	IP	H	R	ER	BB	SO	NP	ERA
Guzman	5	4	4	4	6	1	116	7.20
Leiter W, 1-0	2⅔	4	0	0	1	2	56	0.00
Ward S, 1	1⅓	2	1	0	0	3	30	0.00

West pitched to 2 batters in the 7th.
Inherited runners-scored—West 2-2, Andersen 1-0, DWard 1-0.
IBB—off Andersen (Olerud) 1, off Guzman (Daulton) 1. WP—Guzman. PB—Daulton.
Umpires—Home, Phillips; First, Runge; Second, Johnson; Third, Williams; Left, McClelland; Right, DeMuth.
T—3:27. A—52,011.

How they scored

PHILLIES FIRST (2): Dykstra led off with a walk and stole second. Duncan struck out. Kruk singled, Dykstra scored. Hollins walked, Kruk moved to second. Daulton singled, Kruk scored.
BLUE JAYS SECOND (2): Carter led off with a single. Olerud singled, Carter moved to second. Molitor singled, Carter scored, Olerud moved to third and Olerud to second on a passed ball by Daulton. Molitor singled, Carter scored, Olerud moved to third. Fernandez forced Molitor at second, Olerud scored.
PHILLIES THIRD (1): Duncan led off with a single and stole second. Kruk singled, Duncan scored.

BLUE JAYS THIRD (1): White led off and reached third on an error by Thompson. Alomar popped out. Carter flied out, White scored.
PHILLIES FIFTH (1): Duncan tripled with one out and scored on a wild pitch.
BLUE JAYS FIFTH (1): White homered with two outs.
BLUE JAYS SIXTH (1): Olerud homered with one out.
BLUE JAYS SEVENTH (3): Borders singled with one out. Henderson singled, Borders moved to third. West came in to pitch. White doubled, Borders scored, Henderson moved to third. Alomar doubled, Henderson and White scored.
PHILLIES NINTH (1): Kruk led off with a single and moved to second on an error by Sprague. Hollins and Daulton struck out. Eisenreich singled, Kruk scored.

World Series, Game 2

PHILLIES	005	000	100—6	12	0
Toronto	000	201	010—4	8	0

PHILLIES	AB	R	H	BI	BB	SO	Avg.
Dykstra cf	4	2	2	1	1	0	.375
Duncan 2b	4	1	1	0	1	2	.444
Kruk 1b	5	1	2	3	0	1	.556
Hollins 3b	4	1	2	1	1	2	.250
Batiste 3b	0	0	0	0	0	0	.000
Daulton c	5	0	1	0	0	0	.222
Eisenreich rf	4	1	1	3	1	1	.222
Incaviglia lf	4	0	1	0	0	2	.200
1-Thompson pr-lf	0	0	0	0	0	0	.000
RJordan dh	4	0	1	0	0	0	.222
Stocker ss	3	0	1	0	1	0	.333
Totals	**37**	**6**	**12**	**6**	**5**	**8**	

Toronto	AB	R	H	BI	BB	SO	Avg.
Henderson lf	3	0	0	0	1	1	.167
White cf	4	0	1	0	0	2	.375
Molitor dh	3	2	2	0	1	0	.429
Carter rf	4	1	1	2	0	1	.286
Olerud 1b	3	0	0	1	1	0	.333
Alomar 2b	3	1	1	0	1	1	.286
Fernandez ss	3	0	2	1	1	0	.333
Sprague 3b	4	0	0	0	0	1	.125
2-Griffin pr	0	0	0	0	0	0	.000
Borders c	4	0	1	0	0	0	.250
Totals	**31**	**4**	**8**	**4**	**4**	**6**	

1-ran for Incaviglia in the 8th. 2-ran for Sprague in the 9th.
LOB—PHILLIES 9, Toronto 5. 2B—White (2), Molitor (1), Fernandez (1). HR—Carter (1) off Mulholland, Dykstra (1) off Castillo, Eisenreich (1) off Stewart. RBIs—Dykstra (1), Kruk (3), Hollins (1), Eisenreich 3 (4), Carter 2 (3), Olerud (2), Fernandez (2). SB—Molitor (1), Alomar (2). CS—Stocker (1), Henderson (1), Alomar (1). SF—Olerud. GIDP—Eisenreich, Borders.
Runners left in scoring position—PHILLIES 6 (Kruk 2, DHollins, Eisenreich 2, Stocker); Toronto 2 (Molitor, Sprague).
Runners moved up—Kruk, Daulton 2, RJordan.
DP—PHILLIES 1 (Stocker, Duncan and Kruk); Toronto 1 (Sprague, Alomar and Olerud).

PHILLIES	IP	H	R	ER	BB	SO	NP	ERA
Mulholland W, 1-0	5⅔	7	3	3	2	4	105	4.76
Mason	1⅔	1	1	1	0	2	24	3.38
MtWilliams S, 1	1⅔	0	0	0	2	0	31	0.00

Toronto	IP	H	R	ER	BB	SO	NP	ERA
Stewart L, 0-1	6	6	5	5	4	6	122	7.50
Castillo	1	3	1	1	0	0	21	9.00
Eichhorn	⅓	1	0	0	1	0	15	0.00
Timlin	1⅔	2	0	0	0	2	29	0.00

Inherited runners-scored—Mason 1-0, MtWilliams 1-1, Timlin 2-0.
WP—Stewart. Balk—Stewart.
Umpires—Home, Runge; First, Johnson; Second, Williams; Third, McClelland; Left, DeMuth; Right, Phillips.
T—3:35. A—52,062.

How they scored

PHILLIES THIRD (5): Dykstra led off with a walk and moved to second on a wild pitch by Stewart. Duncan walked. Kruk singled, Dykstra scored, Duncan moved to third. Hollins singled, Duncan scored, Kruk moved to second. Daulton grounded out, Kruk moved to third and Hollins to second. Eisenreich homered, Kruk and Hollins scored in front of him.
BLUE JAYS FOURTH (2): Molitor led off with a single. Carter homered, Molitor scored in front of him.
BLUE JAYS SIXTH (1): Alomar singled with two outs. Fernandez doubled, Alomar scored.
PHILLIES SEVENTH (1): Dykstra led off with a home run.
BLUE JAYS EIGHTH (1): Molitor led off with a double. Carter struck out. Williams came in to pitch. Molitor stole third. Olerud flied out, Molitor scored.

World Series, Game 3

Toronto	301	001	302—10	13	1
PHILLIES	000	001	101— 3	9	0

Toronto	AB	R	H	BI	BB	SO	Avg.
RHenderson lf	4	2	2	0	0	0	.300
White cf	4	2	1	1	1	0	.333
Molitor 1b	4	3	3	3	1	0	.545
Carter rf	4	1	1	1	0	1	.273
RAlomar 2b	5	2	4	2	0	0	.500
TFernandez ss	3	0	2	2	1	0	.444
Sprague 3b	4	0	0	1	0	2	.083
Borders c	4	0	0	0	1	0	.167
Hentgen p	3	0	0	0	0	1	.000
Cox p	1	0	0	0	0	0	.000
DWard p	0	0	0	0	0	0	.000
Totals	36	10	13	10	4	4	

PHILLIES	AB	R	H	BI	BB	SO	Avg.
Dykstra cf	5	0	1	0	0	1	.308
Duncan 2b	5	0	2	1	0	1	.429
Kruk 1b	3	1	2	0	2	1	.583
DHollins 3b	3	0	0	1	1	1	.182
Daulton c	3	0	0	0	1	1	.167
Eisenreich rf	4	0	1	1	0	0	.231
Incaviglia lf	3	0	0	0	0	2	.125
Thigpen p	0	0	0	0	0	0	.000
b-Morandini ph	0	0	0	0	1	0	.000
Andersen p	0	0	0	0	0	0	.000
Stocker ss	4	0	1	0	0	2	.300
DnJackson p	1	0	0	0	0	1	.000
a-Chamberlain ph	1	0	0	0	0	0	.000
Rivera p	0	0	0	0	0	0	.000
MThompson lf	2	2	2	1	0	0	.400
Totals	34	3	9	3	5	10	

a-grounded into double play for DnJackson in the 5th.
b-walked for Thigpen in the 8th.
E—Carter (2). LOB—Toronto 7, PHILLIES 9. 2B—RHenderson (1), Kruk (1). 3B—White (1), Molitor (1), RAlomar (1). HR—MThompson (1) off DWard, Molitor (1) off DnJackson. RBIs—White (3), Molitor 3 (4), Carter (4), RAlomar 2 (4), TFernandez 2 (4), Sprague (1), Duncan (1), Eisenreich (5), MThompson (1). SB—RAlomar 2 (4). SF—Carter, TFernandez, Sprague. GIDP—DHollins, Chamberlain.
Runners left in scoring position—Toronto 3 (Sprague 2, Borders); PHILLIES 6 (DHollins 2, Daulton 2, Incaviglia 2).
DP—Toronto 2 (RAlomar, TFernandez and Molitor), (Molitor, TFernandez and Cox).

Toronto	IP	H	R	ER	BB	SO	NP	ERA
Hentgen W, 1-0	6	5	1	1	3	6	99	1.50
Cox	2	3	1	1	2	2	29	4.50
DWard	1	1	1	1	0	2	18	3.86

PHILLIES	IP	H	R	ER	BB	SO	NP	ERA
Jackson L, 0-1	5	6	4	4	1	1	89	7.20
Rivera	1⅓	4	4	4	2	3	50	27.00
Thigpen	1⅔	0	0	0	1	0	27	0.00
Andersen	1	3	2	2	0	0	28	10.80

Inherited runners-scored—Thigpen 2-1.
HRP—by Thigpen (RHenderson).

Umpires—Home, Johnson; First, Williams; Second, McClelland; Third, DeMuth; Left, Phillips; Right, Runge.

T—3:16. A—62,689.

How they scored

BLUE JAYS FIRST (3): Henderson led off with a single. White walked, Henderson moved to second. Molitor tripled, Henderson and White scored. Carter flied out, Molitor scored.
BLUE JAYS THIRD (1): Molitor homered with two out.
BLUE JAYS SIXTH (1): Alomar led off with a single and stole second and third. Fernandez flied out, Alomar scored.
PHILLIES SIXTH (1): Kruk walked with one out. Hollins flied out. Daulton walked, Kruk moved to second. Eisenreich singled, Kruk scored.
BLUE JAYS SEVENTH (3): Henderson led off with a double. White tripled, Henderson scored. Molitor walked. Carter struck out. Alomar singled, White scored, Molitor went to third. Fernandez walked. Sprague flied out, Molitor scored.
PHILLIES SEVENTH (1): Thompson singled with one out. Dykstra singled, Thompson moved to third. Duncan singled, Thompson scored.
BLUE JAYS NINTH (2): Molitor led off with an infield single. Carter forced Molitor at second. Alomar tripled, Carter scored. Fernandez singled, Alomar scored.
PHILLIES NINTH (1): Thompson led off with a home run.

World Series, Game 4

Toronto	304	002	060—15	18	0
PHILLIES	420	151	100—14	14	0

Toronto	AB	R	H	BI	BB	SO	Avg.
RHenderson lf	5	2	2	2	1	1	.333
White cf	5	3	4	1	1	1	.412
RAlomar 2b	6	1	2	2	0	1	.444
Carter rf	6	2	3	0	0	0	.353
Olerud 1b	4	2	1	0	2	0	.300
Molitor 3b	4	2	2	2	1	0	.467
Griffin 3b	0	0	0	0	0	0	.000
TFernandez ss	6	2	3	5	0	1	.467
Borders c	4	1	1	1	1	0	.188
Stottlemyre p	0	0	0	0	0	1	.000
a-Butler ph	1	1	0	0	0	0	.000
ALeiter p	1	0	1	0	0	0	1.000
Castillo p	1	0	0	0	0	1	.000
d-Sprague ph	1	0	0	0	0	1	.077
Timlin p	0	0	0	0	0	0	.000
DWard p	0	0	0	0	0	0	.000
Totals	44	15	18	15	7	6	

PHILLIES	AB	R	H	BI	BB	SO	Avg.
Dykstra cf	5	4	3	4	1	1	.389
Duncan 2b	6	1	3	1	0	0	.450
Kruk 1b	5	0	0	0	1	2	.412
DHollins 3b	4	3	2	0	2	0	.267
Daulton c	3	2	1	3	1	1	.200
Eisenreich rf	4	2	1	1	1	0	.235
MThompson lf	5	1	3	5	0	0	.500
Stocker ss	4	0	0	0	1	1	.214
TGreene p	1	1	1	0	0	0	1.000
Mason p	1	0	0	0	0	0	.000
b-RJordan ph	1	0	0	0	0	0	.200

West p	0	0	0	0	0	0	.000
c-Chamberlain ph	1	0	0	0	0	1	.000
Andersen p	0	0	0	0	0	0	.000
MtWilliams p	0	0	0	0	0	0	.000
e-Morandini ph	1	0	0	0	0	1	.000
Thigpen p	0	0	0	0	0	0	.000
Totals	**41**	**14**	**14**	**14**	**7**	**7**	

a-grounded into fielder's choice for Stottlemyre in the 3rd. b-grounded out for Mason in the 5th. c-struck out for West in the 6th. d-struck out for Castillo in the 8th. e-struck out for MtWilliams in the 8th.
LOB—Toronto 10, PHILLIES 8. 2B—RHenderson (2), White (3), Carter (1), ALeiter (1), Dykstra (1), DHollins (1), MThompson (1). 3B—White (2), MThompson (1). HR—Dykstra (2) off Stottlemyre, Dykstra (3) off ALeiter, Daulton (1) off ALeiter. RBIs—RHenderson 2 (2), White 4 (7), RAlomar (5), Molitor (5), TFernandez 5 (9), Borders (1), Dykstra 4 (5), Duncan (2), Daulton 3 (4), Eisenreich (6), MThompson 5 (6). SB—RHenderson (1), White (1), Dykstra (2), Duncan (2).
Runners left in scoring position—Toronto 8 (RHenderson, RAlomar 3, TFernandez, Borders 3); PHILLIES 5 (Kruk, MThompson 2, Stocker, Chamberlain).
Runners moved up—Olerud, TFernandez, Butler.

Toronto	IP	H	R	ER	BB	SO	NP	ERA
Stottlemyre	2	3	6	6	4	1	53	27.00
ALeiter	2⅔	8	6	6	0	1	52	10.13
Castillo W, 1-0	2⅓	3	2	2	3	1	54	8.10
Timlin	⅔	0	0	0	0	2	8	0.00
DWard S, 2	1⅓	0	0	0	0	2	14	2.45
PHILLIES	**IP**	**H**	**R**	**ER**	**BB**	**SO**	**NP**	**ERA**
TGreene	2⅓	7	7	7	4	1	66	27.00
Mason	2⅔	2	0	0	1	2	38	1.69
West	1	3	2	2	0	0	19	27.00
Andersen	1⅓	2	3	1	2	0	26	15.00
MtWilliams L, 0-1	⅔	3	3	3	1	1	20	11.57
Thigpen	1	1	0	0	0	0	17	0.00

Inherited runners-scored—Castillo 1-0, Mason 2-2, MtWilliams 2-2.
HBP—by Castillo (Daulton), by West (Molitor).
Umpires—Home, Williams; First, McClelland; Second, DeMuth; Third, Phillips; Left, Runge; Right, Johnson.
T—4:14. A—62,731.

How they scored

BLUE JAYS FIRST (3): Henderson led off with a double. White walked. Alomar popped out. Carter singled, Henderson moved to third and White to second. Olerud popped out. Molitor walked, Henderson scored, White moved to third and Carter to second. Fernandez singled, White and Carter scored.
PHILLIES FIRST (4): Dykstra led off with a walk. Duncan flied out. Dykstra stole second. Kruk struck out. Hollins walked. Daulton walked, Dykstra moved to third and Hollins to second. Eisenreich walked, Dykstra scored, Hollins moved to third and Daulton to second. Thompson tripled, Hollins, Daulton and Eisenreich scored.
PHILLIES SECOND (2): Greene led off with a single. Dykstra homered, Greene scored in front of him.
BLUE JAYS THIRD (4): Olerud walked with one out. Molitor singled, Olerud moved to third. Fernandez singled, Olerud scored, Molitor moved to third. Borders singled, Molitor scored, Fernandez moved to second. Mason came in for Stottlemyre and forced Borders and second, Fernandez moved to third. Henderson walked to load the bases. White singled, Fernandez and Butler scored.
PHILLIES FOURTH (1): Dykstra doubled with two outs. Duncan singled, Dykstra scored.
PHILLIES FIFTH (5): Hollins led off with a single. Daulton homered, Hollins scored in front of him. Eisenreich singled. Thompson doubled, Eisenreich scored. Stocker grounded out. Jordan batted for Mason and grounded out. Dykstra homered, Thompson scored in front of him.

BLUE JAYS SIXTH (2): White led off with a double. Alomar singled, White scored. Carter flied out. Olerud singled, Carter moved to third. Molitor was hit by a pitch to load the bases. Fernandez grounded out, Alomar scored.
PHILLIES SIXTH (1): Hollins led off with a double. Daulton flied out. Eisenreich popped out. Thompson singled, Hollins scored.
PHILLIES SEVENTH (1): Duncan singled with one out. Kruk walked, Duncan moved to second. Hollins walked to load the bases. Daulton was hit by a pitch, Duncan scored.
BLUE JAYS EIGHTH (6): Carter singled with one out. Olerud walked. Molitor doubled, Carter scored, Olerud moved to third. Williams came in to pitch. Fernandez singled, Olerud scored, Molitor moved to third. Borders walked to load the bases. Sprague batted for Castillo and struck out. Henderson singled, Molitor and Fernandez scored, Borders moved to second. White tripled, Borders and Henderson scored.

Series records set and tied in the game

RECORDS SET

Most runs, game: 29; old record 22, Yankees vs. Giants, 1936.

Most runs, first four games: 65; old record 56, Yankees vs. Cubs, 1932.

Longest nine-inning game: Four hours, fourteen minutes; old record three hours, forty-eight minutes, Pirates vs. Orioles, 1979.

Most players, one or more run, both teams: 16; old record, 15, Pirates vs. Yankees, 1960.

RECORDS TIED

Most runs, individual game: 4, Lenny Dykstra, shared by seven others.

Most hits, individual game: 32, shared by Pirates vs. Yankees, 1960.

Most walks, pitcher, one inning: 4, Todd Stottlemyre, shared by four others.

Most at-bats, no hits, game: 5, John Kruk, shared by many.

World Series, Game 5

Toronto	000 000 000—0 5 1
PHILLIES	110 000 00x—2 5 1

Toronto	AB	R	H	BI	BB	SO	Avg.
RHenderson lf	3	0	0	0	1	0	.278
White cf	3	0	0	0	1	2	.350
RAlomar 2b	3	0	1	0	1	0	.429
Carter rf	4	0	0	0	0	1	.286
Olerud 1b	4	0	0	0	0	1	.214
Molitor 3b	4	0	1	0	0	0	.474
TFernandez ss	3	0	0	0	0	1	.389
Borders c	3	0	2	0	0	0	.263
1-Canate pr	0	0	0	0	0	0	.000
Knorr c	0	0	0	0	0	0	.000
Guzman p	2	0	0	0	0	1	.000
a-Butler ph	1	0	1	0	0	0	.500
Cox p	0	0	0	0	0	0	.000
Totals	30	0	5	0	3	6	

PHILLIES	AB	R	H	BI	BB	SO	Avg.
Dykstra cf	2	1	0	0	2	1	.350
Duncan 2b	4	0	0	0	0	1	.375
Kruk 1b	3	0	1	1	1	1	.400
DHollins 3b	3	0	1	0	1	1	.278
Batiste 3b	0	0	0	0	0	0	.000
Daulton c	4	1	1	0	0	1	.211
Eisenreich rf	4	0	0	0	0	1	.190
MThompson lf	3	0	0	0	1	1	.385
Stocker ss	2	0	1	1	1	1	.250
Schilling p	2	0	1	0	0	1	.500
Totals	27	2	5	2	6	9	

a-singled for Guzman in the 8th.
1-ran for Borders in the 8th.
E—Borders (1), Duncan (1). LOB—Toronto 6, Philadelphia 8. 2B—Daulton (1), Stocker (1). RBIs—Kruk (4), Stocker (1). SB—Dykstra (3). CS—RAlomar (2). S—Schilling. GIDP—RAlomar, Guzman, Duncan.
Runners left in scoring position—Toronto 2 (RAlomar 2); PHILLIES 5 (Duncan 2, Daulton, MThompson, Schilling).
Runners moved up—RHenderson, Kruk, Eisenreich.
DP—Toronto 1 (TFernandez and Olerud) and PHILLIES 3 (Kruk, Stocker and Duncan), (Daulton and Duncan), (Duncan, Stocker and Kruk).

Toronto	IP	H	R	ER	BB	SO	NP	ERA
Guzman L, 0-1	7	5	2	1	4	6	101	3.75
Cox	1	0	0	0	2	3	24	3.00

Philadelphia	IP	H	R	ER	BB	SO	NP	ERA
Schilling W, 1-1	9	5	0	0	3	6	148	3.52

IBB—off Guzman (Dykstra) 1.
Umpires—Home, McClelland; First, DeMuth; Second, Phillips; Third, Runge; Left, Johnson; Right, Williams.
T—2:53. A—62,706.

How they scored

PHILLIES FIRST (1): Dykstra led off with a walk, stole second and moved to third on an error by Borders. Duncan flied out. Kruk drove home Dykstra.
PHILLIES SECOND (1): Daulton led off with a double. Eisenreich grounded out, Daulton moved to third. Thompson flied out. Stocker doubled, Daulton scored.

World Series, Game 6

PHILLIES	000 100 500—6 7 0
Toronto	300 110 003—8 10 2

PHILLIES	AB	R	H	BI	BB	SO	Avg.
Dykstra cf	3	1	1	3	2	1	.348
Duncan dh	5	1	1	0	0	1	.345
Kruk 1b	3	0	0	0	2	1	.348
DHollins 3b	5	1	1	1	0	0	.261
Batiste 3b	0	0	0	0	0	0	.000
Daulton c	4	1	1	0	1	0	.217
Eisenreich rf	5	0	2	1	0	0	.231
MThompson lf	3	0	0	0	0	0	.313
a-Incaviglia ph-lf	0	0	0	1	0	0	.125
Stocker ss	3	1	0	0	1	1	.211
Morandini 2b	4	1	1	0	0	1	.200
Totals	35	6	7	6	6	5	

Toronto	AB	R	H	BI	BB	SO	Avg.
RHenderson lf	4	1	0	0	1	2	.227
White cf	4	1	0	0	1	2	.292
Molitor dh	5	3	3	2	0	0	.500
Carter rf	4	1	1	4	0	1	.280
Olerud 1b	3	1	0	0	1	0	.235
1-Griffin pr-3b	0	0	0	0	0	0	.000
RAlomar 2b	4	1	3	1	0	0	.480
TFernandez ss	3	0	0	0	0	1	.333
Sprague 3b-1b	2	0	0	1	1	0	.067
Borders c	4	0	2	0	0	0	.304
Totals	33	8	10	8	4	3	

One out when winning run scored.
a-hit sacrifice fly for MThompson in the 7th.
1-ran for Olerud in the 8th.
E—RAlomar (2), Sprague (2). LOB—PHILLIES 9, Toronto 7. 2B—Daulton (2), Olerud (1), RAlomar (3). 3B—Molitor (2). HR—Molitor (2) off Mulholland, Carter (2) off MtWilliams, Dykstra (4) off Stewart. RBIs—Dykstra 3 (8), DHollins (2), Eisenreich (7), Incaviglia (1), Molitor 2 (8), Carter 4 (8), RAlomar (6), Sprague (5). SB—Dykstra (4), Duncan (3). SF—Incaviglia, Carter, Sprague.
Runners left in scoring position—PHILLIES 4 (Kruk, DHollins 2, Stocker); Toronto 2 (Borders 2).
Runners moved up—RAlomar, TFernandez.

PHILLIES	IP	H	R	ER	BB	SO	NP	ERA
Mulholland	5	7	5	5	1	1	70	6.75
Mason	2⅓	1	0	0	0	2	27	1.17
West	0	0	0	0	1	0	5	27.00
Andersen	⅔	0	0	0	1	0	27	12.27
Williams L, 0-2	⅓	2	3	3	1	0	21	20.25

Toronto	IP	H	R	ER	BB	SO	NP	ERA
Stewart	6	4	4	4	4	2	120	6.75
Cox	⅓	3	2	2	1	1	24	8.10
ALeiter	1⅔	0	0	0	1	2	21	7.71
DWard W, 1-0	1	0	0	0	0	0	7	1.93

Stewart pitched to 3 batters in the 7th, West pitched to 1 batter in the 8th.
Inherited runners-scored—Andersen 1-0, ALeiter 3-1.
HBP—by Andersen (TFernandez).
Umpires—Home, DeMuth; First, Phillips; Second, Runge; Third, Johnson; Left, Williams; Right, McClelland.
T—3:26. A—52,195.

How they scored

BLUE JAYS FIRST (3): White walked with one out. Molitor tripled, White scored. Carter flied out, Molitor scored. Olerud doubled. Alomar singled, Olerud scored.
PHILLIES FOURTH (1): Daulton doubled with two outs. Eisenreich singled, Daulton scored.
BLUE JAYS FOURTH (1): Alomar led off with a double. Fernandez grounded out, Alomar moved to third. Sprague flied out, Alomar scored.
BLUE JAYS FIFTH (1): Molitor homered with one out.
PHILLIES SEVENTH (5): Stocker led off with a walk. Morandini singled, Stocker moved to third. Dykstra homered, Stocker and Morandini scored in front of him. Cox came in to pitch. Duncan singled. Kruk struck out. Duncan stole second. Hollins singled, Duncan scored. Daulton walked, Hollins moved to second. Eisenreich singled, Hollins moved to third and Dalton to second. Leiter came in to pitch. Incaviglia batted for Thompson and flied out, Hollins scored.
BLUE JAYS NINTH (3): Henderson led off with a walk. White flied out. Molitor singled, Henderson moved to second. Carter homered, Henderson and Molitor scored in front of him.

Final World Series composite box score

BATTING SUMMARY

Phillies	G	AB	R	H	2B	3B	HR	RBI	SO	BB	Avg.	PO	A	E	Pct.
Greene p	1	1	1	1	0	0	0	0	0	0	1.000	0	0	0	—
Schilling p	2	2	0	1	0	0	0	0	1	0	.500	0	3	0	1.000
Dykstra cf	6	23	9	8	1	0	4	8	4	7	.348	19	1	0	1.000
Kruk 1b	6	23	4	8	1	0	0	4	7	7	.348	42	3	0	1.000
Duncan 2b-dh	6	29	5	10	0	1	0	2	7	1	.345	10	17	1	.964
Thompson lf-pr	5	16	3	5	1	1	1	6	2	1	.313	10	0	1	.909
Hollins 3b	6	23	5	6	1	0	0	2	5	6	.261	9	9	0	1.000
Eisenreich rf	6	26	3	6	0	0	1	7	4	2	.231	18	0	0	1.000
Daulton c	6	23	4	5	2	0	1	4	5	4	.217	31	4	0	1.000
Stocker ss	6	19	1	4	1	0	0	1	5	5	.211	8	13	0	1.000
Jordan dh-ph	3	10	0	2	0	0	0	0	2	0	.200	0	0	0	—
Morandini ph-2b	3	5	1	1	0	0	0	0	2	1	.200	2	0	0	1.000
Incaviglia ph-lf	4	8	0	1	0	0	0	1	4	0	.125	7	0	0	1.000
Chamberlain ph	2	2	0	0	0	0	0	0	1	0	.000	0	0	0	—
Jackson p	1	1	0	0	0	0	0	0	1	0	.000	0	0	0	—
Mason p	4	1	0	0	0	0	0	0	0	0	.000	0	0	0	—
Andersen p	4	0	0	0	0	0	0	0	0	0	—	0	0	0	—
Batiste 3b	2	0	0	0	0	0	0	0	0	0	—	0	1	0	1.000
Mulholland p	2	0	0	0	0	0	0	0	0	0	—	1	1	0	1.000
Rivera p	1	0	0	0	0	0	0	0	0	0	—	0	0	0	—
Thigpen p	2	0	0	0	0	0	0	0	0	0	—	0	1	0	1.000
West p	3	0	0	0	0	0	0	0	0	0	—	0	0	0	—
Williams, Mt. p	3	0	0	0	0	0	0	0	0	0	—	0	1	0	1.000
Totals	6	212	36	58	7	2	7	35	50	34	.274	157	54	2	.991

Toronto	G	AB	R	H	2B	3B	HR	RBI	SO	BB	Avg.	PO	A	E	Pct.
Leiter p	3	1	0	1	1	0	0	0	0	0	1.000	0	0	0	—
Molitor dh-1b-3b	6	24	10	12	2	2	2	8	0	3	.500	7	3	0	1.000
Butler ph	2	2	1	1	0	0	0	0	0	0	.500	0	0	0	—
Alomar 2b	6	25	5	12	2	1	0	6	3	2	.480	10	21	2	.939
Fernandez ss	6	21	2	7	1	0	0	9	3	3	.333	11	8	0	1.000
Borders c	6	23	2	7	0	0	0	1	1	2	.304	50	2	1	.981
White cf	6	24	8	7	3	2	1	7	7	4	.292	16	0	0	1.000
Carter rf	6	25	6	7	1	0	2	8	4	0	.280	12	0	2	.857
Olerud 1b	5	17	5	4	1	0	1	2	1	4	.235	36	0	0	1.000
Henderson lf	6	22	6	5	2	0	0	2	2	5	.227	8	0	0	1.000
Sprague 3b-ph-1b	5	15	0	1	0	0	0	2	6	1	.067	4	9	2	.867
Hentgen p	1	3	0	0	0	0	0	0	1	0	.000	0	0	0	—
Guzman p	2	2	0	0	0	0	0	0	1	0	.000	0	1	0	1.000
Castillo p	2	1	0	0	0	0	0	0	1	0	.000	0	0	0	—
Cox p	3	1	0	0	0	0	0	0	0	0	.000	1	0	0	1.000
Griffin pr-3b	3	0	0	0	0	0	0	0	0	0	—	0	0	0	—
Canate pr	1	0	0	0	0	0	0	0	0	0	—	0	0	0	—
Eichhorn p	1	0	0	0	0	0	0	0	0	0	—	0	0	0	—
Knorr c	1	0	0	0	0	0	0	0	0	0	—	3	0	0	1.000
Stewart p	2	0	0	0	0	0	0	0	0	0	—	1	1	0	1.000
Stottlemyre p	1	0	0	0	0	0	0	0	0	1	—	0	0	0	—
Timlin p	2	0	0	0	0	0	0	0	0	0	—	0	0	0	—
DWard p	4	0	0	0	0	0	0	0	0	0	—	0	0	0	—
Totals	6	206	45	64	13	5	6	45	30	25	.311	159	45	7	.967

PITCHING SUMMARY

Phillies	G	CG	IP	H	R	BB	SO	HB	WP	W	L	SV	Pct.	ER	ERA
Thigpen	2	0	2⅔	1	0	1	0	1	0	0	0	0	—	0	0.00
Mason	4	0	7⅔	4	1	1	7	0	0	0	0	0	—	1	1.17
Schilling	2	1	15⅓	13	7	5	9	0	0	1	1	0	.500	6	3.52
Mulholland	2	0	10⅔	14	8	3	5	0	0	1	0	0	1.000	8	6.75
Jackson	1	0	5	6	4	1	1	0	0	0	1	0	.000	4	7.20
Andersen	4	0	3⅔	5	5	3	3	1	0	0	0	0	—	5	12.27
Williams, Mt.	3	0	2⅔	5	6	4	1	0	0	0	2	1	.000	6	20.25
Greene	1	0	2⅓	7	7	4	1	0	0	0	0	0	—	7	27.00
Rivera	1	0	1⅓	4	4	2	3	0	0	0	0	0	—	4	27.00
West	3	0	1	5	3	1	0	1	0	0	0	0	—	3	27.00
Totals	**6**	**1**	**52⅓**	**64**	**45**	**25**	**30**	**3**	**0**	**2**	**4**	**1**	**.333**	**44**	**7.57**

Toronto	G	CG	IP	H	R	BB	SO	HB	WP	W	L	SV	Pct.	ER	ERA
Timlin	2	0	2⅓	2	0	0	4	0	0	0	0	0	—	0	0.00
Eichhorn	1	0	⅓	1	0	1	0	0	0	0	0	0	—	0	0.00
Hentgen	1	0	6	5	1	3	6	0	0	1	0	0	1.000	1	1.50
Ward	4	0	4⅔	3	2	0	7	0	0	1	0	2	1.000	1	1.93
Guzman	2	0	12	10	6	8	12	0	1	0	1	0	.000	5	3.75
Stewart	2	0	12	10	9	8	8	0	1	0	1	0	.000	9	6.75
Leiter	3	0	7	12	6	2	5	0	0	1	0	0	1.000	6	7.71
Castillo	2	0	3⅓	6	3	3	1	1	0	1	0	0	1.000	3	8.10
Cox	3	0	3⅓	6	3	5	6	0	0	0	0	0	—	3	8.10
Stottlemyre	1	0	2	3	6	4	1	0	0	0	0	0	—	6	27.00
Totals	**6**	**0**	**53**	**58**	**36**	**34**	**50**	**1**	**2**	**4**	**2**	**2**	**.667**	**34**	**5.77**

SCORE BY INNINGS
Phillies . . . . 736 262 802—36
Toronto . . . . 926 325 675—45
One out when winning run scored (Game 6).
West pitched to 2 batters in the 7th (Game 1), Stewart pitched to 3 batters in the 7th (Game 6), West pitched to 1 batter in the 8th (Game 6).
DP: PHILLIES 5, Toronto 5. LOB: PHILLIES 54, Toronto 39. SB: Dykstra 4, Duncan 3, Alomar 4, Molitor, Henderson, White. CS: Fernandez, Henderson, Stocker, Alomar 2. S: Schilling. SF: Carter 3, Olerud, Fernandez, Sprague 2, Incaviglia.
IBB: off Guzman 2 (Daulton, Dykstra); off Andersen (Olerud). HBP: by Thigpen (Henderson); by West (Molitor); by Castillo (Daulton); by Andersen (Fernandez). Balk: Stewart. PB: Daulton.
Umpires: Phillips (AL), Runge (NL), Johnson (AL), Williams (NL), McClelland (AL), DeMuth (NL).
Time: Game 1 at Toronto, 3:27.
Game 2 at Toronto, 3:35.
Game 3 at Philadelphia, 3:16.
Game 4 at Philadelphia, 4:14.
Game 5 at Philadelphia, 2:53.
Game 6 at Toronto, 3:27.
Attendance: Game 1 at Toronto, 52,011.
Game 2 at Toronto, 52,062.
Game 3 at Philadelphia, 62,689.
Game 4 at Philadelphia, 62,731.
Game 5 at Philadelphia, 62,706.
Attendance: Game 6 at Toronto, 52,195.